GERMAN
pocket
VOCABULARY

New York Chicago San Francisco Lisbon London Madrid Mexico City
Milan New Delhi San Juan Seoul Singapore Sydney Toronto

ISBN 978-0-07-163622-3
MHID 0-07-163622-6

McGraw-Hill books are available at special quantity discounts to use as premiums and sales promotions or for use in corporate training programs. To contact a representative, please visit the Contact Us pages at www.mhprofessional.com.

Translation: Horst Kopleck
Project Editors: Alex Hepworth, Kate Nicholson
With Helen Bleck

Designed by Chambers Harrap Publishers Ltd, Edinburgh
Typeset in Rotis Serif and Meta Plus by Macmillan Publishing Solutions

CONTENTS

CONTENTS

Introduction

This German vocabulary book from Chambers has been compiled
to meet the needs of those who are learning German and is
particularly useful for those taking school examinations. The basic
vocabulary required for these is fully treated in this book.

This new, fully revised edition has been updated and expanded to
contain over 7,500 vocabulary items in 66 subject areas, so users have
all the language needed for a particular topic at their fingertips. Words
are grouped thematically within each section, followed by example
sentences showing vocabulary in context, illustrating tricky structures
and offering some informal phrases (labelled *Inf*). All the vocabulary
items included are entirely relevant to modern German, and spellings
are consistent with the latest reforms. Users will also find a helpful
chapter listing genitive and plural forms for over 1,500 nouns.

Boxed notes draw the user's attention to points of difficulty or
confusion, while brand-new 'Homework help' sections provide
inspiration for essay writing or oral presentations. Finally, this new
edition features a smart, two-colour design to make consultation
even easier and more enjoyable.

An index of approximately 2,000 words has been built up with
specific reference to school exam requirements. This index is given
in English with cross-references to the section of the book where
the German vocabulary item is given.

Abbreviations used in the text:

m	masculine
f	feminine
n	neuter
pl	plural
acc	accusative
dat	dative
gen	genitive
Inf	informal
®	registered trade mark

1 BESCHREIBUNG VON MENSCHEN

DESCRIBING PEOPLE

sein	to be
haben	to have
aussehen	to look
scheinen	to seem
wiegen	to weigh
beschreiben	to describe
die Beschreibung	description
die Erscheinung	appearance
das Aussehen	look
eine Brille	glasses
das Piercing	piercing
die Tätowierung	tattoo
ziemlich	quite, rather
sehr	very
zu	too
jung	young
alt	old
schön	beautiful, good-looking *(woman)*
gut aussehend	good-looking, handsome
hübsch	pretty
hässlich	ugly
elegant	stylish
modisch	trendy
schlampig	scruffy
rechtshändig	right-handed
linkshändig	left-handed

Größe und Gewicht — height and weight

groß	tall
klein	small, short
mittelgroß	of average height
dick	fat
übergewichtig	overweight
fettleibig	obese
dünn	thin, skinny
schlank	thin, slim
kurvenreich	curvy
gut gebaut	well-built
stämmig	stocky
muskulös	muscular
gebrechlich	frail-looking

die Haut — skin

der Teint	complexion
Sommersprossen *(pl)*	freckles
ein Leberfleck *(m)*	mole, beauty spot
ein Pickel *(m)*	spot, pimple
Falten *(pl)*	wrinkles
Grübchen *(pl)*	dimples
sonnengebräunt	sun-tanned
braun gebrannt	tanned
blass	pale
weiß	white
schwarz	black
asiatisch	Asian
orientalisch	Oriental
gemischtrassig	mixed-race
pickelig	spotty
faltig	wrinkled

die Haare — hair

das Haar	hair
der Bart	beard

1 Beschreibung von Menschen

der Schnurrbart	moustache
der Spitzbart	goatee
der Dreitagebart	stubble
er/sie hat ... Haare	he/she has ... hair
lange	long
mittellange	medium-length
schulterlange	shoulder-length
kurze	short
lockige	curly
gewellte	wavy
krause	frizzy
glatte	straight
glänzende	shiny
blonde	blonde/fair
braune	brown
schwarze	black
rote	red/ginger
graue	grey
weiße	white
blond sein	to be blonde/fair-haired
eine Glatze haben	to be bald
einen Pony haben	to have a fringe
eine Glatze tragen	to have a shaved head
Strähnchen tragen	to have highlights
einen Afro-Look tragen	to have an Afro

die Augen

eyes

er/sie hat ... Augen	he/she has ... eyes
blaue	blue
grüne	green
graue	grey
braune	brown
hellbraune	hazel
schwarze	black
graublaue	grey-blue
graugrüne	grey-green

wie ist er/sie?
what's he/she like?

können Sie ihn/sie beschreiben?
can you describe him/her?

wie groß bist du?
how tall are you?

wie viel wiegst du?
how much do you weigh?

er benimmt sich eigenartig
he behaves strangely

er trägt eine Brille
he wears glasses

sie hat langes blondes Haar
she's got long blonde hair

er/sie ist sehr attraktiv
he's/she's very attractive

ein Mann mittlerer Größe
a man of medium height

ich bin 1 Meter 75 groß
I'm 1.75 metres (5 ft 9 in) tall

ich wiege 70 Kilo
I weigh 70 kilos (11 stone)

er sieht etwas seltsam aus
he looks a bit strange

er hat gepiercte Augenbrauen
he's got his eyebrow pierced

sie hat eine gute Figur
she's got a good figure

Inf **sie sieht toll aus**
she's gorgeous

Note

Note that the German word for 'glasses' is singular: die Brille.

See also Sections

2 CLOTHES AND FASHION, 3 HAIR AND MAKE-UP, 4 THE HUMAN BODY, 6 HEALTH, ILLNESSES AND DISABILITIES *and* **63 DESCRIBING THINGS.**

sich anziehen	to dress
sich ausziehen	to undress
anziehen	to put on
ausziehen	to take off
anprobieren	to try on
tragen	to wear
anhaben	to have on
passen	to suit, to fit

die Kleider

clothes

ein Mantel *(m)*	coat, overcoat
ein Regenmantel *(m)*	raincoat
ein Anorak *(m)*	anorak
ein Parka *(m)*	parka
ein Blouson *(n)*	bomber jacket, blouson
eine Jacke	jacket
ein Sakko *(m)*	(sports) jacket
eine Thermoweste	body-warmer
ein Pelzmantel *(m)*	fur coat
ein Blazer *(m)*	blazer
ein Vlies *(n)*	fleece
ein Poncho *(m)*	poncho
ein Anzug *(n)*	suit
ein Kostüm *(n)*	lady's suit
ein Smoking *(m)*	dinner jacket
eine Uniform	uniform
eine Schuluniform	school uniform
eine Hose	trousers
eine Jeans	jeans

Bluejeans *(pl)*	jeans
eine Schlaghose	flares
eine Kampfhose	combat trousers
Leggings *(pl)*	leggings
eine Latzhose	dungarees
ein Overall *(m)*	overalls
ein Trainingsanzug *(m)*	tracksuit
die Shorts *(pl)*	shorts
ein Kleid *(n)*	dress
ein Abendkleid *(n)*	evening dress
ein Rock *(m)*	skirt
ein Minirock *(m)*	mini-skirt
ein Kilt *(m)*	kilt
ein Trägerkleid *(n)*	pinafore dress
eine Burka	burqa
ein Sari *(m)*	sari
ein Pullover *(m)*	jumper, sweater
ein Pulli *(m)*	pullover
ein Kapuzenshirt *(n)*	hoodie, hooded top
ein Rollkragenpullover *(m)*	polo neck (jumper)
ein Pullover *(m)* mit V-Ausschnitt	V-neck jumper
eine Weste	waistcoat
eine Strickjacke	cardigan
ein Hemd *(n)*	shirt
eine Bluse	blouse
ein T-Shirt *(n)*	T-shirt
ein Top *(n)*	top
ein Trägertop *(n)*	vest top
ein Nachthemd *(n)*	nightdress
ein Schlafanzug *(m)*	pyjamas
ein Pyjama *(m)*	pyjamas
ein Bademantel *(m)*	dressing gown, bathrobe
ein Morgenrock *(m)*	dressing gown *(for women)*
ein Bikini *(m)*	bikini
ein Badeanzug *(m)*	swimming costume

die Unterwäsche	underwear
ein Höschen *(n)*	knickers, pants
ein BH *(m)* (Büstenhalter)	bra
ein Unterhemd *(n)*	vest
eine Unterhose	(under)pants
Boxershorts *(pl)*	boxer shorts
ein Tanga *(m)*	thong
ein Unterrock *(m)*	underskirt, petticoat
Strumpfhalter *(pl)*	suspenders
Socken *(pl)*	socks
die Strumpfhose	tights
Netzstrümpfe *(pl)*	fishnet tights
Strümpfe *(pl)*	socks; stockings
Kniestrümpfe	knee-length socks

die Schuhe
shoes

Schuhe *(pl)*	shoes
Stiefel *(pl)*	boots
Gummistiefel	Wellington boots
Kniestiefel *(pl)*	knee-high boots
Turnschuhe	trainers
Skistiefel	ski boots
Sandalen *(pl)*	sandals
Hausschuhe	slippers
der Absatz	heel
flache Absätze	flat heels
Bleistiftabsätze	stiletto heels
Plateauschuhe *(pl)*	platform shoes
ein Paar	a pair of
die Sohle	sole
ein Riemen *(m)*	strap
eine Schnalle	buckle
das Klettband	Velcro®

das Zubehör — accessories

ein Hut *(m)*	hat
ein Strohhut *(m)*	straw hat
ein Sonnenhut *(m)*	sun hat
eine Haube	bonnet
eine Mütze	cap
eine Beanie-Mütze	beanie hat
eine Kappe	cap
ein Schal *(m)*	scarf
ein Kopftuch *(n)*	(head)scarf
Handschuhe *(pl)*	gloves
Fausthandschuhe *(pl)*	mittens
eine Krawatte	tie
ein Schlips *(m)*	tie
eine Fliege	bow tie
Hosenträger *(pl)*	braces
ein Gürtel *(m)*	belt
der Kragen	collar
die Tasche	pocket
ein Knopf *(m)*	button
Manschettenknöpfe *(pl)*	cufflinks
ein Reißverschluss *(m)*	zip
Schnürsenkel *(pl)*	shoelaces
ein Band *(n)*	ribbon
ein Taschentuch *(n)*	handkerchief
ein Regenschirm *(m)*	umbrella
eine Handtasche	handbag
ein Rucksack *(m)*	rucksack
eine Gürteltasche	bumbag

der Schmuck — jewellery

ein Juwel *(n)*	jewel
das Silber	silver
das Gold	gold
ein Edelstein *(m)*	precious stone

eine Perle	pearl
ein Diamant *(m)*	diamond
ein Smaragd *(m)*	emerald
ein Rubin *(m)*	ruby
ein Saphir *(m)*	sapphire
ein Ring *(m)*	ring
Ohrringe *(pl)*	earrings
ein Nasenring *(m)*	nose ring
ein Nasenstecker *(m)*	nose stud
ein Armreif *(m)*	bangle
ein Armband *(n)*	bracelet
ein Armband *(n)* mit Amulett	charm bracelet
ein Freundschaftsband *(n)*	friendship bracelet
eine Brosche	brooch
eine Halskette	necklace
eine Kette	chain
ein Anhänger *(m)*	pendant
eine Armbanduhr	watch
ein Perlenkollier *(n)*	pearl necklace

die Größe — size

klein	small
mittelgroß	medium
groß	large
kurz	short
lang	long
weit	wide, loose-fitting
eng	tight
die Größe	size
die Taille	waist
die Schuhgröße	shoe size
die Kragenweite	collar size
die Hüftweite	hip measurement
die Oberweite	bust/chest measurement

der Stil — style

das Modell	model
die Farbe	colour
die Schattierung	shade
das Muster	pattern, design
uni	plain
bestickt	embroidered
kariert	check(ed)
geblümt	flowered, flowery
gepunktet	with polka-dots, spotted
gestreift	striped
schick	elegant, smart
elegant	elegant
formell	formal
lässig	casual
sportlich	snazzy
schlampig	sloppy
einfach	simple, plain
knallig	loud, gaudy
modisch	fashionable
altmodisch	old-fashioned
dekolletiert	low-cut, low-necked

die Mode — fashion

die Modebranche	fashion industry
die (Winter)kollektion	(winter) collection
die Herrenkonfektion	menswear
die Damenkonfektion	ladieswear
die Schneiderei	dressmaking
die Haute Couture	haute couture, high fashion
die Designerkleidung	designer clothes
ein(e) Schneider(in)	dressmaker
ein(e) Modedesigner(in)	fashion designer
ein(e) Modeschöpfer(in)	fashion designer
das Mannequin	fashion model
ein Dressman *(m)*	male model

eine Modenschau	fashion show
der Laufsteg	catwalk

es ist aus Leder
it's (made of) leather

sie hat ein blaues Kleid an
she has a blue dress on

kann ich die Hose anprobieren?
can I try these trousers on?

ich möchte gern etwas Preiswerteres
I'd like something cheaper

ich möchte einen zu diesem Hemd passenden Rock
I'd like a skirt matching this shirt

welche Größe/Schuhgröße haben Sie?
what is your size/shoe size?

rot steht mir nicht
red doesn't suit me

diese Hose steht Ihnen gut
these trousers suit you

ich muss mich erst noch umziehen
I have to get changed first

diese Jacke sitzt gut
this jacket is a good fit

sie ist sehr gut gekleidet
she's very well dressed

Note

★ *False friend:* the German word die Weste means 'waistcoat'. The word for a vest is das Unterhemd (lit. 'undershirt').

★ Note that some items of clothing which are plural in English are singular in German, eg eine Hose:

ich habe eine neue Hose
I have a new pair of trousers

ich habe zwei Hosen gekauft
I bought two pairs of trousers

The same applies to eine Jeans, ein Pyjama, ein Höschen, eine Unterhose.

See also Sections

13 LIKES AND DISLIKES, 18 SHOPPING, 64 COLOURS *and* **65 MATERIALS.**

3 HAARE UND MAKE-UP
HAIR AND MAKE-UP

kämmen	to comb
bürsten	to brush
schneiden	to cut
nachschneiden	to trim
sich frisieren	to do one's hair
sich *(dat)* (die Haare) kämmen	to comb one's hair
sich *(dat)* die Haare bürsten	to brush one's hair
sich *(dat)* die Haare färben	to dye one's hair
sich *(dat)* die Haare blondieren	to bleach one's hair
sich *(dat)* die Haare schneiden lassen	to have a hair-cut
sich *(dat)* die Haare färben lassen	to have one's hair dyed
sich Strähnchen machen lassen	to have highlights put in
sich *(dat)* die Haare föhnen lassen	to have a blow-dry
sich die Haare glätten lassen	to have one's hair straightened
sich eine Dauerwelle machen lassen	to have a perm
sich die Haare verlängern lassen	to have extensions put in
sich schminken	to put one's make-up on
ein Makeover machen	to have a makeover
eine Gesichtsbehandlung machen lassen	to have a facial
sich *(dat)* die Fingernägel lackieren	to paint one's nails
eine Maniküre machen lassen	to have a manicure
eine Pediküre machen lassen	to have a pedicure
sich rasieren	to shave
sich die Beine rasieren	to shave one's legs
wachsen	to wax

sich die Beine wachsen lassen	to have one's legs waxed
sich die Augenbrauen zupfen	to pluck one's eyebrows

Frisuren — hairstyles

... Haar haben	to have ... hair
dichtes	thick
gefärbtes	dyed
fettiges	greasy
trockenes	dry
der (Haar)schnitt	(hair-)cut
eine Dauerwelle	perm
eine Locke	curl
der Scheitel	parting
Strähnchen *(pl)*	highlights
ein Pony *(m)*	fringe
ein Pferdeschwanz *(m)*	pony tail
ein Zopf *(m)*	plait, pigtail
ein Kamm *(m)*	comb
eine Haarbürste	hairbrush
eine Haarspange	hairslide
ein Lockenwickler *(m)*	roller, curler
ein Haartrockner *(m)*	hairdryer
ein Lockenstab *(m)*	tongs
ein Haarglätter *(m)*	hair straighteners
eine Perücke	wig
das (Haar)shampoo	shampoo
das Haarwaschmittel	shampoo
das Gel	gel
das Haarspray	hair spray
das Wachs	wax
die Schuppen *(pl)*	dandruff

das Make-up — make-up

die Schönheit	beauty
die Gesichtscreme	face cream
die Feuchtigkeitscreme	moisturizer

der Lippenfettstift	lip balm
die Gesichtspackung	face pack
das Puder	powder
die Puderdose	compact
die Grundierungscreme	foundation
der Lippenstift	lipstick
der Lipgloss	lip gloss
der Lippenkonturenstift	lip liner
die Wimperntusche	mascara
der Lidschatten	eye-shadow
der Eyeliner	eyeliner
eine Pinzette	tweezers
der Make-up-Entferner	make-up remover
die Reinigungscreme	cleanser
das Gesichtswasser	toner
der Nagellack	nail varnish
der Nagellackentferner	nail-varnish remover
das Parfüm	perfume
das Kölnischwasser	cologne
der Deodorant	deodorant
das Deospray	deodorant (spray)
die Bräunungscreme	fake tan
die Sonnenbank	sunbed

die Rasur — shaving

der Bart	beard
der Schnurrbart	moustache
das Rasiermesser	razor
der Rasierapparat	shaver
der Elektrorasierer	electric shaver
die Rasierklinge	razor blade
die Rasiercreme	shaving foam
das Rasierwasser	aftershave
Haare (pl)	hair (on face, body)
das Wachsen	waxing

er hat Schuppen he has dandruff	**sie trägt Zöpfe** she wears her hair in plaits
sie trägt viel Make-up she wears a lot of make-up	**ich gehe auf die Sonnenbank** I go on a sunbed

See also Section

1 DESCRIBING PEOPLE.

4 DER KÖRPER
THE HUMAN BODY

Körperteile	**parts of the body**
der Kopf	head
der Hals	neck
die Kehle	throat
der Nacken	nape of the neck
die Schulter	shoulder
die Brust	chest
der Busen	bust
Brüste *(pl)*	breasts
der Bauch	stomach
der Rücken	back
der Arm	arm
der Ell(en)bogen	elbow
die Hand	hand
das Handgelenk	wrist
die Faust	fist
der Finger	finger
der Daumen	thumb
der Zeigefinger	index finger
der Mittelfinger	middle finger
der Ringfinger	ring finger
der kleine Finger	little finger
der Nagel	nail
die Taille	waist
die Hüfte	hip
der Hintern	behind, bottom
das Gesäß	buttocks
das Bein	leg
der Schenkel	thigh
das Knie	knee

die Wade	calf
der Knöchel	ankle
der Fuß	foot
die Ferse	heel
die Zehe	toe
ein Organ *(n)*	organ
ein Glied *(n)*	limb
ein Muskel *(m)*	muscle
ein Knochen *(m)*	bone
das Skelett	skeleton
das Rückgrat	spine
eine Rippe	rib
das Fleisch	flesh
die Haut	skin
das Herz	heart
die Lunge	lungs
der Magen	stomach
die Leber	liver
Nieren *(pl)*	kidneys
die Blase	bladder
das Blut	blood
die Ader	vein
die Vene	vein
die Arterie	artery

der Kopf — the head

der Schädel	skull
das Gehirn	brain
das Haar	hair
das Gesicht	face
Gesichtszüge *(pl)*	features
die Stirn	forehead
Augenbrauen *(pl)*	eyebrows
Wimpern *(pl)*	eyelashes
das Auge	eye
(Augen)lider *(pl)*	eyelids

die Pupille	pupil
die Nase	nose
das Nasenloch	nostril
die Backe	cheek
die Wange	cheek
der Backenknochen	cheekbone
die Schläfe	temple
der Kiefer	jaw
der Mund	mouth
Lippen *(pl)*	lips
die Zunge	tongue
ein Zahn *(m)*	tooth
ein Milchzahn *(m)*	milk tooth
ein Weisheitszahn *(m)*	wisdom tooth
das Kinn	chin
das Ohr	ear
das Ohrläppchen	ear lobe

See also Sections

6 HEALTH, ILLNESSES AND DISABILITIES *and* **7 MOVEMENTS AND GESTURES.**

5 WIE GEHT ES IHNEN?

HOW ARE YOU FEELING?

sich fühlen	to feel
hungrig	hungry
durstig	thirsty
satt	full
schläfrig	sleepy
fit	fit
in Hochform	on top form
müde	tired
erschöpft	exhausted
atemlos	out of breath
träge	lethargic
stark	strong
schwach	weak
gebrechlich	frail
gesund	in good health
krank	sick, ill
wach	awake, alert
erregt	agitated
im Halbschlaf	half asleep
durchnässt	soaked
durch(ge)froren	frozen

er ist müde	**er sieht müde aus**
he is/feels tired	he looks tired
er schläft	**was hast du?**
he's asleep	what's wrong?

mir ist nicht wohl
I don't feel well

ich habe Hunger/Durst
I'm hungry/thirsty

mir ist (zu) warm/kalt
I'm (too) hot/cold

mir reicht's
I've had enough

Inf **er ist in Topform**
he's on top form

ich fühle mich schwach
I feel weak

ich sterbe vor Hunger!
I'm starving!

ich bin eiskalt!
I'm freezing!

ich bin am Ende meiner Kräfte
I'm worn out

Inf **ich fühle mich ziemlich mies**
I feel quite rough

Note

Look out for expressions such as:

er hat sich das Bein gebrochen
he broke his leg

A reflexive verb is used to emphasise the idea of breaking *his own* leg, not someone else's. Note that German uses a definite article (**das Bein**) where English would use a possessive pronoun ('his leg').

See also Section

6 HEALTH, ILLNESSES AND DISABILITIES.

6 GESUNDHEIT, KRANKHEITEN UND BEHINDERUNGEN

HEALTH, ILLNESSES AND DISABILITIES

gesund sein	to be well
krank sein	to be ill
krank werden	to fall ill
bekommen	to catch
Magenschmerzen *(pl)*	stomach ache
Kopfschmerzen *(pl)*	headache
Halsschmerzen *(pl)*	sore throat
Rückenschmerzen *(pl)*	backache
Zahnschmerzen *(pl)*	toothache
sich krank fühlen	to feel sick
Schmerzen haben	to be in pain
leiden an *(+dat)*	to suffer from
erkältet sein	to have a cold
ein Herzleiden *(n)* haben	to have a heart condition
Brust-/Haut-/Lungenkrebs haben	to have breast/skin/lung cancer
Diabetiker sein	to have diabetes
sich *(dat)* den Arm/das Bein brechen	to break one's leg/arm
sich *(dat)* den Knöchel verstauchen	to sprain one's ankle
seine Periode haben	to have one's period
Menstruationsbeschwerden haben	to have period pain

sich an der Hand verletzen	to hurt one's hand
verletzen	to hurt
bluten	to bleed
wehtun	to hurt
erbrechen	to vomit
husten	to cough
niesen	to sneeze
schwitzen	to sweat
zittern	to shake, to shiver
Fieber haben	to have a temperature
in Ohnmacht fallen	to faint
ohnmächtig sein	to be in a coma
behandeln	to treat
pflegen	to nurse
sich kümmern um	to look after
rufen	to call
kommen lassen	to send for
sich anmelden	to make an appointment
untersuchen	to examine
verschreiben	to prescribe
operieren	to operate
operiert werden	to have an operation
sich die Mandeln entfernen lassen	to have one's tonsils taken out
sich den Blinddarm entfernen lassen	to have one's appendix taken out
sich einen Zahn ziehen lassen	to have a tooth taken out
entbinden	to give birth
röntgen	to X-ray
verbinden	to dress *(wound)*
amputieren	to amputate
entfernen	to remove
eine Wiederbelebung durchführen	to perform CPR
brauchen	to need
einnehmen	to take

heilen	to heal, to cure
einreiben	to rub in
eine Diät machen	to be on a diet
sich ausruhen	to rest
sich erholen	to recover
sich verschlimmern	to get worse
sterben	to die
krank	ill, sick
unwohl	unwell
schwach	weak
gesund	healthy
fit	fit
lebendig	alive
schwanger	pregnant
allergisch gegen	allergic to
anämisch	anaemic
epileptisch	epileptic
diabetisch	diabetic
verstopft	constipated
betrunken	drunk
schmerzhaft	painful, sore
ansteckend	contagious
ernst	serious
schlimm	bad
infiziert	infected
geschwollen	swollen
gebrochen	broken
verstaucht	sprained

Krankheiten

illnesses

eine Krankheit	illness
ein Leiden (n)	disease
der Schmerz	pain
eine Epidemie	epidemic
ein Anfall (m)	fit, attack
eine Wunde	wound

eine Verstauchung	sprain
ein Bruch *(m)*	fracture
eine Blutung	bleeding
das Fieber	fever, temperature
der Schluckauf	hiccups
der Husten	cough, coughing
der Schock	shock
der Puls	pulse
die Temperatur	temperature
die Atmung	respiration, breathing
die Blutgruppe	blood group
der Blutdruck	blood pressure
ein Abszess *(m)*	abscess
Aids	Aids
die Allergie	allergy
eine Angina	angina
die Arthritis	arthritis
das Asthma	asthma
eine Blasenentzündung	cystitis
die Blinddarmentzündung	appendicitis
die Bronchitis	bronchitis
das Downsyndrom	Down's Syndrome
der Durchfall	diarrhoea
die Epilepsie	epilepsy
eine Erkältung	cold
eine Gehirnerschütterung	concussion
eine Geschlechtskrankheit	STI
ein Geschwür *(n)*	ulcer
die Grippe	flu
ein Herzinfarkt *(m)*	heart attack
das Heufieber	hay fever
eine Infektion	infection
ein Kater *(m)*	hangover

die Kinderlähmung	polio
das Kopfweh	headache
der Krebs	cancer
die Leukämie	leukaemia
eine Lungenentzündung	pneumonia
eine Magenverstimmung	upset stomach, indigestion
die Masern *(pl)*	measles
die Migräne	migraine
der Mumps	mumps
der Rheumatismus	rheumatism
die Röteln *(pl)*	German measles
ein Schnupfen *(m)*	cold
ein Sonnenstich *(m)*	sunstroke
die Tollwut	rabies
die Tuberkulose	TB
der Typhus	typhoid
die Verstopfung	constipation
die Vogelgrippe	bird flu
die Windpocken *(pl)*	chickenpox
die Periode	period
Wehen *(pl)*	labour
die Geburt	childbirth
ein Kaiserschnitt *(m)*	Caesarean (section)
eine Fehlgeburt	miscarriage
eine Abtreibung	abortion
die In-vitro-Fertilisation	IVF
ein Retortenbaby *(n)*	test-tube baby

Hautverletzungen   skin complaints

eine Verbrennung	burn
eine Schnittverletzung	cut
ein Kratzer *(m)*	scratch
ein Insektenstich *(m)*	insect bite
ein Jucken *(n)*	itch
ein Ausschlag *(m)*	rash
die Akne	acne

Pickel *(pl)*	spots
Krampfadern *(pl)*	varicose veins
eine Warze	wart
ein Hühnerauge *(n)*	corn
eine Blase	blister
ein blauer Fleck	bruise
eine Narbe	scar
ein Sonnenbrand *(m)*	sunburn

die Behandlung — treatment

die Medizin	medicine
die Hygiene	hygiene
die Gesundheit	health
die Empfängnisverhütung	contraception
die Familienberatungsstelle	family planning clinic
die Behandlung	(course of) treatment
die Erste Hilfe	first aid
ein Krankenhaus *(n)*	hospital
eine Klinik	clinic
eine Kur	health cure
die Diät	diet
die Sprechstunde	surgery hours
das Wartezimmer	waiting room
eine Arztpraxis	doctor's surgery
das Sprechzimmer	(doctor's) surgery
die private Gesundheitsfürsorge	private health care
die staatliche Gesundheitsfürsorge	state health care
die Krankenkasse	health insurance scheme
der Krankenschein	medical card
ein Termin *(m)*	appointment
ein Rezept *(n)*	prescription
die Genesung	convalescence
die Erholung	recovery
der Tod	death
ein Notfall *(m)*	emergency
ein Krankenwagen *(m)*	ambulance

eine Trage	stretcher
die Watte	cotton wool
ein Pflaster *(n)*	plaster
ein Verband *(m)*	bandage, dressing
eine Armbinde	sling
ein Gipsverband *(m)*	plaster cast
das Heftpflaster	sticking plaster
eine Damenbinde	sanitary towel
ein Tampon *(n)*	tampon
Krücken *(pl)*	crutches
eine Operation	operation
die Narkose	anaesthetic
eine Bluttransfusion	blood transfusion
eine Röntgenaufnahme	X-ray
eine Chemotherapie	chemotherapy
eine Strahlentherapie	radiotherapy
eine Schönheitsoperation	cosmetic surgery
eine Gesichtsoperation	plastic surgery
eine Nasenkorrektur	nose job
ein Facelifting *(n)*	facelift
eine Brustvergrößerung	breast implants
das Fettabsaugen	liposuction
der Arzt, die Ärztin	doctor
ein Hausarzt, eine Hausärztin	GP
ein Spezialist *(m)*	specialist
eine Krankenschwester	nurse *(female)*
ein Pfleger *(m)*	nurse *(male)*
ein Kranker, eine Kranke	sick person
ein(e) Patient(in)	patient

Medikamente

medicines

das Medikament	medicine
eine Apotheke	(dispensing) chemist's
eine Drogerie	chemist's
die Antibiotika *(pl)*	antibiotics
ein Schmerzmittel *(n)*	painkiller

eine Kopfschmerztablette	aspirin
ein Beruhigungsmittel *(n)*	tranquillizer
eine Schlaftablette	sleeping pill
ein Abführmittel *(n)*	laxative
Vitamine *(pl)*	vitamins
der Hustensaft	cough mixture
eine Tablette	tablet
die Tropfen *(pl)*	drops
ein Antiseptikum *(n)*	antiseptic
die Salbe	ointment
eine Spritze	injection
die Impfung	vaccination
die Pille	(contraceptive) pill
die Pille danach	morning-after pill
ein Kondom *(n)*	condom

beim Zahnarzt — at the dentist's

ein Zahnarzt *(m)*	dentist
eine Zahnarztpraxis	dental surgery
ein Zahn *(m)*	tooth
eine Plombe	filling
ein Gebiss *(n)*	dentures
der Zahnersatz	dentures
die Karies	caries
der Zahnbelag	plaque
ein Mundgeschwür *(n)*	mouth ulcer
eine Zahnspange	brace

Behinderungen — disabilities

behindert	disabled
körperbehindert	physically disabled
geistig behindert	mentally disabled
blind	blind
einäugig	one-eyed
farbenblind	colour-blind
kurzsichtig	short-sighted
weitsichtig	long-sighted

33

schwerhörig	hard of hearing
taub	deaf
taubstumm	deaf-mute
gelähmt	lame
ein Behinderter, eine Behinderte	disabled person
ein Lernbehinderter, eine Lernbehinderte	person with a learning disability
ein Blinder, eine Blinde	blind person
ein Stock *(m)*	stick
ein Rollstuhl *(m)*	wheelchair
ein Hörgerät *(n)*	hearing aid
eine Brille	glasses
Kontaktlinsen *(pl)*	contact lenses

was fehlt Ihnen?
what's wrong with you?

wie fühlen Sie sich?
how are you feeling?

ich fühle mich nicht sehr gut
I don't feel very well

mir ist schlecht/schwindlig
I feel sick/dizzy

wo tut es weh?
where does it hurt?

ich habe Halsschmerzen
I've got a sore throat

meine Nase ist verstopft/läuft
I've got a blocked-up/runny nose

mein Knie tut weh
my knee hurts

es ist nichts Ernstes
it's nothing serious

sie leisteten ihm Erste Hilfe
they gave him first aid

ich habe Fieber gemessen
I took my temperature

er hat 38 Fieber
he's got a temperature of 101

er liegt im Koma
he's in a coma

sie ist im Krankenhaus
she's in hospital

sie ist im sechsten Monat (schwanger)
she's six months pregnant

sie ist an den Augen operiert worden
she had an eye operation

ich muss mich am Knie operiern lassen
I'm going to have an operation on my knee

haben Sie etwas gegen ...?   **gute Besserung!**
have you got anything for ...?   get well soon!

es geht mir heute schon viel besser
I'm feeling a lot better today

Inf **ich habe mir mit irgendwas den Magen verdorben**
I've got a bit of a dodgy tummy

Inf **ich musste Höllenqualen ausstehen!**
I was in agony!

Note

★ Note this commonly used informal expression:

er ist wieder auf dem Damm
he's back on his feet again
(lit. 'back on the dyke')

★ The word **das Rezept** can mean both 'recipe' and 'prescription'.

See also Section

4 THE HUMAN BODY.

7 BEWEGUNGEN UND GESTEN

MOVEMENTS AND GESTURES

das Kommen und Gehen	comings and goings
anhalten	to stop
ankommen	to arrive
auf und ab gehen	to pace up and down
auftauchen	to turn up
ausrutschen	to slip
aussteigen aus	to get off *(train, bus etc)*
bleiben	to stay, to remain
davoneilen	to rush away
einsteigen in *(+acc)*	to get on *(train, bus etc)*
erscheinen	to appear
fahren	to drive; to ride; to go
folgen	to follow
gehen	to go, to walk
gehen durch	to go through
herauskommen aus	to come out of
hereinkommen in *(+acc)*	to come in(to)
hereinstürzen	to rush in
herunterkommen	to come down(stairs)
hinaufgehen	to go up(stairs)
hinausgehen aus	to go out of
hineingehen in *(+acc)*	to go in(to)
hinuntergehen	to go down(stairs)
holen gehen	to go and get, to fetch
humpeln	to limp
hüpfen	to hop
kommen	to come
laufen	to run

losgehen	to set off
näher kommen	to come closer
rasen	to belt along
rennen	to run
rückwärts gehen	to walk backwards
schleichen	to slide
schreiten	to stride
sich ausruhen	to rest
sich beeilen	to hurry
sich *(dat)* die Beine vertreten	to go for a stroll
sich hinlegen	to lie down
sich verstecken	to hide
spazieren gehen	to go for a walk
springen	to jump
stolpern	to trip
taumeln	to stagger
trödeln	to dawdle
überqueren	to cross
verschwinden	to disappear
vorbeigehen	to pass, to go past
weggehen	to go away
weitergehen	to continue, to go on
wie angewurzelt dastehen	to be rooted to the spot
wiederkommen	to return, to come back
zu/ins Bett gehen	to go to bed
zurückgehen	to go back (in/home)
zurückkommen	to come back (in/home)
die Ankunft	arrival
die Abreise	departure
der Anfang	start
der Beginn	beginning
das Ende	end
der Eingang	entrance
der Ausgang	exit, way out
die Rückkehr	return

die Überquerung	crossing
ein Spaziergang *(m)*	walk, stroll
die Gangart	way of walking
ein Schritt *(m)*	step
eine Pause	rest
der Sprung	jump
Schritt für Schritt	step by step

Handlungen

actions

anfangen	to start
auffahren	to give a start, to jump
aufhören	to stop
aufmachen	to open
aufstehen	to stand up; to get up
beenden	to finish
beginnen	to begin
berühren	to touch
bewegen	to move
drücken	to push, to squeeze
entfernen	to remove
fallen lassen	to drop
fangen	to catch
festhalten	to hold tight
halten	to hold
herunterlassen	to lower
hochheben	to lift, to raise
legen	to put
nehmen	to take
öffnen	to open
schließen	to close
setzen	to put, to place
sich ausruhen	to (have a) rest
sich ausstrecken	to stretch out
sich bücken	to stoop
sich hinhocken	to squat down
sich hinknien	to kneel down

sich hinlegen	to lie down
sich hinsetzen	to sit down
sich lehnen (gegen/auf)	to lean (against/on)
sich lehnen (über)	to lean (over)
sich umdrehen	to turn round
stellen	to put
stoßen	to hit, to knock
verschließen	to close, to lock
verstecken	to hide
werfen	to throw
ziehen	to pull, to drag
zumachen	to shut

die Haltung · posture, position

kauernd	squatting
hingehockt	squatting
kniend	kneeling
auf Knien	on one's knees
liegend	lying down
ausgestreckt	stretched out
gelehnt (auf/gegen)	leaning (on/against)
auf allen vieren	on all fours
sitzend	sitting, seated
stehend	standing
angelehnt	leaning
regungslos	motionless

Gesten · gestures

treten	to kick
boxen	to punch
schlagen	to slap
das Gesicht verziehen	to make a face
ein Zeichen (n) geben	to make a sign
ein Handzeichen (n) geben	to signal with one's hand
die Stirn runzeln	to frown
die Schultern zucken	to shrug (one's shoulders)
nicken	to nod

blicken	to glance
einen Blick werfen	to cast a glance
aufblicken	to look up, to raise one's eyes
die Augen senken	to look down, to lower one's eyes
blinzeln	to blink
zwinkern	to wink
zeigen auf *(+acc)*	to point at
lachen	to laugh
den Kopf schütteln	to shake one's head
lächeln	to smile
grinsen	to grin
lachen	to laugh
gähnen	to yawn
ein Achselzucken *(n)*	shrug
eine Bewegung	movement
ein Blick *(m)*	look, glance
ein Gähnen *(n)*	yawn
eine Geste	gesture
eine Grimasse	grimace
ein Grinsen *(n)*	grin
ein Kopfschütteln *(n)*	shake of the head
ein Lächeln *(n)*	smile
das Lachen	laugh
ein Nicken *(n)*	nod
ein Schlag *(m)*	punch, blow
ein Schulterzucken *(n)*	shrug
ein Tritt *(m)*	kick
ein Zeichen *(n)*	sign, signal, gesture
ein Zwinkern *(n)*	wink

wir sind mit dem Auto hingefahren
we went there by car

ich gehe zu Fuß zur Schule
I walk to school

er lief nach unten
he ran downstairs

ich rannte hinaus
I ran out

sie rannte über die Straße
she ran across the street

er kommt morgen zurück
he'll be back tomorrow

Note

Note that the verb gehen ('to go') is only used when going somewhere on foot. If any kind of transport is involved, the verb is fahren.

8 IDENTITÄT UND ALTER
IDENTITY AND AGE

der Name	**name**
nennen	to name, to call
taufen	to christen
heißen	to be called
unterschreiben	to sign
buchstabieren	to spell
die Identität	identity
die Unterschrift	signature
der Name	name
der Familienname	family name
der Nachname	surname
der Zuname	surname
der Vorname	first name
der Mädchenname	maiden name
der Spitzname	nickname
der Geburtsort	place of birth
die Staatsangehörigkeit	nationality
die Initialen *(pl)*	initials
Herr Martin	Mr Martin
Frau Müller	Mrs Müller
Fräulein (Frl.) Schröder	Miss Schröder
Herren	gentlemen
Damen	ladies
das Alter	**age**
die Geburt	birth
das Leben	life
die Jugend	youth

die Jugendzeit	adolescence
das Alter	old age
das Geburtsdatum	date of birth
der Geburtstag	birthday
ein Baby *(n)*	baby
ein Kind *(n)*	child
ein Teenager *(m)*	teenager
ein Erwachsener, eine Erwachsene	adult
ein Jugendlicher *(m)*	young person
junge Leute	young people
eine junge Frau	young woman
ein junges Mädchen	young girl
ein junger Mann	young man
eine alte Frau	old woman
eine ältere Dame	elderly woman
ein alter Mann	old man
ein älterer Herr	elderly man
ein(e) Rentner(in)	pensioner
alte Leute	old people
die Alten *(pl)*	the old
jung	young
alt	old

das Geschlecht — sex

eine Frau	woman
eine Dame	lady
ein Mädchen *(n)*	girl
ein Mann *(m)*	man
ein Herr *(m)*	gentleman
ein Junge *(m)*	boy
männlich	masculine, male
weiblich	feminine, female

der Familienstand	marital status
geboren werden	to be born
sterben	to die
heiraten	to marry
sich verloben	to get engaged
sich scheiden lassen	to get divorced
die Verlobung lösen	to break off one's engagement

ledig	single
unverheiratet	unmarried
verheiratet	married
verlobt	engaged
geschieden	divorced
getrennt lebend	separated
verwitwet	widowed
verwaist	orphaned

ein Junggeselle *(m)*	bachelor
eine Junggesellin	unmarried woman
eine alte Jungfer	spinster
der Ehemann	husband
die Ehefrau	wife
der Mann	husband
die Frau	wife
der Exmann	ex-husband
die Exfrau	ex-wife
der (die) Verlobte	fiancé(e)
der Bräutigam	bridegroom
die Braut	bride
die Jungverheirateten *(pl)*	newly-weds
ein Witwer *(m)*, eine Witwe	widower/widow
eine Waise	orphan *(male and female)*

die Zeremonie	ceremony
die Geburt	birth
die Taufe	christening

der Tod	death
die Beerdigung	funeral
die Hochzeit	wedding
die Verlobung	engagement
die Scheidung	divorce

die Adresse — address

leben	to live
wohnen	to live *(in a place)*
mieten	to rent
vermieten	to let

die Adresse	address
der Wohnort	place of residence
die Etage	floor, storey
die Postleitzahl	postcode
die (Haus)nummer	number
die Telefonnummer	phone number
das Telefonbuch	telephone directory
der Hauswirt	owner, landlord
der Vermieter	landlord
der Mieter	tenant
der Nachbar	neighbour

bei Klaus	at Klaus's
in der Stadt	in town
am Stradtrand	in the suburbs
auf dem Lande	in the country

die Religion — religion

katholisch	Catholic
protestantisch	Protestant
evangelisch	Protestant
anglikanisch	Anglican
moslemisch	Muslim
jüdisch	Jewish
atheistisch	atheist

8 IDENTITÄT UND ALTER

wie heißt du/heißen Sie?
what is your name?

ich heiße Paul Schmidt
my name is Paul Schmidt

wie heißt du/heißen Sie mit Vornamen?
what is your first name?

er heißt Rainer
his name is Rainer

wie schreibt man das?
how do you spell that?

wie schreiben Sie sich?
how do you spell/write your name?

wo wohnst du/wohnen Sie?
where do you live?

ich wohne in Köln/in Österreich
I live in Cologne/in Austria

es ist im dritten Stock
it's on the third floor

ich wohne (in der) Stephanstraße (Nummer) 27
I live at 27, Stephanstraße

ich wohne seit einem Jahr hier
I've been living here for a year

wie alt bist du/sind Sie?
how old are you?

ich bin 20 Jahre (alt)
I'm 20 years old

wann bist du geboren?
when were you born?

am ersten März 1990
on the first of March 1990

in welchem Jahr sind Sie geboren?
what year were you born in?

ich bin 1968 in Stuttgart geboren
I was born in Stuttgart in 1968

ein einen Monat altes Baby
a one-month old baby

ein achtjähriges Kind
an eight year old child

ein sechzehnjähriges Mädchen
a sixteen year old girl

mit 20
at the age of 20

eine Frau von dreißig Jahren
a woman of thirty

ein Mann mittleren Alters
a middle-aged man

er sieht etwa sechzehn Jahre alt aus
he looks about sixteen

sie ist in den Dreißigern	**er muss Ende fünfzig sein**
she's in her thirties	he must be in his late fifties
ein Herr im reiferen Alter	*Inf* **sie ist uralt!**
an elderly gentleman	she's ancient!

Note

Note the construction mit + age:

mit 18 darf man wählen
at (the age of) 18 you can vote

See also Section

31 FAMILY AND FRIENDS.

9 ARBEIT UND BERUF

JOBS AND WORK

arbeiten	to work
vorhaben	to intend
werden	to become
studieren	to study
einen Lehrgang besuchen	to go on a training course
ehrgeizig sein	to be ambitious
Erfahrung haben	to have experience
keine Erfahrung haben	to have no experience
arbeitslos sein	to be unemployed
erwerbslos sein	to be unemployed
Arbeit suchen	to look for work
sich für eine Stelle bewerben	to apply for a job
ablehnen	to reject
annehmen	to accept
einstellen	to take on
eine Stelle finden	to find a job
Dienst haben	to be on duty
Erfolg haben	to be successful
seinen Lebensunterhalt verdienen	to earn a living
verdienen	to earn
bekommen	to get
bezahlen	to pay
Urlaub nehmen	to take a holiday
einen Tag frei nehmen	to take a day off
entlassen	to dismiss
kündigen	to resign
kündigen *(+dat)*	to dismiss
seine Stelle aufgeben	to leave (job)
sich zur Ruhe setzen	to retire

streiken	to be on strike
in Streik treten	to go on strike
schwer	difficult
leicht	easy
interessant	interesting
aufregend	exciting
reizvoll	challenging
anstrengend	demanding
lohnend	rewarding
wichtig	important
nützlich	useful
langweilig	boring
gefährlich	dangerous
stressig	stressful

Berufstätige

people at work

ein Angestellter, eine Angestellte	employee
ein(e) Anstreicher(in)	painter and decorator
ein(e) Apotheker(in)	chemist
ein(e) Arbeiter(in)	(factory) worker
ein(e) Architekt(in)	architect
ein Arzt, eine Ärztin	doctor
ein(e) Astronaut(in)	astronaut
ein(e) Astronom(in)	astronomer
ein(e) Ausbilder(in)	instructor
eine Aushilfskraft	temp
ein(e) Babysitter(in)	childminder
ein(e) Bäcker(in)	baker
ein Bankangestellter, eine Bankangestellte	bank clerk
ein(e) Bauarbeiter(in)	builder
ein Bauer, eine Bäuerin	farmer
ein Beamter, eine Beamtin	civil servant
ein(e) Berater(in)	consultant
ein Bergmann *(m)*	miner
ein(e) Berufsberater(in)	careers adviser

ein(e) Blumenhändler(in)	florist
ein(e) Botschafter(in)	ambassador
ein(e) Buchhalter(in)	accountant
ein(e) Buchhändler(in)	bookseller
ein Büroangestellter, eine Büroangestellte	office worker
ein(e) Busfahrer(in)	bus driver
ein(e) Chefsekretär(in)	PA
ein(e) Chirurg(in)	surgeon
ein(e) Direktor(in)	manager, director
ein Discjockey *(m)*	DJ
ein(e) Dolmetscher(in)	interpreter
ein(e) Dozent(in)	lecturer
ein(e) Drogist(in)	pharmacist
ein(e) Elektriker(in)	electrician
ein(e) Entwicklungshelfer(in)	aid worker
ein(e) Fahrer(in)	driver
ein Feuerwehrmann *(m)*	firefighter
ein(e) Fernsehmoderator(in)	TV presenter
ein(e) Fischer(in)	fisherman
ein(e) Fischhändler(in)	fishmonger
ein(e) Fitnesstrainer(in)	personal trainer
ein(e) Fleischer(in)	butcher
ein(e) Flugbegleiter(in)	flight attendant
ein(e) Fotograf(in)	photographer
ein Fotomodell *(n)*	model *(male and female)*
ein freiwilliger Helfer, eine freiwillige Helferin	volunteer
ein(e) Fremdenführer(in)	tourist guide
ein Friseur, eine Friseuse	hairdresser
ein(e) Gärtner(in)	gardener
ein Geistlicher *(m)*	priest
eine Geschäftsfrau	businesswoman
ein(e) Geschäftsführer(in)	manager, company director
ein(e) Geschäftsinhaber(in)	shopkeeper
ein Geschäftsmann *(m)*	businessman

ein(e) Grafiker(in)	graphic designer
ein(e) Grundschullehrer(in)	primary-school teacher
ein(e) Händler(in)	trader
ein Hausmeister *(m)*	caretaker
eine Hebamme	midwife
ein(e) Hilfsarbeiter(in)	labourer, unskilled worker
ein(e) Hochschullehrer(in)	university teacher
ein(e) Immobilienmakler(in)	estate agent
ein(e) Ingenieur(in)	engineer
ein(e) Innenausstatter(in)	interior decorator
ein(e) Installateur(in)	plumber
ein(e) Journalist(in)	journalist
ein(e) Jugendarbeiter(in)	youth worker
ein(e) Juwelier(in)	jeweller
ein Kaufmann, eine Kauffrau	shopkeeper; clerk
ein(e) Kellner(in)	waiter/waitress
ein(e) Kfz-Mechaniker(in)	garage mechanic
ein(e) Kindergärtner(in)	kindergarten teacher
ein Kindermädchen *(n)*	nanny
ein(e) Klempner(in)	plumber
ein Koch, eine Köchin	cook
ein Krankenpfleger *(m)*	(male) nurse
eine Krankenschwester	(female) nurse
ein(e) Künstler(in)	artist
ein(e) Lastwagenfahrer(in)	lorry driver
ein(e) Lebensmittelhändler(in)	grocer
ein(e) Lehrer(in)	teacher
ein(e) Lkw-Fahrer(in)	lorry driver
ein(e) Maler(in)	painter
ein(e) Manager(in)	executive
ein Mannequin *(n)*	model *(female)*
ein Matrose *(m)*	sailor
ein(e) Mechaniker(in)	mechanic
ein(e) Metzger(in)	butcher
ein Möbelpacker *(m)*	removal man
ein(e) Moderator(in)	presenter *(on television, radio)*

ein(e) Modeschöpfer(in)	dressmaker, fashion designer
ein Mönch *(m)*	monk
ein Müllmann *(m)*	dustman
ein(e) Musiker(in)	musician
eine Nonne	nun
ein Ober *(m)*	waiter
ein Offizier *(m)*	(army) officer
ein(e) Pastor(in)	minister
ein(e) Personalberater(in)	recruitment consultant
ein(e) Pfarrer(in)	vicar
ein(e) Physiker(in)	physicist
ein(e) Pilot(in)	pilot
ein(e) Platzanweiser(in)	usher
ein(e) Politiker(in)	politician
ein Polizist, eine Polizistin	police officer
ein Popstar *(m)*	popstar
ein Postbote, eine Postbotin	postman/woman
ein(e) Pressesprecher(in)	press officer
ein Priester *(m)*	priest
ein(e) Programmierer(in)	computer programmer
ein(e) Psychiater(in)	psychiatrist
ein Psychologe, eine Psychologin	psychologist
eine Putzfrau	cleaner
ein(e) Rabbiner(in)	rabbi
ein Rechtsanwalt, eine Rechtsanwältin	lawyer, solicitor
ein(e) Redakteur(in)	editor
ein(e) Reiseveranstalter(in)	travel agent
ein(e) Reporter(in)	reporter
ein(e) Richter(in)	judge
ein(e) Sänger(in)	singer
ein(e) Sanitäter(in)	ambulance man/woman
ein(e) Schäfer(in)	(ticket) inspector
ein(e) Schauspieler(in)	actor/actress
ein(e) Schneider(in)	tailor
ein(e) Schriftsteller(in)	writer

ein(e) Schuhmacher(in)	cobbler
ein(e) Schulleiter(in)	headteacher
ein Seemann *(m)*	sailor
eine Sekretärin	secretary *(female)*
ein(e) Soldat(in)	soldier
ein(e) Sozialarbeiter(in)	social worker
eine Sprechstundenhilfe	(doctor's) receptionist
ein(e) Steward(ess)	flight attendant, steward(ess)
ein(e) Student(in)	student
ein Studienrat, eine Studienrätin	secondary-school teacher
ein(e) Taxifahrer(in)	taxi driver
ein(e) Techniker(in)	technician
ein Tierarzt, eine Tierärztin	vet
ein(e) Übersetzer(in)	translator
ein(e) Uhrmacher(in)	watchmaker
ein(e) Verkäufer(in)	shop assistant, salesperson
ein(e) Versicherungsmakler(in)	insurance broker
ein(e) Vertreter(in)	sales representative
ein(e) Webdesigner(in)	web designer
ein(e) Wissenschaftler(in)	scientist
ein Zahnarzt, eine Zahnärztin	dentist
ein(e) Zeitungshändler(in)	newsagent
ein Zimmermann *(m)*	carpenter
ein Zimmermädchen *(n)*	chambermaid
ein Zollbeamter, eine Zollbeamtin	customs officer

die Arbeitswelt

the world of work

ein(e) Arbeiter(in)	worker
ein Arbeitsloser, eine Arbeitslose	unemployed person
ein Arbeitssuchender, eine Arbeitssuchende	jobseeker
ein(e) Arbeitgeber(in)	employer
ein(e) Chef(in)	boss
die Geschäftsleitung	management
der Vorstand	board
ein(e) Arbeitnehmer(in)	employee
das Personal	staff, personnel

ein Kollege, eine Kollegin	colleague
ein Lehrling *(m)*	trainee, apprentice *(male and female)*
ein Auszubildender, eine Auszubildende	trainee, apprentice
die Aushilfskraft	temp
ein Streikender, eine Streikende	striker
ein(e) Rentner(in)	retired person, pensioner
ein(e) Gewerkschafter(in)	trade unionist
die Zukunft	the future
eine Laufbahn	career
ein Beruf *(m)*	profession, occupation
die Branche	profession, line
eine Beschäftigung	job
Aussichten *(pl)*	prospects
Möglichkeiten *(pl)*	openings
eine Stelle	post
ein Lehrgang *(m)*	training course
die Lehrzeit	apprenticeship
die Ausbildung	training
die Weiterbildung	continuing education
ein Abschluss *(m)*	qualification, degree
eine Bescheinigung	certificate, diploma
eine Arbeit	job, employment
ein Job *(m)*	temporary job
eine Teilzeitarbeit	part-time job
eine Halbtagsbeschäftigung	part-time job
eine Ganztagsstelle	full-time job
die Überstunden *(pl)*	overtime
die Berufsberatung	careers advice
der Bereich	sector
die Industrie	industry
die Geschäftswelt	business
ein Unternehmen *(n)*	company

ein Betrieb *(m)*	firm, factory
eine Firma	firm
ein Büro *(n)*	office
eine Fabrik	factory
eine Werkstatt	workshop
ein Geschäft *(n)*	shop
ein Labor *(n)*	laboratory
eine Abteilung	department
der Verkauf	sales
das Marketing	marketing
die Personalabteilung	HR
die Buchhaltung	accounts
die Finanzabteilung	finance
die Geschäftsleitung	management
der Kundendienst	customer service
die Öffentlichkeitsarbeit	PR
die Informationstechnik	IT
die Forschung	research
die Arbeit	work, job
die Mittagspause	lunch break
der Feierabend	end of the day
der Urlaub	holidays
der Jahresurlaub	annual holiday
die Betriebsferien	company holidays
der Mutterschaftsurlaub	maternity leave
der Vaterschaftsurlaub	paternity leave
ein (Arbeits)vertrag *(m)*	contract (of employment)
eine Bewerbung	job application
eine Online-Bewerbung	online application
ein Formular *(n)*	form
eine Anzeige	ad(vertisement)
Stellenangebote *(pl)*	situations vacant
das Begleitschreiben	covering letter
das Vorstellungsgespräch	interview
Fähigkeiten *(pl)*	skills

| das Wissen | knowledge |
| das Können | ability |

motiviert	motivated
fleißig	hard-working
erfahren	experienced
zuverlässig	reliable
gewissenhaft	conscientious
kreativ	creative
dynamisch	dynamic

die Teamarbeit	teamwork
Aufgaben *(pl)*	duties
Pflichten *(pl)*	responsibilities
eine Tätigkeitsbeschreibung	job description
das Gehalt	salary, wages
der (Arbeits)lohn	pay, wages
Vergünstigungen *(pl)*	perks
eine Essensmarke	luncheon voucher
ein Firmenwagen *(m)*	company car
ein Reisekostenzuschuss *(m)*	travel allowance
der lockere Freitag	dress-down Friday
eine Beförderung	promotion
die gleitende Arbeitszeit	flexitime
die 40-Stunden-Woche	forty hour week
Überstunden *(pl)*	overtime
die Arbeitsplatzsicherheit	job security
Steuern *(pl)*	taxes
eine Gehaltserhöhung	pay rise
ein Bonus *(m)*	bonus
eine Geschäftsreise	business trip
die Einstellung	appointment
die Entlassung	dismissal
die Rente	pension
die Gewerkschaft	trade union
der Streik	strike
der Bummelstreik	go-slow

ein Computer *(m)*	computer
ein Drucker *(m)*	printer
ein Fax *(n)*	fax machine
die Vermittlung	switchboard
ein Fotokopierer *(m)*	photocopier
das Büromaterial	stationery

was ist sie von Beruf? — **er ist Arzt**
what does she do for a living? — he's a doctor

was möchtest du einmal werden? — **was sind Ihre Zukunftspläne?**
what do you want to be? — what are your plans for the future?

ich wäre gern ein Künstler — **ich will Medizin studieren**
I'd like to be an artist — I intend to study medicine

er ist krankgeschrieben — **Feierabend machen**
he's off sick — to finish work

ich verbringe den Feierabend mit Freunden
after work I get together with my friends

er arbeitet in der Werbung/im Versicherungswesen
he works in advertising/insurance

dieser Job hat eine gute Zukunft
this job has good prospects

mangelnde Arbeitsplatzsicherheit ist ein Problem
lack of job security is a problem

Inf **mein Job stresst mich total** — *Inf* **sie arbeiten für einen Hungerlohn**
my job really stresses me out — they get paid peanuts

Note

A German job application would normally include a photo of the applicant.

Homework help

Your ambitions

I'd like to be a...	I'm going to be a...
Ich möchte ... werden.	**Ich werde später einmal...**

I'd like to work with children.
Ich möchte mit Kindern arbeiten.

I'd like a job where I can help people/travel the world.
Ich möchte eine Arbeit, wo ich Menschen helfen/die Welt sehen kann.

I want to use my languages.
Ich möchte meine Sprachkenntnisse nutzen.

I like a challenge.
Ich möchte eine Arbeit, wo ich gefordert bin.

It's important to have nice colleagues/a good salary.
Es ist wichtig, nette Kollegen/ein gutes Gehalt zu haben.

I want to be rich/famous.
Ich möchte reich/berühmt werden.

Happiness is more important than money.
Zufriedenheit ist wichtiger als Geld.

Job applications
  Asking for work

I would like to apply for the position of...
Ich möchte mich für die Stelle als ... bewerben.

I would like to apply for a work placement.
Ich möchte mich für ein Praktikum bewerben.

I am writing to see if you have any vacancies.
Ich schreibe um zu erfahren, ob Sie freie Stellen haben.

Please find enclosed my CV.
Mein Lebenslauf ist beigefügt.

I am available for an interview.
Ich stehe für ein Vorstellungsgespräch zur Verfügung.

Your skills and abilities

I am well organized/a good communicator.
Ich habe gute Organisations-/Kommunikationsfähigkeiten.

I am very reliable/motivated.
Ich bin sehr zuverlässig/motiviert.

I work well under pressure.
Ich kann gut unter Druck arbeiten.

I like meeting people.
Ich gehe gern mit Menschen um.

I enjoy working as part of a team.
Ich arbeite gern im Team.

I have excellent IT skills.
Ich habe sehr gute Computerkenntnisse.

I speak fluent English/German.
Ich spreche fließend Englisch/Deutsch.

Your experience

I have experience of working in a shop/looking after children.
Ich habe Arbeitserfahrung in Geschäften/in der Kinderbetreuung.

I have a Saturday job in a café.
Ich habe einen Samstagsjob in einem Café.

I write for our school magazine.
Ich schreibe für unsere Schulzeitung.

I have designed my own website.
Ich habe meine eigene Website erstellt.

10 CHARAKTER UND BENEHMEN

CHARACTER AND BEHAVIOUR

sich benehmen	to behave
sich verhalten	to behave
sich beherrschen	to control oneself
gehorchen	to obey
erlauben	to allow
lassen	to let
verhindern	to prevent
verbieten	to forbid
billigen	to approve of
missbilligen	to disapprove of
ausschimpfen	to scold
ausgeschimpft werden	to be told off
sich aufregen	to get angry
sich entschuldigen	to apologize
vergeben	to forgive
bestrafen	to punish
belohnen	to reward
wagen	to dare
die Arroganz	arrogance
das Benehmen	behaviour
der Charakter	character
der Charme	charm
die Ehrlichkeit	honesty
die Eifersucht	jealousy
die Einsicht	understanding
die Eitelkeit	vanity
eine Entschuldigung	excuse, apology

die Erlaubnis	permission
die Faulheit	laziness
die Frechheit	insolence
die Freude	joy, delight
die Fröhlichkeit	cheerfulness
die Geduld	patience
die Gehässigkeit	spite
der Gehorsam	obedience
die Geschicklichkeit	skilfulness
die Grausamkeit	cruelty
die Grobheit	coarseness
die Güte	goodness, kindness
die Höflichkeit	politeness
der Instinkt	instinct
die Intelligenz	intelligence
die Intoleranz	intolerance
die Laune	mood
die Liebenswürdigkeit	kindness
der Neid	envy
die Prahlerei	boastfulness
die Rücksichtslosigkeit	heedlessness
die Schlauheit	craftiness
die Schüchternheit	shyness, timidity
die Stimmung	mood
der Stolz	pride
die Strafe	punishment
die Trauer	sadness
die Ungeduld	impatience
die Ungezogenheit	nastiness, naughtiness
die Unhöflichkeit	rudeness
das Verhalten	behaviour
die Verlegenheit	embarrassment
die Verrücktheit	madness
die Vorsicht	caution
aktiv	active
amüsant	amusing

angeberisch	pretentious
angenehm	nice, pleasant
anständig	decent
arm	poor
arrogant	arrogant
bescheiden	modest
besitzergreifend	possessive
blöd	silly, stupid
böse	angry
boshaft	mischievous
charmant	charming
doof	silly, stupid
dumm	stupid
ehrbar	respectable
ehrlich	honest
eifersüchtig	jealous
einsichtig	understanding
eitel	vain
ernst	serious
erstaunlich	surprising
faul	lazy
frech	cheeky
freundlich	friendly
froh	glad
fröhlich	joyful, cheerful
geduldig	patient
gehorsam	obedient
geistreich	witty
geschickt	skilful
gesprächig	talkative
glücklich	happy
grausam	cruel
grob	rude, coarse
gut	good
gut gelaunt	cheerful
gütig	kind

hartnäckig	obstinate
herrlich	terrific
hetero	straight, heterosexual
hinterhältig	devious, shifty
höflich	polite
impulsiv	impulsive
intelligent	intelligent
intolerant	intolerant
komisch	funny
kontaktfreudig	outgoing
langweilig	boring
lästig	annoying
launisch	moody
liebevoll	affectionate
lustig	funny
mutig	courageous
naiv	naive
natürlich	natural
neidisch	envious
nett	kind, nice
neugierig	curious
optimistisch	optimistic
pessimistisch	pessimistic
prahlerisch	boastful
raffiniert	shrewd
respektvoll	respectful
ruhig	quiet, calm
sanftmütig	gentle
scharfsinnig	astute
schlau	wily
schlecht	bad
schlecht gelaunt	in a bad mood
schüchtern	shy, timid
schwul	gay
seltsam	strange
sensibel	sensitive

10 CHARAKTER UND BENEHMEN

stolz	proud
störrisch	stubborn
sympathisch	nice, pleasant
tolerant	tolerant
toll	terrific
tollpatschig	clumsy
traurig	sad
unangenehm	nasty
ungeduldig	impatient
unfreundlich	unfriendly
ungehorsam	disobedient
ungeschickt	clumsy
ungesellig	unsociable
ungezogen	mischievous, naughty
unglücklich	unhappy
unhöflich	rude
unordentlich	untidy
unverschämt	insolent
unzugänglich	unapproachable
unzuverlässig	unreliable
verlegen	embarrassed
vernünftig	sensible
verrückt	mad
verschwiegen	discreet
vorsichtig	cautious, careful
zerfahren	scatterbrained
zerstreut	absent-minded
zufrieden	pleased
zuverlässig	reliable
zuversichtlich	confident

ich finde sie sehr nett
I think she's very nice

er ist gutmütig/übellaunig
he is good/ill-natured

er hat gute/schlechte Laune
he's in a good/bad mood

er hat eine zurückhaltende Art
he is shy and retiring

sie ist von Natur aus sehr schüchtern
she is very shy by nature

er ist ein Angeber
he's a show-off

es tut mir (sehr) leid
I'm (really) sorry

ich bitte vielmals um Entschuldigung
I do apologize

er entschuldigte sich beim Lehrer für seine Frechheiten
he apologized to the teacher for being cheeky

Inf **sie platzte vor Neid, als sie meine neuen Kleider sah!**
she was green with envy when she saw my new outfit!

Note

★ The word **stolz** ('proud') is used with the preposition **auf**:

   er ist stolz auf seine Tochter
   he is proud of his daughter

★ The word **komisch** is similar to the English word 'funny', in that it can mean either 'amusing' or 'strange':

   zurzeit benimmt er sich sehr komisch
   he's acting very strangely at the moment

★ *False friend*: when used about a person, the word **raffiniert** means 'smart, shrewd', not 'refined' or 'elegant'.

11 GEFÜHLE
EMOTIONS

die Wut	**anger**
wütend werden	to get angry
die Fassung verlieren	to lose one's temper
böse sein	to be angry
wütend sein	to be fuming
mürrisch sein	to be sullen
sich ärgern	to be/get angry
verärgert sein	to be angry/annoyed
sich entrüsten	to be/get indignant
sich aufregen	to get excited/worked up
schreien	to shout
brüllen	to yell
schlagen	to hit
ohrfeigen	to slap (on the face)
die Wut	anger
die Entrüstung	indignation
der Ärger	anger
die Spannung	tension
der Schrei	cry, shout
der Schlag	blow
die Ohrfeige	slap (on the face)

die Trauer	**sadness**
weinen	to cry
in Tränen ausbrechen	to burst into tears
schluchzen	to sob
seufzen	to sigh
Sorge bereiten *(+dat)*	to distress
schockieren	to shock

bestürzen	to dismay
enttäuschen	to disappoint
beunruhigen	to disconcert
deprimieren	to depress
berühren	to move, to affect, to touch
bekümmern	to trouble
Mitleid haben	to take pity
trösten	to comfort, to console
die Sorge	grief, sorrow
die Trauer	sadness
die Enttäuschung	disappointment
die Depression	depression
das Heimweh	homesickness
die Melancholie	melancholy
das Leiden	suffering
das Versagen	failure
das Pech	bad luck
das Unglück	misfortune, bad luck
eine Träne	tear
ein Schluchzen *(n)*	sob
ein Seufzer *(m)*	sigh
traurig	sad
mitgenommen	shattered
enttäuscht	disappointed
deprimiert	depressed
frustriert	frustrated
bekümmert	distressed, sorry
berührt	moved, touched
melancholisch	gloomy
missmutig	sullen
unglücklich	unhappy

Angst und Sorge

fear and worry

Angst haben (vor)	to be frightened (of)
fürchten	to fear

erschrecken	to frighten
Angst machen *(+dat)*	to frighten
sich sorgen wegen	to worry about
zittern	to tremble

die Angst	fear
die Furcht	fear
der Schrecken	fright
der Schauer	shiver
der Schock	shock
der Ärger	trouble
die Ängste *(pl)*	anxieties
ein Problem *(n)*	problem
eine Sorge	worry

furchtsam	fearful
ängstlich	afraid
erschreckt	frightened
besorgt	worried, anxious
nervös	nervous

Glück und Freude

joy and happiness

sich amüsieren	to enjoy oneself
erfreut sein über *(+acc)*	to be delighted about
lachen (über + acc)	to laugh (at)
in Gelächter ausbrechen	to burst out laughing
kichern	to have the giggles
lächeln	to smile

das Glück	happiness
die Freude	joy
die Zufriedenheit	satisfaction
die Liebe	love
das Glück	luck
der Erfolg	success
die Überraschung	surprise
das Lachen	laugh

das Gelächter	laughter
ein Lachanfall *(m)*	fit of laughter
eine Lachsalve	burst of laughter
ein Lächeln *(n)*	smile

zufrieden	pleased
erfreut	happy
hocherfreut	overjoyed
verliebt	in love

---

er hat sie erschreckt
he frightened them/her

er hat Angst vor Hunden
he's frightened of dogs

er war starr vor Schrecken
he was petrified

ich habe keine Lust dazu
I don't feel like it

es tut mir leid, das zu hören
I'm sorry to hear that

sie hat Glück
she's lucky

sein Bruder fehlt ihm
he misses his brother

ich habe Heimweh
I'm homesick

er ist in Monika verliebt
he's in love with Monika

Inf **mein Vater ging an die Decke**
my dad hit the roof

Inf **seine Witze machen mich total fertig!**
his jokes crack me up!

Note

★ The word verliebt ('in love') is used with the preposition in:

er ist in Monika verliebt
he's in love with Monika

★ Do not confuse the words das Lächeln ('smile') and das Lachen ('laugh').

12 DIE SINNE
THE SENSES

die Sicht	sight
sehen	to see
betrachten	to look at, to watch
beobachten	to observe, to watch
untersuchen	to examine, to study closely
erblicken	to catch sight of
blicken (auf + acc)	to look at
einen Blick werfen auf *(+acc)*	to glance at
starren auf *(+acc)*	to stare at
gucken auf *(+acc)*	to peek at
fernsehen	to watch TV
das Licht anmachen	to switch on the light
das Licht ausmachen	to switch off the light
blenden	to dazzle, to blind
erscheinen	to appear
verschwinden	to disappear
wieder auftauchen	to reappear
der Blick	view
der Gesichtssinn	sight *(sense)*
der Anblick	sight *(seen)*
das Sehvermögen	sight, vision *(faculty)*
das Auge	eye
eine Brille	glasses
eine Sonnenbrille	sun glasses
Kontaktlinsen *(pl)*	contact lenses
eine Lupe	magnifying glass
ein Vergrößerungsglas *(n)*	magnifying glass
ein Fernglas *(n)*	binoculars
ein Mikroskop *(n)*	microscope

ein Teleskop *(n)*	telescope
die Blindenschrift	Braille
die Farbe	colour
das Licht	light
die Helligkeit	brightness
die Dunkelheit	darkness
hell	bright, light
blendend	dazzling
dunkel	dark
finster	dark

das Gehör
hearing

hören	to hear
zuhören *(+dat)*	to listen to
flüstern	to whisper
singen	to sing
summen	to hum
brummen	to drone
pfeifen	to whistle
rascheln	to rustle
knistern	to crackle
knarren	to creak
läuten	to ring
donnern	to thunder
surren	to hum *(engine)*
die Tür zuknallen	to slam the door
still sein	to be silent
das Ohr	ear
das Geräusch	noise, sound
der Ton	sound
der Lärm	racket
das Echo	echo
das Flüstern	whisper
das Lied	song
das Summen	buzzing

das Rascheln	rustling
das Knistern	crackling
die Explosion	explosion
das Knarren	creaking
das Läuten	ringing
der Donner	thunder
der Lautsprecher	loudspeaker
eine Gegensprechanlage	intercom
Kopfhörer *(pl)*	earphones, headset
Lautsprecher *(pl)*	speakers
ein CD-Player *(m)*	CD player
ein MP3-Player *(m)*	MP3 player
der Walkman®	personal stereo
das Radio	radio
die Sirene	siren
das Morsealphabet	Morse code
das Ohropax®	earplugs
ein Hörgerät *(n)*	hearing aid
laut	noisy, loud
leise	quiet
still	silent
schwach	faint
ohrenbetäubend	deafening
taub	deaf
schwerhörig	hard of hearing

der Tastsinn

touch

berühren	to touch
streicheln	to stroke
fühlen	to feel
kitzeln	to tickle
reiben	to rub
stoßen	to knock
schlagen	to hit
kratzen	to scratch

die Berührung	touch
Fingerspitzen *(pl)*	fingertips
der Händedruck	handshake
die Kälte	cold
die Wärme	warm
das Streicheln	stroke
der Stoß	knock
der Schlag	blow
glatt	smooth
rau	rough
weich	soft
hart	hard
warm	warm
heiß	hot
kalt	cold

der Geschmack taste

probieren	to taste
trinken	to drink
essen	to eat
lecken	to lick
schlürfen	to sip
verschlingen	to gobble up
kosten	to savour
schlucken	to swallow
kauen	to chew
salzen	to put salt on/in
pfeffern	to put pepper on/in
zuckern	to put sugar on/in
süßen	to sweeten
würzen	to spice (up)
der Mund	mouth
die Zunge	tongue
der Speichel	saliva
Geschmacksknospen *(pl)*	taste buds

der Appetit	appetite
der Hunger	hunger
appetitlich	appetizing
köstlich	delicious
scheußlich	horrible
süß	sweet
zuckrig	sugary
salzig	salted, salty
herb	tart
sauer	sour
bitter	bitter
scharf	spicy, hot
streng	pungent, strong
fade	tasteless
lecker	delicious

der Geruch — smell

riechen (nach)	to smell (of)
schnüffeln	to sniff
stinken	to stink
parfümieren	to perfume
gut/schlecht riechen	to smell nice/horrible
der Geruchssinn	sense of smell
die Nase	nose
Nasenlöcher *(pl)*	nostrils
der Duft	scent
das Parfüm	perfume
das Aroma	aroma, fragrance
der Gestank	stench, stink
der Rauch	smoke
parfümiert	fragrant, scented
stinkend	stinking
verräuchert	smoky *(room)*
geruchlos	odourless

im Keller ist es dunkel
it's dark in the cellar

es fühlt sich weich an
it feels soft

ich höre dich nicht
I can't hear you

ich habe das Kind singen hören
I heard the child singing

dabei läuft mir das Wasser im Mund zusammen
it makes my mouth water

dieser Kaffee schmeckt nach Seife
this coffee tastes of soap

hier ist es stickig
it's stuffy in here

es riecht gut/schlecht
it smells good/bad

Inf **ohne meine Kontaktlinsen bin ich total blind**
I'm as blind as a bat without my contacts

Inf **du musst schon schreien, er ist stocktaub**
you'll have to shout, he's as deaf as a post

Inf **diese Socken stinken!**
these socks stink!

Inf **ihre Wohnung stinkt nach Rauch**
their flat stinks of smoke

Note

Note that the German word for 'binoculars' is singular: das Fernglas.

See also Sections

4 THE HUMAN BODY, 6 HEALTH, ILLNESSES AND DISABILITIES,
15 FOOD *and* 64 COLOURS.

13 VORLIEBEN UND ABNEIGUNGEN

LIKES AND DISLIKES

mögen	to like
gern haben	to like
lieben	to love
schwärmen für	to adore, to be mad about
brauchen	to need
benötigen	to need
wollen	to want, to wish for
(sich) wünschen	to wish for
hoffen	to hope
nicht mögen	to dislike
verabscheuen	to detest
hassen	to hate
verachten	to despise
vorziehen	to prefer
lieber mögen	to prefer
wählen	to choose
beschließen	to decide
vergleichen	to compare
die Liebe	love
der Geschmack	taste
die Vorliebe	liking, preference
das Interesse	interest
das Bedürfnis	need
der Wunsch	wish, desire
die Abneigung	strong dislike
der Hass	hate

die Verachtung	scorn
die Wahl	choice
der Vergleich	comparison
das Gegenteil	contrary, opposite
der Kontrast	contrast
der Unterschied	difference
die Ähnlichkeit	similarity
Lieblings-	favourite
vergleichbar (mit)	comparable (to)
verschieden (von)	different (from)
anders (als)	different (from)
identisch (mit)	identical (to)
dasselbe (wie)	the same (as)
das Gleiche (wie)	the same (as)
ähnlich	similar
wie	like
im Vergleich zu	in comparison with
in Bezug auf *(+acc)*	in relation to
mehr	more
weniger	less
viel	a lot
eine Menge	enormously, a great deal
viel mehr/weniger	a lot more/less
sehr viel mehr/weniger	quite a lot more/less
besser	better

mir/ihnen gefällt dieses Buch
I/they like this book

ich mag lieber Tee als Kaffee
I prefer tea to coffee

ich möchte gern ausgehen
I'd like to go out

es freut mich, Sie zu sehen
I'm pleased to see you

Inf **ich kann diesen Typen nicht ausstehen**
I can't stand that guy

Inf **wollen wir einen trinken gehen?**
fancy going for a drink?

rot ist meine Lieblingsfarbe
red is my favourite colour

das gefällt mir gar nicht
I don't like that at all

ich bleibe lieber zu Hause
I'd rather stay at home

hoffentlich kommt er bald
I hope he comes soon

Inf **bist du scharf auf ihn?**
do you fancy him?

14 TAGESABLAUF UND SCHLAF

DAILY ROUTINE AND SLEEP

aufwachen	to wake up
erwachen	to wake up
aufstehen	to get up
sich strecken	to stretch
gähnen	to yawn
sich ausschlafen	to have a long lie-in
verschlafen	to oversleep
die Vorhänge öffnen	to open the curtains
auf die Toilette gehen	to go to the toilet
sich waschen	to wash
sich *(dat)* das Gesicht waschen	to wash one's face
sich *(dat)* die Hände waschen	to wash one's hands
sich *(dat)* die Zähne putzen	to brush one's teeth
sich *(dat)* die Haare waschen	to wash one's hair
duschen	to have a shower
baden	to have a bath
sich einseifen	to soap oneself
sich abtrocknen	to dry oneself
sich rasieren	to shave
sich anziehen	to get dressed
sich *(dat)* die Haare kämmen	to comb one's hair
sich *(dat)* die Haare bürsten	to brush one's hair
sich schminken	to put one's make-up on
das Bett machen	to make the bed
frühstücken	to have breakfast
die Katze/den Hund füttern	to feed the cat/dog

die Blumen gießen	to water the plants
sich fertig machen	to get ready
das Haus verlassen	to leave the house
zur Schule gehen	to go to school
ins Büro gehen	to go to the office
zur Arbeit gehen	to go to work
mit dem Bus/der Straßenbahn fahren	to take the bus/tram
nach Hause gehen/kommen	to go/come home
aus der Schule (zurück)kommen	to come back from school
von der Arbeit (zurück)kommen	to come back from work
die Hausaufgaben machen	to do one's homework
sich ausruhen	to have a rest
ein Nickerchen *(n)* machen	to have a nap
fernsehen	to watch television
lesen	to read
spielen	to play
zu Mittag essen	to have lunch
zu Abend essen	to have dinner
die Tür abschließen	to lock the door
sich ausziehen	to undress
die Vorhänge zuziehen	to draw the curtains
zu Bett gehen	to go to bed
sich zudecken	to tuck oneself up
den Wecker stellen	to set the alarm clock
das Licht ausmachen	to switch the light off
einschlafen	to fall asleep
schlafen	to sleep
träumen	to dream
an Schlaflosigkeit leiden	to suffer from insomnia
eine schlaflose Nacht verbringen	to have a sleepless night
schlafwandeln	to sleepwalk

gewöhnlich	usually
morgens	in the morning
mittags	at lunchtime
abends	in the evening
nachts	at night
dann	then

das Waschen — washing

die Seife	soap
das Handtuch	towel
das Bade(hand)tuch	bath towel
das Händehandtuch	hand towel
der Waschlappen	flannel
ein Schwamm *(m)*	sponge
eine Bürste	brush
ein Kamm *(m)*	comb
eine Zahnbürste	toothbrush
die Zahnpasta	toothpaste
das Shampoo	shampoo
ein Duschgel *(n)*	shower gel
das Schaumbad	bubble bath
das Deo	deodorant
eine Körperlotion	body lotion
das Toilettenpapier	toilet paper
der Haartrockner	hairdryer
der Föhn	hairdryer
die Waage	scales

---

ich stelle den Wecker auf sieben Uhr
I set my alarm clock for seven

ich bin kein Nachtschwärmer; ich gehe früh zu Bett
I'm not a night owl; I go to bed early

ich habe geschlafen wie ein Bär
I slept like a log

> **er kommt immer zu spät zur Schule**
> he's always late for school
>
> **ich bin nicht ausgeschlafen**
> I didn't get enough sleep/I haven't woken up yet
>
> *Inf* **ich bin total kaputt**   *Inf* **ich habe kein Auge zugetan**
> I'm shattered   I didn't sleep a wink

 Homework help

First... **Zuerst...**	Then... **Dann...**
Next... **Als Nächstes...**	After that... **Danach...**
I always... **Ich ... immer**	I usually... **Ich ... gewöhnlich**
I sometimes... **Ich ... manchmal**	I never... **Ich ... nie**
Before school... **Vor der Schule...**	At lunchtime... **In der Mittagspause...**
After school... **Nach der Schule...**	On Mondays... **Montags...**
At the weekend... **Am Wochenende...**	I have to... **Ich muss...**

I'm allowed to/not allowed to...
Ich darf/darf nicht...

See also Sections

> **15 FOOD, 17 HOUSEWORK, 23 MY ROOM** *and* **56 ADVENTURES AND DREAMS.**

15 DAS ESSEN
FOOD

essen	to eat
trinken	to drink
probieren	to taste, to try
kochen	to cook
machen	to make
Vegetarier(in) sein	to be vegetarian
Veganer(in) sein	to be vegan
eine Diät machen	to be on a diet
ein Rezept *(n)*	recipe
Biolebensmittel *(pl)*	organic food
die Reformkost	health foods
fettarm	low-fat
kalorienarm	low-calorie

Mahlzeiten — mealtimes

das Frühstück	breakfast
das Mittagessen	lunch
das Abendessen	dinner
ein Imbiss *(m)*	snack; snack bar
die Zwischenmahlzeit	snack
das Picknick	picnic
ein Fertiggericht *(n)*	ready meal
ein Menü *(n)*	set menu
ein Kinderteller *(m)*	children's portion
eine Portion	portion, helping

Gänge

	courses
die Vorspeise	starter
das Hauptgericht	main course
das Tagesgericht	today's special *(in a restaurant)*
der Nachtisch	dessert
die Nachspeise	dessert

Getränke

	drinks
das Wasser	water
das Mineralwasser	mineral water
die Milch	milk
der Tee	tea
der Pfefferminztee	mint tea
der Kamillentee	camomile tea
der Kaffee	coffee
ein Kakao *(m)*	hot chocolate
ein Softdrink *(m)*	soft drink
ein Fruchtsaft *(m)*	fruit juice
ein Orangensaft *(m)*	orange juice
ein Apfelsaft *(m)*	apple juice
eine Apfelschorle	fizzy apple juice
eine Cola	Coke®
eine Limonade	lemonade
ein Getränk *(n)* mit Kohlensäure	fizzy drink
ein Energy-Drink *(m)*	energy drink
ein alkoholisches Getränk *(n)*	alcoholic drink
ein Bier *(n)*	beer
ein Pils *(n)*	pils
ein Malzbier *(n)*	malt beer *(northern Germany)*
dunkles Bier	dark beer
ein Weizenbier *(n)*	wheat beer
ein Alsterwasser *(n)*	shandy
ein Radler *(n)*	shandy *(southern Germany)*
ein Cidre *(m)*	cider
der Wein	wine
der Rotwein	red wine
der Weißwein	white wine

der Rosé	rosé
der Sekt	sparkling wine
der Champagner	champagne
eine Weinschorle	white wine spritzer
ein Cocktail *(m)*	cocktail
Spirituosen *(pl)*	spirits
ein Aperitif *(m)*	aperitif
ein Likör *(m)*	liqueur
ein Schnaps *(m)*	schnapps
ein Kognak *(m)*	cognac
ein Weinbrand *(m)*	brandy

Gewürze — seasonings and herbs

das Salz	salt
der Pfeffer	pepper
der Zucker	sugar
der Senf	mustard
der Essig	vinegar
das Öl	oil
der Knoblauch	garlic
die Zwiebel	onion
Kräuter *(pl)*	herbs
die Petersilie	parsley
ein Lorbeerblatt *(n)*	bay leaf
der Muskat	nutmeg
eine Gewürznelke	clove
der Ingwer	ginger
eine Paprika	paprika
eine Peperoni	chilli
die Soße	sauce
die Mayonnaise	mayonnaise

Frühstück — breakfast

das Brot	bread
das Weißbrot	white bread
das Graubrot	brown bread
ein Brötchen *(n)*	roll

der Zwieback	rusk
das Knäckebrot	crispbread
ein Butterbrot *(n)*	piece of bread and butter
ein Käsebrot *(n)*	piece of bread and cheese
der Toast	toast
die Butter	butter
die Margarine	margarine
die Marmelade	jam
die Konfitüre	jam
die Orangenmarmelade	marmalade
der Honig	honey
die Erdnussbutter	peanut butter
die Cornflakes®	cornflakes
das Müsli	muesli
das Joghurt	yoghurt

Obst — fruit

eine Frucht	piece of fruit
ein Apfel *(m)*	apple
eine Birne	pear
eine Aprikose	apricot
ein Pfirsich *(m)*	peach
eine Pflaume	plum
eine Melone	melon
eine Ananas	pineapple
eine Banane	banana
eine Orange	orange
eine Apfelsine	orange
eine Pampelmuse	grapefruit
eine Mandarine	tangerine
eine Zitrone	lemon
eine Erdbeere	strawberry
eine Himbeere	raspberry
eine Brombeere	blackberry
eine Rote Johannisbeere	redcurrant
eine Schwarze Johannisbeere	blackcurrant

eine Kirsche	cherry
(Wein)trauben *(pl)*	grapes

Gemüse und Beilagen

vegetables and sides

ein Gemüse *(n)*	vegetable
Erbsen *(pl)*	peas
grüne Bohnen *(pl)*	green beans
der Lauch	leek
der Porree	leek
eine Kartoffel	potato
die Salzkartoffeln *(pl)*	boiled potatoes
die Pommes frites *(pl)*	chips
die Chips *(pl)*	crisps
der Kartoffelsalat	potato salad
das Kartoffelpüree	mashed potatoes
Pellkartoffeln *(pl)*	unpeeled boiled potatoes
in der Schale gebackene Kartoffel *(f)*	baked potato
Knödel *(pl)*	dumplings
der Reis	rice
eine Möhre	carrot
der Kohl	cabbage
der Weißkohl	white cabbage
das Sauerkraut	sauerkraut
der Rotkohl	red cabbage
der Wirsing	savoy cabbage
der Blumenkohl	cauliflower
der Rosenkohl	Brussels sprouts
der Kopfsalat	lettuce
der Spinat	spinach
Pilze *(pl)*	mushrooms
ein Champignon *(m)*	button mushroom
eine Artischocke	artichoke
der Spargel	asparagus
eine (grüne/rote) Paprikaschote	(green/red) pepper
eine Aubergine	aubergine
die Brokkoli *(pl)*	broccoli

die Zucchini *(pl)*	courgettes
eine Zwiebel	onion
der Mais	corn
die Radieschen *(pl)*	radishes
eine Tomate	tomato
eine Gurke	cucumber
ein gemischter Salat	mixed salad
eine kalte Platte	salad

Fleisch — meat

das Schweinefleisch	pork
das Kalbfleisch	veal
das Rindfleisch	beef
das Lammfleisch	lamb
das Hammelfleisch	mutton
das Rehfleisch	venison
ein Hähnchen *(n)*	chicken
ein Brathähnchen *(n)*	roast chicken
ein Truthahn *(m)*	turkey
eine Ente	duck
eine Gans	goose
das Geflügel	poultry
ein Hase *(m)*	hare
ein Kaninchen *(n)*	rabbit
das Wild	game
ein Steak *(n)*	steak
ein Beefsteak *(n)*	steak
ein Kotelett *(n)*	chop
ein Schnitzel *(n)*	escalope
ein Wiener Schnitzel *(n)*	Wiener schnitzel
ein Braten *(m)*	joint
ein Schweinebraten *(m)*	roast pork
das Roastbeef	roast beef
das Ragout	stew
der Gulasch	goulash
das Hackfleisch	mince

die Frikadelle	meatball
der Hamburger	hamburger
Nieren *(pl)*	kidneys
die Leber	liver
die Leberpastete	liver pâté
der Aufschnitt	slices of cold meat
die Wurst	sausage
die Leberwurst	liver sausage
die Blutwurst	black pudding
eine Bratwurst	sausage *(fried or grilled)*
eine Currywurst	curried sausage
ein Würstchen *(n)*	frankfurter
der Schinken	ham
der Speck	bacon

Fisch — fish

der Kabeljau	cod
Ölsardinen *(pl)*	sardines
die Scholle	sole
der Thunfisch	tuna
die Forelle	trout
der Lachs	salmon
der Räucherlachs	smoked salmon
Fischstäbchen *(pl)*	fish fingers
die Meeresfrüchte *(pl)*	seafood
der Hummer	lobster
der Klebs	crab
Austern *(pl)*	oysters
Krabben *(pl)*	prawns
Muscheln *(pl)*	mussels

Eier — eggs

ein Ei *(n)*	egg
ein gekochtes Ei	boiled egg
ein Speigelei *(n)*	fried egg
Rühreier *(pl)*	scrambled eggs
verlorene Eier *(pl)*	poached eggs
ein Omelett *(n)*	omelette

15 Das Essen

Nudeln
die Spaghetti *(pl)*
die Makkaroni *(pl)*
die Spätzle *(pl)*

pasta
spaghetti
macaroni
type of home-made pasta

warme Gerichte
die Suppe
ein Auflauf *(m)*
ein Pfannkuchen *(m)*
das Eisbein
der Sauerbraten
gekocht
durchgebraten
englisch
paniert
am Spieß
gefüllt
gebraten
gebacken
überbacken

hot dishes
soup
soufflé
pancake
knuckle of pork
marinated pot roast
cooked, boiled
well done *(meat)*
rare *(meat)*
fried in breadcrumbs
spit-roast
stuffed
roasted
baked
baked in the oven with cheese

Nachtisch
eine Apfeltorte
die Sahne
die Schlagsahne
ein Eis *(n)*
ein Vanilleeis *(n)*
ein Pudding *(m)*
der Schokoladenpudding
die Vanillesoße
der Käse

dessert
apple tart
cream
whipped cream
ice-cream
vanilla ice-cream
blancmange, jelly *etc*
chocolate pudding
custard
cheese

Süßigkeiten
die Schokolade
eine Tafel Schokolade
Pralinen *(pl)*
Plätzchen *(pl)*
Kekse *(pl)*

sweet things
chocolate
chocolate bar
chocolates
biscuits
biscuits

ein Kuchen *(m)*	cake
eine Torte	gateau, tart
eine Schwarzwälder Kirschtorte	Black Forest gateau
ein Käsekuchen *(m)*	cheesecake
ein Eis *(n)* am Stiel	ice lolly
Bonbons *(pl)*	sweets
Pfefferminzbonbons	mints
der Kaugummi	chewing gum

Geschmacksrichtungen

tastes

der Geschmack	taste
das Aroma	aroma
süß	sweet
salzig	salty
bitter	bitter
sauer	sour
würzig	spicy
pikant	savoury
scharf	hot
fade	tasteless

was nimmst du?	**ich nehme...**
what are you having?	I'll have...
Pommes frites sind nicht gut für dich	
chips are bad for you	
Obst ist gut für dich	**ich habe eine Nussallergie**
fruit is good for you	I'm allergic to nuts
ich esse kein Fleisch/keinen Fisch	
I don't eat meat/fish	
Inf **ich sterbe vor Hunger!**	*Inf* **ich bin total satt**
I'm starving!	I'm stuffed

Note

Do not confuse the words das Obst and die Frucht (*pl.* Früchte), which can both be translated as 'fruit':

das Obst refers to fruit in general:

| **Obst und Gemüse** | **eine Schale Obst** |
| fruit and vegetables | a bowl of fruit |

die Frucht is used for the fruits growing on a particular tree:

| **die Früchte reifen** | **der Baum trägt Früchte** |
| the fruits are ripening | the tree is bearing fruit |

 Homework help

We should eat more/less....
Wir sollten mehr/weniger ... essen.

It's important... **Es ist wichtig, ...**	to eat healthy food. **gesund zu essen.**
	to eat five portions of fruit and vegetables a day. **fünf Portionen Obst und Gemüse am Tag zu essen.**
	to have a balanced diet. **ausgewogen zu essen.**
	to know how to cook. **dass man kochen kann.**
But... **Aber...**	children don't like vegetables. **Kinder mögen kein Gemüse.**
	people don't have time to cook. **man hat keine Zeit zum Kochen.**

I don't know how to cook.
ich kann nicht kochen.

organic food is too expensive.
organische Lebensmittel sind zu teuer.

I like junk food.
ich mag Junkfood.

too much salt/fat isn't healthy.
zu viel Salz/Fett ist ungesund.

I think...
Ich denke, ...

we should learn to cook at school.
wir sollten in der Schule kochen lernen.

buying ready meals is lazy.
Fertiggerichte kauft man nur aus Faulheit.

school dinners are awful.
das Schulessen ist schrecklich.

it's ok to eat junk food occasionally.
es ist okay, manchmal Junkfood zu essen.

I'm vegetarian because...
Ich bin Vegetarier(in), weil...

it's cruel to kill animals.
es grausam ist, Tiere zu töten.

I don't like meat.
ich kein Fleisch mag.

vegetarian food is healthier.
vegetarisches Essen gesünder ist.

eating meat is against my religion.
es gegen meine Religion ist, Fleisch zu essen.

I don't eat chocolate because... **Ich esse keine Schokolade, weil...**	it's fattening. **das dick macht.**
	I'm on a diet. **ich eine Diät mache.**
	I don't like sweet things. **ich keine Süßigkeiten mag.**

See also Sections

5 HOW ARE YOU FEELING?, 17 HOUSEWORK, 22 EVENINGS OUT, 62 QUANTITIES *and* **63 DESCRIBING THINGS.**

16 RAUCHEN
SMOKING

rauchen	to smoke
anzünden	to light
ausdrücken	to stub out
eine Zigarette	cigarette
eine Fluppe	fag
eine Selbstgedrehte	roll-up
eine Zigarettenkippe	cigarette end
eine Zigarre	cigar
eine Pfeife	pipe
ein Streichholz *(n)*	match
die Streichholzschachtel	box of matches
ein Feuerzeug *(n)*	cigarette lighter
eine Schachtel Zigaretten	packet of cigarettes
ein Päckchen *(n)* Tabak	packet of tobacco
das Zigarettenpapier	cigarette papers
die Asche	ash
ein Aschenbecher *(m)*	ashtray
der Rauch	smoke
ein(e) Raucher(in)	smoker
ein(e) Nichtraucher(in)	non-smoker
Nichtraucher-	non-smoking
der Raucherbereich	smoking area
das Rauchverbot	smoking ban
eine Zigarettenpause	cigarette break
das Passivrauchen	passive smoking

haben Sie Feuer?
have you got a light?

Raucher oder Nichtraucher?
smoking or non-smoking?

Rauchen ist im Restaurant nicht gestattet
smoking is not permitted in the restaurant

Inf **hat jemand Fluppen bei sich?**
has anyone got any fags?

Homework help

I don't smoke.
Ich rauche nicht.

I want to give up smoking.
Ich will das Rauchen aufgeben.

I smoke about ... cigarettes a day/a week.
Ich rauche etwa ... Zigaretten am Tag/in der Woche.

I'm in favour of/against the smoking ban.
Ich bin für/gegen das Rauchverbot.

Some people... **Manche...**	think smoking is cool. **denken, dass Rauchen cool ist.**
	smoke because their friends do. **rauchen, weil ihre Freunde es tun.**
	say the smoking ban is unfair. **sagen, dass das Rauchverbot unfair ist.**
But... **Aber...**	smoking is bad for your health. **Rauchen schadet der Gesundheit.**
	smoking can cause cancer. **vom Rauchen kann man Krebs bekommen.**

passive smoking is dangerous.
Passivrauchen ist gefährlich.

cigarettes are expensive.
Zigaretten sind teuer.

In my opinion...
Meiner Meinung nach...

cigarettes smell horrible.
stinken Zigaretten furchtbar.

smoking should be banned in pubs.
sollte das Rauchen in Kneipen verboten werden.

people should be allowed to smoke where they want.
sollte man rauchen dürfen, wo man will.

See also Section

34 TOPICAL ISSUES.

17 HAUSHALT
HOUSEWORK

die Hausarbeit machen	to do the housework
sauber machen	to clean
kehren	to sweep
wegwerfen	to throw away
Staub putzen	to dust
Staub saugen	to vacuum
aufräumen	to tidy up
das Bett machen	to make the bed
(Wäsche) waschen	to do the washing
bügeln	to iron
nähen	to sew
sich kümmern um *(+dat)*	to look after
helfen	to help
zur Hand gehen *(+dat)*	to give a hand
ordentlich sein	to be tidy
unordentlich sein	to be messy
kochen	to cook
das Essen zubereiten	to prepare a meal
vorbereiten	to prepare
schneiden	to cut
in Scheiben schneiden	to slice
reiben	to grate
schälen	to peel
kochen	to cook; to boil
braten	to fry; to roast
backen	to bake
grillen	to grill
rösten	to roast
toasten	to toast

den Tisch decken	to set the table
den Tisch abräumen	to clear the table
abwaschen	to do the washing-up
spülen	to do the washing-up
abtrocknen	to do the drying-up

im Haus Beschäftigte

people who work in the house

die Hausfrau	housewife
die Putzfrau	cleaner
ein Dienstmädchen *(n)*	maid
ein Au-pair-Mädchen *(n)*	au pair
ein(e) Babysitter(in)	baby sitter

Haushaltsgeräte

household appliances

ein Gerät *(n)*	gadget
ein Staubsauger *(m)*	vacuum-cleaner
eine Waschmaschine	washing machine
eine Wäscheschleuder	spin-dryer
ein Trockenautomat *(m)*	tumbledryer
ein Bügeleisen *(n)*	iron
eine Nähmaschine	sewing machine
eine Küchenmaschine	food processor
ein Mixer *(m)*	mixer, blender
eine Küchenmaschine	food processor
eine Kaffeemühle	coffee grinder
eine Kaffeemaschine	coffee machine
ein Wasserkessel *(m)*	kettle
ein Toaster *(m)*	toaster
ein Sandwichtoaster *(m)*	sandwich toaster
eine Küchenwaage	kitchen scales
ein Mikrowellenherd *(m)*	microwave
ein Kühlschrank *(m)*	fridge
eine Tiefkühltruhe	freezer
eine (Geschirr)spülmaschine	dishwasher
ein Herd *(m)*	cooker
ein Elektroherd *(m)*	electric cooker
ein Gasherd *(m)*	gas cooker

der Backofen	oven
ein Grill *(m)*	grill
der Gas	gas
der Strom	electricity, power

Zubehör

utensils

ein Bügelbrett *(n)*	ironing board
ein Besen *(m)*	broom
ein Mopp *(m)*	mop
ein Kehrblech *(n)* und ein Handfeger *(m)*	brush and dustpan
ein Abfalleimer *(m)*	(rubbish) bin
eine Bürste	brush
eine Toilettenbürste	toilet brush
ein Lappen *(m)*	rag
ein Putzlappen *(m)*	floorcloth
ein Staubtuch *(n)*	cloth, duster
ein Spültuch *(n)*	dish cloth
ein Geschirrtuch *(n)*	dish towel
ein Waschbecken *(n)*	washbasin
die Spüle	sink
eine Spülschüssel	basin
ein Topfhandschuh *(m)*	oven glove
ein Wäscheständer *(m)*	clothes horse
Wäscheklammern *(pl)*	clothes pegs
ein Wäschekorb *(m)*	laundry basket
Reinigungsmittel *(pl)*	cleaning products
das (Geschirr)spülmittel	washing-up liquid
das Waschpulver	washing powder
der Weichspüler	fabric softener
das Raumspray	air freshener
ein Kochtopf *(m)*	saucepan
eine (Brat)pfanne	frying pan
eine Kasserolle	casserole dish
eine Kuchenform	cake tin
ein Dampfkochtopf *(m)*	pressure cooker

ein Schnellkochtopf *(m)*	pressure cooker
eine Fritteuse	deep-fat fryer
eine Teigrolle	rolling pin
ein Brett *(n)*	chopping board
ein Dosenöffner *(m)*	tin opener
ein Flaschenöffner *(m)*	bottle opener
ein Korkenzieher *(m)*	corkscrew
eine Knoblauchpresse	garlic press
ein Schälmesser *(n)*	peeler
ein Schneebesen *(m)*	whisk
ein Bratenheber *(m)*	spatula
ein Holzlöffel *(m)*	wooden spoon
ein Tablett *(n)*	tray

das Besteck — cutlery

ein Löffel *(m)*	spoon
ein Kaffeelöffel *(m)*	teaspoon
ein Esslöffel *(m)*	soupspoon, tablespoon
eine Gabel	fork
ein Messer *(n)*	knife
ein Küchenmesser *(n)*	kitchen knife
ein Brotmesser *(n)*	bread knife

das Geschirr — dishes

ein Set *(n)*	place mat
ein Teller *(m)*	plate
eine Untertasse	saucer
eine Tasse	cup
ein Becher *(m)*	mug
ein Glas *(n)*	glass
ein Weinglas *(n)*	wine glass
eine Suppenschüssel	soup tureen
eine Schale	dish, bowl (shallow)
eine Schüssel	dish, bowl (large)
ein Salzstreuer *(m)*	salt cellar
eine Pfeffermühle	peppermill
eine Zuckerdose	sugar bowl

eine Teekanne	teapot
eine Kaffeekanne	coffeepot
ein Milchkännchen *(n)*	milk jug
ein Eierbecher *(m)*	egg cup

mein Vater spült das Geschirr
my father does the dishes

meine Eltern teilen sich die Hausarbeit
my parents share the housework

du bist dran mit dem Tischdecken/Abräumen
it's your turn to set/clear the table

Inf **dein Zimmer sieht wie ein Schweinestall aus!**
your room is a total pigsty!

Note

Note that the verb kochen can mean both 'to cook' and 'to boil':

sie kocht gut
she's a good cook
(lit. 'she cooks well')

er wird Kaffee kochen
he's going to make some coffee
(lit. 'to boil some coffee')

See also Sections

15 FOOD *and* **24 THE HOUSE.**

18 EINKAUFEN
SHOPPING

kaufen	to buy
kosten	to cost
ausgeben	to spend
umtauschen	to exchange
(be)zahlen	to pay
Wechselgeld herausgeben	to give change
verkaufen	to sell
einkaufen gehen	to go shopping
einkaufen	to do the shopping
ein Geschäft *(n)*	shop
ein Laden *(m)*	shop
eine Handlung	shop
ein Kunde, eine Kundin	customer
ein(e) Verkäufer(in)	shop assistant
ein Schnäppchen *(n)*	bargain
billig	cheap
preiswert	inexpensive
günstig	good value
teuer	expensive
gratis	free
kostenlos	free
zum Mitnehmen	to take away
reduziert	reduced
heruntergesetzt	reduced
im Sonderangebot	on special offer
gebraucht	second-hand
ausverkauft	sold out

der Umtausch	exchange
die Selbstbedienung	self-service
der Sonderpreis	special price
der Ausverkauf	clearance sale
die Geschäftszeiten	business hours
die Öffnungszeiten	opening times
geöffnet	open
geschlossen	closed

Geschäfte — shops

die Apotheke	(dispensing) chemist's
die Bäckerei	baker's
die Blumenhandlung	florist's
die Boutique	boutique
die Buchhandlung	bookshop
die chemische Reinigung	dry cleaner's
die Drogerie	chemist's
das Einkaufszentrum	shopping centre
der Feinkostladen	delicatessen
das Fischgeschäft	fishmonger's
die Fleischerei	butcher's
der Juwelierladen	jeweller's
das Kaufhaus	department store
der Kiosk	kiosk
die Konditorei	confectioner's and cake shop
das Lebensmittelgeschäft	grocer's
die Lederwarenhandlung	leather-goods shop
der Markt	market
die Metzgerei	butcher's
das Musikgeschäft	music shop, CD shop
die Obst- und Gemüsehandlung	greengrocer's
der Optiker	optician's
das Reisebüro	travel agent's
der Schnellimbiss	takeaway
die Schreibwarenhandlung	stationer's
der Schuhmacher	cobbler's

der Souvenirladen	souvenir shop
die Spielwarenhandlung	toy shop
das Sportgeschäft	sports shop
der Supermarkt	supermarket
der Süßwarenladen	confectioner's
der Tabakwarenladen	tobacconist's
die Tierhandlung	pet shop
das Warenhaus	department store
die Wäscherei	laundry
der Waschsalon	launderette
die Wein- und Spirituosenhandlung	off-licence
der Wohltätigkeitsladen	charity shop
der Zeitungsladen	newsagent's
eine Packung	packet
eine Dose	tin
eine Büchse	tin
ein Einkaufswagen *(m)*	trolley
ein Einkaufskorb *(m)*	shopping basket
eine Tasche	bag
eine Tüte	plastic/paper bag
die Einkäufe *(pl)*	shopping
das Onlineshopping	online shopping
eine Bestellung	order
eine Lieferung	delivery
die Theke	counter
der Ladentisch	counter
die Kasse	till
die Schlange	queue
der Preis	price
das Wechselgeld	(small) change
der Kassenzettel	receipt
eine Kreditkarte	credit card
eine PIN-Nummer	PIN code
eine Pay-back-Karte	reward card

eine Kundenkarte	loyalty card
die Abteilung	department
die Auswahl	selection, range
das Schaufenster	shop window
die Größe	size
die Gebrauchsanweisung	instructions for use

ich gehe einkaufen
I'm going shopping

das ist aber günstig!
that's a bargain!

was darf es sein?
can I help you?

was für Brot haben Sie?
what sort of bread do you have?

ich hätte gern zwei Pfund Äpfel
I'd like two pounds of apples please

sonst noch etwas?
will there be anything else?

danke, das ist alles
that's all, thank you

wie viel macht das?
how much is it?

das macht zusammen 30 Euro
that comes to 30 euros

haben Sie das Geld passend?
have you got the right change?

soll ich es als Geschenk einpacken?
do you want it gift-wrapped?

kann ich mit Kreditkarte bezahlen?
can I pay by credit cart?

ich mache gern einen Schaufensterbummel
I love window-shopping

ich kaufe meist im Internet
I do most of my shopping online

geben Sie Ihre Kartennummer ein
enter your card details

in den Warenkorb legen
add to basket

zur Kasse gehen
proceed to checkout

Inf **ich habe heute ein Vermögen ausgegeben!**
I've spent a fortune today!

See also Sections

2 CLOTHES AND FASHION, 9 JOBS AND WORK *and* **33 MONEY.**

19 DER SPORT
SPORT

trainieren	to exercise, to work out
fit werden	to get fit
sich fit halten	to keep fit
sich trimmen	to get into shape
sich aufwärmen	to warm up
sich abkühlen	to cool down
Liegestütze machen	to do press-ups
Bauchgymnastik machen	to do sit-ups
sich strecken	to stretch
laufen	to run
joggen	to jog
schwimmen	to swim
tauchen	to dive
springen	to jump
werfen	to throw
Ski laufen/fahren	to ski
zum Skilaufen gehen	to go skiing
Inliner fahren	to go rollerblading
Skateboard fahren	to skateboard
skateboarden	to skateboard
surfen	to surf
Snowboard fahren	to snowboard
snowboarden	to snowboard
fischen	to fish
angeln	to fish
trainieren	to train
üben	to practise
reiten	to ride
spielen	to play
auf die Jagd gehen	to go hunting

ein Tor (n) schießen	to score a goal
gewinnen	to win
verlieren	to lose
in Führung sein	to be in the lead
schlagen	to beat
einen neuen Rekord aufstellen	to set a new record
aufschlagen	to serve
schießen	to shoot
ein Profi (m)	professional
ein Amateur (m)	amateur

Sportarten — types of sport

das Aerobic	aerobics
der American Football	American football
das Angeln	fishing
das Badminton	badminton
das Ballett	ballet
der Basketball	basketball
das Bauchtanzen	belly dancing
das Bergsteigen	mountaineering
das Boxen	boxing
das Breakdancing	breakdancing
das Drachenfliegen	hang-gliding
das Eishockey	ice hockey
der Eiskunstlauf	figure skating
das Eisschießen	curling
der Extremsport	extreme sports
das Fallschirmspringen	parachuting
das Fechten	fencing
der Federball	badminton
das Fischen	fishing
das Fitnesstraining	fitness training
der Fußball	football
das Gesellschaftstanzen	ballroom dancing
das Gewichtheben	weight-lifting
das Golf	golf

der Handball	handball
der Hochsprung	high jump
das Hockey	hockey
das Inlineskating	rollerblading
das Jagen	hunting
der Jazztanz	jazz (dance)
das Jogging	jogging
das Judo	judo
das Kanufahren	canoeing
das Karate	karate
das Kickboxen	kick boxing
das Kricket	cricket
das Kugelstoßen	shot-put
das Laufen	running
die Leichtathletik	athletics
das Mountainbiking	mountain biking
das Pilates	pilates
das Radfahren	cycling
das Reiten	horse riding
das Ringen	wrestling
das Rudern	rowing
das Rugby	rugby
das Schießen	shooting
das Schlittschuhlaufen	skating
die Schwerathletik	weight-lifting, wrestling *etc*
das Schwimmen	swimming
das Segelfliegen	gliding
das Segeln	sailing
das Skateboarding	skateboarding
das Skifahren	skiing
der Skilanglauf	cross-country skiing
das Snowboarding	snowboarding
das Speerwerfen	javelin
das Squash	squash
der Stabhochsprung	pole vault
das Steppaerobic	step aerobics

das Steppen	tap dancing
das Tai-Chi	tai chi
das Tauchen	diving
das Tennis	tennis
das Tischtennis	table tennis
das Turnen	PE, gymnastics
der Volleyball	volleyball
das Wandern	rambling
der Wasserball	water polo
das Wasserski	water-skiing
der Weitsprung	long jump
das Windsurfen	windsurfing
der Wintersport	winter sports
das Yoga	yoga

Ausrüstung und Gerät · equipment

ein Ball *(m)*	ball
eine Kugel	bowl, ball *(small)*
die Sportkleidung	sportswear
eine Badekappe	swimming cap
eine Taucherbrille	swimming goggles
ein Schnorchel *(m)*	snorkel
Schwimmflossen *(pl)*	flippers
Turnschuhe *(pl)*	trainers
Fußballschuhe *(pl)*	football boots
Ballettschuhe *(pl)*	ballet shoes
ein Schweißleder *(n)*	sweatband
ein Sport-BH *(m)*	sports bra
Boxhandschuhe *(pl)*	boxing gloves
ein Helm *(m)*	helmet
Knieschützer *(pl)*	knee pads
Schienbeinschützer *(pl)*	shin pads
Gewichte *(pl)*	weights
der Barren	parallel bars
ein Tennisschläger *(m)*	tennis racket
ein Netz *(n)*	net

ein Schläger *(m)*	bat
ein Golfschläger *(m)*	golf club
eine Angel(rute)	fishing rod
ein Sattel *(m)*	saddle
ein Fahrrad *(n)*	bicycle
Rollerblades *(pl)*	Rollerblades®
Schlittschuhe *(pl)*	ice skates
Skier *(pl)*	skis
Skistiefel *(pl)*	ski boots
ein Skistock *(m)*	ski pole
ein Snowboard *(n)*	snowboard
ein Skateboard *(n)*	skateboard
ein Surfbrett *(n)*	surfboard
ein Kanu *(n)*	canoe
ein Ruderboot *(n)*	rowing boat
ein Segelboot *(n)*	sailing boat
eine Stoppuhr	stopwatch

Sportstätten — places

das Spielfeld	pitch, field
der Sportplatz	sports ground
ein Tennisplatz *(m)*	tennis court
ein Golfplatz *(m)*	golf course
ein Stadion *(n)*	stadium
der Ring	ring
eine Schlittschuhbahn	ice-rink
eine Skipiste	(ski) slope
ein Fahrradweg *(m)*	cycle track
ein Sportzentrum *(n)*	sports centre
ein Fitnessstudio *(n)*	gym
ein Studio *(n)*	studio
ein Schwimmbad *(n)*	swimming pool
ein Freibad *(n)*	open-air pool
ein Hallenbad *(n)*	indoor pool
eine Sauna	sauna
ein Dampfraum *(m)*	steam room
ein Whirlpool *(m)*	jacuzzi

eine Dusche	shower
der Umkleideraum	changing room
der Wettbewerb	**competition**
das Training	training
der Work-out	workout
das Aufwärmen	warm-up
das Abkühlen	cooldown
ein Team *(n)*	team
eine Mannschaft	team
der Sieger, die Siegerin	winner
der Verlierer, die Verliererin	loser
ein Rennen *(n)*	race
ein Spurt *(n)*	sprint
ein Spiel *(n)*	match, game
die Halbzeit	half-time
ein Tor *(n)*	goal
der Spielstand	score
das Ergebnis	result
ein Unentschieden *(n)*	draw
die Verlängerung	extra time
ein Freistoß *(m)*	free kick
der Elfmeter	penalty kick
das Elfmeterschießen	penalty shoot-out
das Golden Goal	golden goal
das Abseits	offside
eine Gelbe/Rote Karte	yellow/red card
ein Marathonlauf *(m)*	marathon
die Meisterschaft	championship
ein Turnier *(n)*	tournament
das Viertelfinale	quarter finals
das Halbfinale	semi-finals
das Endspiel	final
das Finale	final
der Rekord	record
der Weltrekord	world record
die Weltmeisterschaft	world cup

die Olympischen Spiele	Olympic Games
die Bundesliga	German Football League
eine Medaille	medal
ein Pokal *(m)*	cup, trophy

Teilnehmer — people

ein(e) Sportler(in)	sportsperson, athlete
ein Fußballspieler *(m)*	footballer
der Torwart	goalkeeper
ein Verteidiger *(m)*	defender
ein Stürmer *(m)*	striker
ein(e) Bergsteiger(in)	mountaineer
ein(e) Leichtathlet(in)	athlete
ein Boxer *(m)*	boxer
ein(e) Läufer(in)	runner
ein Radrennfahrer *(m)*	racing cyclist
ein(e) Radfahrer(in)	cyclist
ein(e) Tennisspieler(in)	tennis player
ein(e) Schlittschuhläufer(in)	ice-skater
ein(e) Eiskunstläufer(in)	figure-skater
ein(e) Inlineskater(in)	rollerblader
ein(e) Taucher(in)	diver
ein(e) Skifahrer(in)	skier
ein(e) Snowboarder(in)	snowboarder
ein(e) Surfer(in)	surfer

der Schiedsrichter	referee
der Trainer	manager
ein(e) Meister(in)	champion
ein(e) Rekordinhaber(in)	record holder
ein(e) Lehrer(in)	instructor
ein(e) Anhänger(in)	supporter
ein(e) Zuschauer(in)	spectator
ein Fan *(m)*	fan

er treibt viel Sport he does a lot of sport	**es steht eins zu null** the score is one-nil

die beiden Mannschaften haben unentschieden gespielt
the two teams drew

das Spiel musste verlängert werden
they had to go into extra time

auf die Plätze, fertig, los! on your marks, get set, go!	**Achtung, fertig, los!** ready, steady, go!

Inf **ich bin total geschafft** I'm shattered	*Inf* **wir haben sie fertiggemacht** we thrashed them

Inf **er hat einen tollen Waschbrettbauch**
he's got a great six-pack

Note

Note that 'to do/play sport' is translated using the verb treiben:
er treibt viel Sport
he does a lot of Sport

This verb can have various other meanings depending on the context, including 'to drive', 'to dig', 'to produce' or 'to get up to'.

 Homework help

My favourite sport is...
Mein Lieblingssport ist...

I like playing/watching...
ich spiele/sehe gern...

I'm good/not very good at sports. **ich bin gut/nicht sehr gut im Sport.**	
Some people... **Manche...**	find sport boring. **finden Sport langweilig.**
	say footballers get paid too much. **sagen, dass Fußballer zu viel verdienen.**
	don't do enough exercise. **treiben zu wenig Sport.**
I think... **Ich glaube, ...**	it's important to keep fit. **es ist wichtig, fit zu bleiben.**
	we should do more/less sport at school. **wir sollten in der Schule mehr/ weniger Sport treiben.**
However... **Aber...**	I don't have time to exercise. **ich habe keine Zeit, um Sport zu treiben.**
	we need better sports facilities. **wir brauchen bessere Sporteinrichtungen.**
	going to a gym is too expensive. **Fitnessstudios sind zu teuer.**
	I don't like competitive sports. **ich mag keinen Leistungssport.**

See also Section

2 CLOTHES AND FASHION.

LEISURE AND HOBBIES

sich interessieren für	to be interested in
sich amüsieren	to enjoy oneself
sich langweilen	to be bored
lesen	to read
zeichnen	to draw
malen	to paint
bauen	to build
machen	to make
fotografieren	to take photographs (of)
sammeln	to collect
kochen	to cook
nähen	to sew
stricken	to knit
Kreuzworträtsel lösen	to do crosswords
tanzen	to dance
singen	to sing
schauspielern	to act
spielen	to play
fernsehen	to watch TV
DVDs sehen	to watch DVDs
Videospiele spielen	to play video games
im Internet surfen	to surf the Internet
online chatten	to chat online
teilnehmen an *(+dat)*	to take part in
gewinnen	to win
verlieren	to lose
schlagen	to beat
wetten	to bet

Sport treiben	to keep fit
spazieren gehen	to go for walks
bummeln	to stroll
klettern	to climb
eine Radtour machen	to go for a bike ride
Rad fahren	to cycle
angeln gehen	to go fishing
Freiwilligenarbeit machen	to do voluntary work
Abendkurse besuchen	to go to evening classes
lernen	to learn
interessant	interesting
spannend	exciting
faszinierend	fascinating
langweilig	boring
ein Hobby *(n)*	hobby
ein Zeitvertreib *(m)*	pastime
die Freizeit	free time
ein Treffpunkt *(m)*	meeting place
ein Klub *(m)*	club
ein Verein *(m)*	club
ein Jugendklub *(m)*	youth club
die Pfadfinder *(pl)*	boy scouts/girl guides
ein Mitglied *(n)*	member *(male and female)*
das Lesen	reading
ein Buch *(n)*	book
ein Roman *(m)*	novel
ein Taschenbuch *(n)*	paperback
ein Comic(strip) *(m)*	(strip) cartoon
ein Magazin *(n)*	magazine
die Zeichnung	drawing
das Gemälde	painting
ein Pinsel *(m)*	brush
die Töpferei	pottery

das Heimwerken	DIY
der Modellbau	model-making
ein Hammer *(m)*	hammer
ein Schraubenzieher *(m)*	screwdriver
ein Nagel *(m)*	nail
eine Schraube	screw
ein Bohrer *(m)*	drill
eine Säge	saw
die Fotografie	photography
eine Kamera	camera
ein Fotoapparat *(m)*	camera
eine Digitalkamera	digital camera
ein Film *(m)*	film
ein Foto *(n)*	photograph
eine Videokamera	video camera
das Video	video
die Computertechnik	computing
ein Computer *(m)*	computer
Computerspiele *(pl)*	computer games
das Internet	Internet
eine Website	website
ein Chatroom *(m)*	chatroom
das Briefmarkensammeln	stamp collecting
eine Briefmarke	stamp
ein Album *(n)*	album, scrapbook
die Sammlung	collection
das Kochen	cooking
ein Rezept *(n)*	recipe
das Schneidern	dressmaking
die Nähmaschine	sewing machine
eine Nadel	needle
ein Faden *(m)*	thread
das Stricken	knitting
eine Stricknadel	knitting needle
das Theater	acting, drama
das Tanzen	dancing

das Ballett	ballet
die Musik	music
die klassische Musik	classical music
die Popmusik	pop music
der Gesang	singing
ein Lied *(n)*	song
ein Chor *(m)*	choir
das Klavier	piano
die Geige	violin
das Cello	cello
die Klarinette	clarinet
die Flöte	flute
die Blockflöte	recorder
eine Gitarre	guitar
das Schlagzeug	drums
ein Spiel *(n)*	game
ein Spielzeug *(n)*	toy
ein Brettspiel *(n)*	board game
das Schach	chess
das Damespiel	draughts
ein Puzzle *(n)*	jigsaw
Karten *(pl)*	cards
ein Kartenspiel *(n)*	game/deck of cards
ein Würfel *(m)*	dice
eine Wette	bet
ein Spaziergang	walk
eine Wanderung	hike
ein Ausflug *(m)*	excursion, outing
das Radfahren	cycling
das Fahrrad	bicycle
die Vogelbeobachtung	birdwatching
das Angeln	fishing

ich lese/stricke gern	**Klaus kann gut basteln**
I like reading/knitting	Klaus is good with his hands
Erika ist eine begeisterte Kinogängerin	
Erika is very keen on the cinema	
ich spiele Klavier	**du bist dran**
I play the piano	it's your turn
ich mache einen Abendkurs in Fotografie	
I'm taking an evening class in photography	
wir laden gern andere zu uns ein	*Inf* **er ist ein Computergenie**
we enjoy entertaining	he's a whizz with computers
Inf **sie treibt sich mit ihren Freundinnen herum**	
she's hanging out with her friends	

Note

Note that the reflexive verb sich interessieren is used with the preposition für:

ich interessiere mich für Kunst/Skifahren
I'm interested in art/skiing

See also Sections

19 SPORT, 21 MEDIA, 22 EVENINGS OUT, 39 COMPUTERS AND THE INTERNET *and* **46 CAMPING, CARAVANNING AND YOUTH HOSTELS.**

21 DIE MEDIEN

THE MEDIA

hören	to listen to
sehen	to watch
fernsehen	to watch television
lesen	to read
einschalten	to switch on
anmachen	to switch on
ausschalten	to switch off
ausmachen	to switch off
herunterladen	to download

das Radio

radio

ein Radio *(n)*	radio
das Digitalradio	digital radio
eine (Radio)sendung	(radio) broadcast, programme
Nachrichten *(pl)*	news
ein Interview *(n)*	interview
der Rundfunk	radio
ein Rundfunkquiz *(n)*	radio quiz
die Hitparade	charts
eine Single	single
ein Werbespot *(m)*	commercial
ein Jingle *(m)*	jingle
ein Discjockey *(m)*	DJ
ein(e) Moderator(in)	presenter
ein(e) Zuhörer(in)	listener
ein Sender *(m)*	station
die Frequenz	frequency

der Empfang	reception
eine Störung	interference
ein Piratensender *(m)*	pirate radio station
ein Podcast *(m)*	podcast

das Fernsehen

television

der Fernseher	TV, television set
das Fernsehgerät	television (set)
der Fernsehapparat	television (set)
der Bildschirm	screen
eine Antenne	aerial
eine Fernbedienung	remote control
der Kanal	channel
das Programm	channel
eine Sendung	programme
ein Programm *(n)*	programme
eine Livesendung	live broadcast
ein Studio *(n)*	studio
eine Nachrichtensendung	news bulletin
die Fernsehnachrichten *(pl)*	television news
die Tagesschau	television news
eine Eilmeldung	breaking news
ein Film *(m)*	film
ein Dokumentarbericht *(m)*	documentary
eine Fernsehserie	serial, soap opera
eine Sitcom	sitcom
eine Talkshow	chat show
eine Talentshow	talent show
eine Quizshow	quiz show
das Reality-TV	reality TV
eine Werbepause	commercial break
ein Werbespot *(m)*	commercial
ein Slogan *(m)*	slogan

ein Sponsor *(m)*	sponsor
ein(e) Nachrichten-sprecher(in)	newsreader
ein Fernsehstar *(m)*	TV star
ein(e) Zuschauer(in)	viewer
das Kabelfernsehen	cable TV
das Satellitenfernsehen	satellite TV
eine Satellitenschüssel	satellite dish
das Pay-per-View	pay-per-view
die Fernsehgebühr	TV licence
eine Fernsehzeitschrift	TV guide
ein DVD-Player	DVD player
eine DVD	DVD
ein Videorekorder *(m)*	video recorder
eine Videokassette	video

die Presse — press

eine Zeitung	newspaper
eine Tageszeitung	daily paper
eine Morgen-/Abendzeitung	morning/evening paper
eine Boulevardzeitung	tabloid
eine Gratiszeitung	free newspaper
eine Wochenzeitung	weekly
eine Illustrierte	magazine
eine Zeitschrift	magazine
ein Nachrichtenmagazin *(n)*	news magazine
ein Promimagazin *(n)*	celebrity magazine
eine Frauen-/Männerzeitschrift	women's/men's magazine
eine Jugendzeitschrift	teen magazine
ein Modemagazin *(n)*	fashion magazine
ein Comicheft *(n)*	comic
die Regenbogenpresse	popular press
eine Newssite	news site

21 Die Medien

ein(e) Journalist(in)	journalist
ein(e) Reporter(in)	reporter
Paparazzi *(pl)*	paparazzi
der Chefredakteur	editor-in-chief
die Titelseite	front page
eine Reportage	press report
ein Artikel *(m)*	article
Schlagzeilen *(pl)*	headlines
der Leitartikel	editorial
eine Rubrik	(regular) column
der Sportteil	sports section
der Kummerkasten	agony column
Kontaktanzeigen *(pl)*	lonely hearts column
eine Farbbeilage	colour supplement
die Reklame	advertisement, advertising
Kleinanzeigen *(pl)*	classified ads
die Onlinewerbung	online advertising
eine Pressekonferenz	press conference
eine Nachrichtenagentur	news agency

im Radio/Fernsehen **live aus Frankfurt**
on the radio/on television live from Frankfurt

'wir schalten um nach Köln'
'we're going over to Cologne'

was gibt es heute Abend im Fernsehen?
what's on television tonight?

im zweiten Programm läuft ein Film
there's a film on channel 2

die Flugzeugentführung kam in die Schlagzeilen
the hijacking made the headlines

 Homework help

I think... **Ich denke, ...**	there are too many reality shows on TV these days. **es gibt heutzutage im Fernsehen zu viele Realityshows.**
	there's too much violence on TV. **es wird zu viel Gewalt im Fernsehen gezeigt.**
	it's important to watch the news. **es ist wichtig, die Nachrichten anzusehen.**
Young people... **Junge Leute...**	don't watch the news. **sehen sich keine Nachrichten an.**
	watch too much television. **sehen zu viel fern.**
	get information on the Internet. **bekommen ihre Informationen im Internet.**
	spend a lot of money on magazines. **geben viel Geld für Zeitschriften aus.**

It annoys me when...
Es ärgert mich, wenn...

shows have lots of ad breaks.
Shows viele Werbepausen haben.

people keep channel-hopping.
Leute ständig umschalten.

some people don't care about what's happening in the world.
es manchen Leuten egal ist, was in der Welt geschieht.

22 ABENDUNTERHALTUNG
EVENINGS OUT

ausgehen	to go out
tanzen gehen	to go dancing
Clubs besuchen	to go clubbing
in die Kneipe gehen	to go to the pub
einen trinken gehen	to go for a drink
betrunken werden	to get drunk
auf eine Party gehen	to go to a party
eine Party machen	to have a party
eine Party feiern	to party
besuchen	to visit
jemanden treffen	to meet somebody
einladen	to invite
sich mit jemandem verabreden	to ask somebody out
jemanden anmachen	to chat somebody up
ein Date haben	to go on a date
geben	to give
reservieren	to book
applaudieren	to applaud
mitbringen	to bring
schenken	to give
begleiten	to accompany
bestellen	to order
empfehlen	to recommend
nach Hause gehen/kommen	to go/come home
allein	alone
zusammen	together

Veranstaltungen	shows
das Theater	theatre
ein Kostüm *(n)*	costume
die Bühne	stage
der Vorhang	curtain
das Parkett	stalls
der erste Rang	dress circle
die Loge	box
die Galerie	gods, balcony
die Reihe	row
die Pause	interval
ein Programm *(n)*	programme
eine Aufführung	show
ein Stück *(n)*	play
ein Schauspiel *(n)*	play
eine Komödie	comedy
eine Tragödie	tragedy
eine Oper	opera
ein Musical *(n)*	musical
ein Ballett *(n)*	ballet
ein Konzert *(n)*	concert
ein Rockkonzert *(n)*	rock concert
eine Vorstellung	performance
das Orchester	orchestra
das Feuerwerk	fireworks
das Publikum	audience
ein(e) Zuschauer(in)	audience member
ein(e) Platzanweiser(in)	usher
ein(e) Schauspieler(in)	actor/actress
ein(e) Tänzer(in)	dancer
der Dirigent	conductor
ein(e) Musiker(in)	musician

das Kino | the cinema

ein (Spiel)film *(m)*	film
ein Kino *(n)*	cinema
die Kasse	ticket office
die Vorstellung	showing
eine (Eintritts)karte	ticket
die Leinwand	screen
der Projektor	projector
ein Zeichentrickfilm *(m)*	cartoon
ein Horrorfilm *(m)*	horror film
ein Science-Fiction-Film *(m)*	science fiction film
ein Western *(m)*	Western
ein Krimi *(m)*	detective film
Untertitel *(pl)*	subtitles
ein(e) Regisseur(in)	director
ein Filmstar *(m)*	film star *(male and female)*

Tanz und Diskotheken | dances and clubs

ein Tanz *(m)*	dance
ein Tanzsaal *(m)*	dance hall
eine Diskothek	disco
ein Nachtklub *(m)*	(night)club
ein Klub *(m)*	club
ein Rave *(m)*	rave
eine Bar	bar
eine (Schall)platte	record
die Tanzfläche	dance floor
der Rock	rock-and-roll
eine Popgruppe	pop group
ein(e) Sänger(in)	singer
der Discjockey	DJ
Lautsprecher *(pl)*	speakers
Plattenteller *(pl)*	decks
der Rausschmeißer	bouncer
ein Ausweis *(m)*	ID
ein Handzettel *(m)*	flyer

essen gehen	**eating out**
ein Restaurant *(n)*	restaurant
ein Café *(n)*	café
eine Gaststätte	restaurant
ein Lokal *(n)*	pub
eine Kneipe	pub
eine Wirtschaft	pub
eine Imbissstube	snack bar
ein Schnellimbiss *(m)*	fast-food restaurant, takeaway
ein(e) Kellner(in)	waiter/waitress
der Oberkellner	head waiter
die Speisekarte	menu
die Weinkarte	wine list
die Rechnung	bill
das Trinkgeld	tip
ein Chinarestaurant *(n)*	Chinese restaurant
ein italienisches Restaurant	Italian restaurant
eine Pizzeria	pizzeria
Einladungen	**invitations**
Gäste *(pl)*	guests
der (die) Gastgeber(in)	host(ess)
ein Geschenk *(n)*	present
ein Drink *(m)*	drink
eine Party	party
eine Feier	celebration
der Geburtstag	birthday
das Privatleben	social life
ein Date *(n)*	date
eine Partneragentur	dating agency
die Partnersuche im Internet	online dating
das Speed Dating	speed dating
ein Singleabend *(m)*	singles' night
ein Anmachspruch *(m)*	chat-up line

Herr Ober, ich möchte zahlen waiter, can I pay please?	**Sonntags Ruhetag** 'closed on Sundays'
es ist ausverkauft it's sold out	**Zugabe!** encore!
hast du heute Abend schon etwas vor? are you doing anything tonight?	
bei ihr ist eine Party there's a party at her place	**möchten Sie mit mir tanzen?** would you like to dance?
sie haben ein sehr ausgefülltes Privatleben they've got a great social life	
Inf **er macht ständig Mädchen an** he's always chatting up girls	*Inf* **sie ist eine echte Partymaus** she's a real party animal

See also Section

15 FOOD.

der (Fuß)boden	floor
der Teppich	carpet
der Teppichboden	fitted carpet
die Decke	ceiling
die Tür	door
das Fenster	window
Vorhänge *(pl)*	curtains
Fensterläden *(pl)*	shutters
Jalousien *(pl)*	blinds
die Tapete	wallpaper

die Möbel — **furniture**

ein Möbelstück *(n)*	piece of furniture
das Bett	bed
ein Einzelbett *(n)*	single bed
ein Doppelbett *(n)*	double bed
ein Etagenbett *(n)*	bunk beds
zwei Einzelbetten *(pl)*	twin beds
ein Sofabett *(n)*	sofa bed
ein Futon *(m)*	futon
eine Matratze	mattress
ein Kopfkissen *(n)*	pillow
eine Nackenrolle	bolster
die Bettwäsche	bed linen
ein (Bett)laken *(n)*	sheet
die Bettdecke	blanket
das Federbett	duvet
eine Steppdecke	quilt
die Tagesdecke	bedspread
der Nachttisch	bedside table

die Kommode	chest of drawers
die Frisierkommode	dressing table
der Kleiderschrank	wardrobe
der Schrank	cupboard
der Schreibtisch	desk
ein Stuhl *(m)*	chair
ein Hocker *(m)*	stool
ein Sessel *(m)*	armchair
ein Sitzsack *(m)*	beanbag
Regale *(pl)*	shelves
ein Bücherregal *(n)*	bookcase

Gegenstände — objects

ein Schlafanzug *(m)*	pyjamas
ein Bademantel *(m)*	dressing gown
Hausschuhe *(pl)*	slippers
eine Wärmflasche	hot-water bottle
eine Lampe	lamp
eine Nachttischlampe	bedside lamp
der Lampenschirm	lampshade
ein Wecker *(m)*	alarm clock
ein Radiowecker *(m)*	radio alarm
eine Stereoanlage	stereo
ein Computer *(m)*	computer
ein Läufer *(m)*	rug
ein Kissen *(n)*	cushion
ein Poster *(n)*	poster
ein Plakat *(n)*	poster
ein Bild *(n)*	picture
ein Foto *(n)*	photo
ein Bilderrahmen *(m)*	picture frame
eine Kerze	candle
ein Spiegel *(m)*	mirror
ein großer Spiegel	full-length mirror
ein Buch *(n)*	book
ein Tagebuch *(n)*	diary

ein Spiel *(n)*	game
ein Spielzeug *(n)*	toy
ein Teddy *(m)*	teddy bear

> **es ist Zeit zum Aufstehen**
> it's time to get up
>
> **es ist Schlafenszeit**
> it's bedtime
>
> **er ist noch im Bett**
> he's still in bed

 ## Homework help

My room is big/small/tidy/messy. **Mein Zimmer ist groß/klein/aufgeräumt/unaufgeräumt.**	
My duvet/carpet is... **Meine Bettdecke/mein Teppich ist...**	My curtains/walls are... **Meine Vorhänge/Wände sind...**
The bed is next to... **Das Bett steht neben...**	Under the bed are... **Unter dem Bett sind...**
On the bed is... **Auf dem Bett ist...**	In the cupboard I have... **Im Schrank habe ich...**
The shelves are above... **Die Regale sind über...**	The desk is opposite... **Der Schreibtisch steht gegenüber...**
The TV is on top of... **Das Fernsehen steht auf...**	The lamp is on... **Die Lampe ist auf...**
The mirror is below... **Der Spiegel ist unter...**	My photos are in front of... **Meine Fotos sind vor...**
I keep... **Ich bewahre...**	my clothes in the wardrobe. **meine Kleider im Kleiderschrank auf.**

my books on a shelf.
meine Bücher auf einem Regal auf.

my toys under the bed.
mein Spielzeug unter dem Bett auf.

my CDs in a box.
meine CDs in einem Karton auf.

See also Sections

14 DAILY ROUTINE AND SLEEP *and* **24 THE HOUSE.**

24 DAS HAUS
THE HOUSE

wohnen	to live
umziehen	to move (house)
gelegen	situated
gemütlich	cosy, pleasant
die Miete	rent
die Hypothek	mortgage
der Eigentümer	owner
ein(e) Mieter(in)	tenant
ein(e) Mitbewohner(in)	housemate, flatmate
der Hausmeister	caretaker
der Möbelpacker	removal man
ein Haus *(n)*	house
ein Einfamilienhaus *(n)*	detached house
ein Bungalow *(m)*	bungalow
eine Villa	villa
ein Reihenhaus *(n)*	terraced house
ein Doppelhaus *(n)*	semi-detached
eine Wohnung	flat
eine Sozialwohnung	council flat
ein Altbau *(m)*	old house
ein Neubau *(n)*	new build
der Wohnblock	block of flats
ein Apartment *(n)*	studio flat
eine möblierte Wohnung	furnished flat

Teile des Hauses
parts of the house

das Souterrain	basement
das Erdgeschoss	ground floor

das Obergeschoss	upper storey
der erste Stock	first floor
der Dachboden	loft
der Keller	cellar
ein Zimmer *(n)*	room
die Ecke	corner
der Stock	floor, storey
die Etage	floor, storey
der Flur	landing
das Treppenhaus	staircase
die Treppe	stairs
eine Stufe	step
das Geländer	banisters
der Aufzug	lift
der Fahrstuhl	lift
eine Wand	wall
das Dach	roof
der Kamin	chimney; fireplace
das Kaminsims	mantelpiece
eine Tür	door
die Eingangstür	front door
die Hintertür	back door
ein Fenster *(n)*	window
eine Balkontür	French window
ein Dachfenster *(n)*	skylight
der Balkon	balcony
der Wintergarten	conservatory
die Garage	garage
innen	inside
außen	outside
oben	upstairs
unten	downstairs

die Zimmer — the rooms

die Diele	entrance, hall
der Flur	landing
die Küche	kitchen
das Esszimmer	dining room
das Wohnzimmer	living room, lounge
das Arbeitszimmer	study
das Schlafzimmer	bedroom
das Gästezimmer	spare room, guestroom
das Kinderzimmer	children's room
das Badezimmer	bathroom
das Bad	bathroom
die Toilette	toilet
das WC	toilet
das Klo	loo

die Möbel — furniture

eine Anrichte	dresser
ein Badezimmerschrank *(m)*	bathroom cabinet
ein Bücherregal *(n)*	bookcase
ein Kleiderschrank *(m)*	wardrobe
Regale *(pl)*	shelves
ein Schaukelstuhl *(m)*	rocking chair
ein Schrank *(m)*	cupboard
ein Schreibtisch *(m)*	desk
ein Sessel *(m)*	armchair
ein Sideboard *(n)*	sideboard
ein Sofa *(n)*	sofa
ein Stuhl *(m)*	chair
ein Tisch *(m)*	table

Gegenstände und Einrichtungen — objects and fittings

ein Abfalleimer *(m)*	bin
eine Antenne	aerial
ein Aschenbecher *(m)*	ashtray

eine Badematte	bathmat
eine Badewanne	bathtub
ein Bidet *(n)*	bidet
ein Bild *(n)*	picture
der Briefkasten	letterbox
die Dusche	shower
ein Foto *(n)*	photo
eine Fußmatte	doormat
die Garderobe	coat rack
der Hahn	tap
der Heizkörper	radiator
die Heizung	heating
Kacheln *(pl)*	tiles
der Kamin	fireplace
eine Kerze	candle
ein Kerzenhalter *(m)*	candlestick
ein Kissen *(n)*	cushion
eine Klinke	door-handle
ein Kohleofen *(m)*	coal-burning stove
eine Lampe	lamp
eine Glühbirne	lightbulb
ein Läufer *(m)*	rug
ein Papierkorb *(m)*	wastepaper basket
ein Poster *(n)*	poster
ein Rahmen *(m)*	frame
ein Schirmständer *(m)*	umbrella stand
ein Schlüssel *(m)*	key
das Schlüsselloch	keyhole
ein Spiegel *(m)*	mirror
die Spüle	kitchen sink
die Steckdose	socket
der Stecker	plug
eine Stehlampe	standard lamp
die Tapete	wallpaper
der Teppich(boden)	(fitted) carpet
ein Tisch *(m)*	table

die Türklingel	doorbell
eine Türklinke	door-handle
eine Vase	vase
Vorhänge *(pl)*	curtains
ein Waschbecken *(n)*	washbasin
die Zentralheizung	central heating
der Zierrat	ornament
Zimmerpflanzen *(pl)*	house plants
ein Telefon *(n)*	telephone
ein Radio *(n)*	radio
eine Stereoanlage	stereo
ein Tonbandgerät *(n)*	tape-recorder
eine CD	CD
eine Kassette	tape
eine (Schall)platte	record
ein Computer *(m)*	computer
ein DVD-Player *(m)*	DVD player
ein Videorekorder *(m)*	video (recorder)

der Garten — the garden

der Vorgarten	front garden
der Hof	yard
der Hinterhof	back yard
der Rasen	lawn
das Gras	grass
die Terrasse	terrace
ein Deck *(n)*	decking
Blumenbeete *(pl)*	flowerbeds
ein Gemüsebeet *(n)*	vegetable patch
ein Zaun *(m)*	fence
ein Gartenschuppen *(m)*	garden shed
ein Sonnenschirm *(m)*	parasol
ein Terrassenstrahler *(m)*	patio heater
ein Grill *(m)*	barbecue
ein Gartenzwerg *(m)*	garden gnome

ein Teich *(m)*	pond
ein Planschbecken *(n)*	paddling pool
eine Schaukel	swings
ein Rasenmäher *(m)*	lawnmower
eine Gießkanne	watering can
ein Schlauch *(m)*	hose

sie hat eine Sozialwohnung she lives in a council flat	*Inf* **sie haben eine** **Riesenwohnung** their place is massive

 Homework help

I live in a house/a flat.
Wir haben ein Haus/eine Wohnung.

Our house is big/small/old/modern.
Unser Haus ist groß/klein/alt/modern.

In our house we have...
In unserem Haus haben wir...

Upstairs/downstairs there is...
Oben/unten gibt es...

The living room is next to...
Das Wohnzimmer ist neben...

My bedroom is above...
Mein Zimmer ist über...

The bathroom is opposite...
Das Badezimmer ist gegenüber...

See also Sections

8 IDENTITY AND AGE, 17 HOUSEWORK *and* **23 MY ROOM.**

25 DIE STADT
THE CITY

eine Stadt	town, city
eine Großstadt	big city
eine Kleinstadt	small town
ein Dorf (n)	village
ein Ort (m)	place
ein Stadtteil (m)	district, part of town
eine Vorstadt	suburbs, outskirts
ein Vorort (m)	suburb
ein Bezirk (m)	area
ein Viertel (n)	district, part of town
das Industriegebiet	industrial area
die Wohngegend	residential district
ein Slum (m)	slum
die Altstadt	old town
die Stadtmitte	town/city centre
die City	city centre
die Umgebung	surroundings
eine Allee	avenue
eine Baustelle	building site
eine Fußgängerzone	pedestrian precinct
eine Gasse	narrow street
eine Geschäftsstraße	shopping street
die Hauptstraße	main road, high street
ein Kreisverkehr (m)	roundabout
ein Platz (m)	square
eine Sackgasse	cul-de-sac
eine Unterführung	underpass, subway
eine Stadtautobahn	expressway

eine Straße	road, street
eine Umgehungsstraße	ring road
ein Stadtplan *(m)*	street map
die Fahrbahn	road
der Bürgersteig	pavement
ein Parkplatz *(m)*	car park
ein Parkhaus *(n)*	multi-storey car park
eine Tiefgarage	underground car park
eine Park-and-ride-Anlage	park-and-ride
ein Park *(m)*	park
ein Friedhof *(m)*	cemetery
eine Brücke	bridge
der Marktplatz	market place
die Stadtmauer	city walls
der Hafen	harbour
der Flughafen	airport
der Bahnhof	railway station
ein Busbahnhof *(m)*	bus station
eine U-Bahn-Station	underground station
belebt	busy
lebhaft	lively
überfüllt	overcrowded
friedlich	peaceful
verschmutzt	polluted
sauber	clean
gefährlich	dangerous
sicher	safe

Gebäude

buildings

ein Haus *(n)*	house, building
ein Gebäude *(n)*	building
ein Hochhaus *(n)*	high-rise
ein Wolkenkratzer *(m)*	skyscraper

ein Wahrzeichen *(n)*	landmark
das Rathaus	town hall
der Gerichtshof	Law Courts
das Fremdenverkehrsbüro	tourist information office
das Verkehrsamt	tourist office
das Postamt	post office
die Post	post office
eine Bücherei	library
eine Polizeiwache	police station
das Polizeipräsidium	police headquarters
die Feuerwache	fire station
eine Schule	school
eine Oberschule	high school
eine Universität	university
ein Gefängnis *(n)*	prison
eine Fabrik	factory
ein Bürogebäude *(n)*	office block
ein Krankenhaus *(n)*	hospital
ein Altenheim *(n)*	old people's home
das Jugendzentrum	youth centre
das Arbeitsamt	job centre, employment office
ein Hotel *(n)*	hotel
ein Theater *(n)*	theatre
ein Kino *(n)*	cinema
die Oper	opera house
ein Museum *(n)*	museum
eine Galerie	art gallery
ein Schloss *(n)*	castle
eine Burg	castle
ein Turm *(m)*	tower
eine Kathedrale	cathedral
ein Dom *(m)*	cathedral
eine Kirche	church
ein Kirchturm *(m)*	church tower, steeple
eine Kapelle	chapel
ein Tempel *(m)*	temple

eine Moschee	mosque
eine Synagoge	synagogue
ein Denkmal *(n)*	memorial, monument
ein Kriegerdenkmal *(n)*	war memorial
eine Statue	statue
ein Brunnen *(m)*	fountain

Menschen — people

ein(e) Städter(in)	city dweller
ein(e) Einwohner(in)	inhabitant
ein Einheimischer, eine Einheimische	local
ein(e) Immigrant(in)	immigrant
ein(e) Passant(in)	passer-by
ein(e) Pendler(in)	commuter
ein Stadtstreicher *(m)*	tramp

---

sie wohnt in der Stadt/am Stadtrand
she lives in town/in the suburbs

wir gehen in die Stadt
we're going into town

die Stadt München
the city of Munich

Inf **die Straßen waren brechend voll**
the streets were heaving

Inf **sie wohnen am Ende der Welt**
they live in the middle of nowhere

Inf **sei vorsichtig, dort herrschen raue Sitten**
be careful, it's a rough area

 Homework help

I live in... **Ich wohne in...**	It's near... **Es ist in der Nähe von...**
It's famous for... **Es ist berühmt für...**	You should go to... **Du solltest nach ... gehen**

My town is big/small/pretty.
Meine Stadt ist groß/klein/hübsch.

> ## Note
>
> There are two words for 'castle' in German: die Burg refers to
> a medieval fortress, while das Schloss is more like a palace or
> 'fairytale castle'.
>
> There are also two words for 'cathedral': der Dom is the most
> commonly used for German cathedrals, while die Kathedrale tends
> to be used for French, Spanish or British ones.

See also Sections

**18 SHOPPING, 22 EVENINGS OUT, 26 CARS, 44 PUBLIC
TRANSPORT, 48 GEOGRAPHICAL TERMS** *and* **66 DIRECTIONS.**

26 AUTOS
CARS

fahren	to drive, to go *(car)*
sich anschnallen	to put one's seat belt on
starten	to start (up)
schneller fahren	to drive faster
langsamer fahren	to slow down
bremsen	to brake
beschleunigen	to accelerate
anhalten	to stop
parken	to park
abschließen	to lock
abbiegen	to turn off
überholen	to overtake
wenden	to do a U-turn
das Licht einschalten	to switch on one's lights
das Licht ausschalten	to switch off one's lights
die Lichthupe betätigen	to flash one's headlights
überqueren	to cross, to go through
überprüfen	to check
Abstand halten	to keep one's distance
Vorfahrt gewähren *(+dat)*	to give way
Vorfahrt haben	to have right of way
hupen	to hoot
schleudern	to skid
abschleppen	to tow
reparieren	to repair
eine Panne haben	to break down
kein Benzin mehr haben	to run out of petrol
volltanken	to fill up
ein Rad wechseln	to change a wheel

sich strafbar machen	to commit an offence
einen Strafzettel bekommen	to get a ticket
einen Strafzettel wegen Falschparken bekommen	to get a parking ticket
einen Strafzettel wegen Geschwindigkeitsüberschreitung bekommen	to get a speeding ticket
eine rote Ampel überfahren	to jump a red light
ein Stoppschild nicht beachten	to ignore a stop sign
langsam	slow
schnell	fast
erlaubt	allowed
verboten	forbidden
untersagt	prohibited

Fahrzeuge — vehicles

ein Auto *(n)*	car
ein Wagen *(m)*	car
ein Pkw *(m)*	car
ein Fahrzeug *(n)*	vehicle
ein Automatikwagen *(m)*	automatic
ein Auto *(n)* mit Handschaltung	manual car
eine Klapperkiste	old banger
ein Gebrauchtwagen *(m)*	second-hand car
ein zweitüriger/viertüriger Wagen *(m)*	two-/four-door car
ein Kombi(wagen) *(m)*	estate car
eine Limousine	saloon
ein Kabriolett *(n)*	convertible
ein Rennauto *(n)*	racing car
ein Sportwagen *(m)*	sports car
ein Hybridauto *(n)*	hybrid car
ein Leihwagen *(m)*	rented car
ein Wagen *(m)* mit Rechtssteuerung/Linkssteuerung	right-/left-hand drive car
das Modell	model

das Fabrikat	make
ein Lastwagen *(m)*	lorry
ein Lkw *(m)*	lorry
ein Sattelschlepper *(m)*	articulated lorry
ein Lieferwagen *(m)*	van
ein Motorrad *(n)*	motorbike
ein Moped *(n)*	moped
ein Mofa *(n)*	small moped
ein Motorroller *(m)*	scooter

Verkehrsteilnehmer road users

der Fahrer, die Fahrerin	driver
ein(e) Autofahrer(in)	motorist
ein Verkehrsrowdy *(m)*	reckless driver
ein(e) Fahrschüler(in)	learner driver
ein(e) Mitfahrer(in)	passenger
ein(e) Lastwagenfahrer(in)	lorry driver
ein(e) Lkw-Fahrer(in)	lorry driver
ein(e) Motorradfahrer(in)	motorcyclist
ein(e) Radfahrer(in)	cyclist
ein(e) Anhalter(in)	hitch-hiker
ein(e) Tramper(in)	hitch-hiker
ein(e) Fußgänger(in)	pedestrian

Autoteile car parts

die Antenne	aerial
das Armaturenbrett	dashboard
der Auspuff	exhaust
das Autoradio	car radio
die Batterie	battery
die Benzinuhr	petrol gauge
der Blinker	indicator
Bremsen *(pl)*	brakes
der Dachgepäckträger	roof rack
der Ersatzreifen	spare wheel
ein Ersatzteil *(n)*	spare part
das Fenster	window

Gänge *(pl)*	gears
der erste Gang	first gear
der zweite Gang	second gear
der dritte Gang	third gear
der vierte Gang	fourth gear
der fünfte Gang	fifth gear
der Rückwärtsgang	reverse
der Leerlauf	neutral
das Gaspedal	accelerator
der Geschwindigkeitsmesser	speedometer
das Getriebe	gears
die Handbremse	handbrake
die Hupe	horn
die Karosserie	body
der Kofferraum	boot
der Kühler	radiator
die Kupplung	clutch
das Lenkrad	steering wheel
der Motor	engine
die Motorhaube	bonnet
das Nummernschild	number plate
das Pedal	pedal
ein Rad *(n)*	wheel
eine Radkappe	hub cap
der Reifen	tyre
Rücklichter *(pl)*	rear lights
der Rücksitz	back seat
der Rückspiegel	(rearview) mirror
ein Satellitennavigationssystem *(n)*	satnav
der Schalthebel	gear lever
ein Scheibenwischer *(m)*	windscreen wiper
das Schloss	lock
der Seitenspiegel	wing mirror
der Sicherheitsgurt	seat belt
das Standlicht	sidelights

die Stoßstange	bumper
der Tank	tank
die Tür	door
das Verdeck	hood, soft top
der Vordersitz	front seat
der Wagenheber	jack
die Windschutzscheibe	windscreen
die Zündung	ignition
das Benzin	petrol
das Super(benzin)	four-star (petrol)
das bleifreie Benzin	unleaded petrol
der Kraftstoff	fuel
das Diesel	diesel
das Öl	oil
das Frostschutzmittel	antifreeze

Schwierigkeiten — problems

die Reparatur	repair
eine (Reparatur)werkstatt	garage
eine Tankstelle	petrol station
eine SB-Tankstelle	self-service petrol station
die Zapfsäule	petrol pump
der Tankwart	petrol pump attendant
der Kfz-Mechaniker	car mechanic
die Versicherung	insurance
die Versicherungspolice	insurance policy
eine Vollkaskoversicherung	comprehensive insurance
eine Teilkaskoversicherung	third-party insurance
der Führerschein	driving licence
der Fahrzeugschein	registration document
die grüne Karte	green card *(insurance)*
die Straßenverkehrsordnung	Highway Code
eine Fahrstunde	driving lesson
die Fahrprüfung	driving test
der Verkehrsunfall	road accident

eine Beule	dent
die Geschwindigkeit	speed
die Geschwindigkeits-überschreitung	speeding
ein Blitzer *(m)*	speed camera
ein Vergehen *(n)*	offence
ein Strafzettel *(m)*	parking ticket
eine Geldbuße	fine
die Vorfahrt	right of way
das Parkverbot	no parking (area)
ein Parkschein *(m)*	carpark ticket
eine Einfahrt	entrance
die Reifenpanne	flat tyre
die Panne	breakdown
der ADAC	breakdown service, AA
ein Abschleppwagen *(m)*	breakdown lorry
ein Stau *(m)*	traffic jam
die Umleitung	diversion
die Straßenbauarbeiten *(pl)*	roadworks
das Glatteis	black ice
ein Loch *(n)*	(pot)hole
die Sicht	visibility

Straßenführung   routes

der Verkehr	traffic
die Straßenkarte	road map
die Straße	road
die Hauptverkehrsstraße	main road
die Nebenstraße	B road
eine Autobahn	motorway
die Umgehungsstraße	bypass
eine Landstraße	country road
der Bürgersteig	pavement
die Ampel	traffic lights
ein Verkehrszeichen *(n)*	road sign
eine Einbahnstraße	one-way street

ein Stoppschild (n)	stop sign
ein Fußgängerüberweg (m)	pedestrian crossing
ein Zebrastreifen (m)	zebra crossing
ein Bahnübergang (m)	level crossing
die Kurve	bend
die Kreuzung	crossroads
der Kreisverkehr	roundabout
ein Autobahndreieck (n)	motorway junction
die Spur	lane
eine Busspur	bus lane
ein Fahrradweg (m)	cycle lane
der Mittelstreifen	central reservation
die Ausfahrt	exit
die Gebühr	toll
eine Raststätte	service area
eine Parkuhr	parking meter
ein Parkplatz (m)	parking place
ein(e) Verkehrspolizist(in)	traffic police officer
eine Politesse	traffic warden
ein Schülerlotse (m)	lollipop man/lady

---

welches Fabrikat ist es?
what make is it?

es ist ein Volkswagen
it's a Volkswagen

schalten Sie in den dritten Gang!
change into third gear!

der Motor ist kaputt
the engine's had it

sie fuhr 100 Kilometer in der Stunde
she was doing 62 miles an hour

in England fährt man links
in England they drive on the left

bei Rot/Gelb/Grün
on a red/amber/green light

ihm ist der Führerschein entzogen worden
he lost his driving licence

Sie haben sich verfahren you've gone the wrong way	**ich hole dich um 5 Uhr ab** I'll pick you up at 5

fahren Sie bis zur dritten Querstraße rechts
drive on to the third turning on the right

'Anlieger frei' 'residents only'	**'Schritt fahren'** 'drive at walking speed'

wir haben einen Anhalter mitgenommen
we picked up a hitch-hiker

Inf **du fährst wie ein** **Wahnsinniger!** you drive like a maniac!	*Inf* **der Verkehr war mörderisch** the traffic was murder

Inf **sie fährt immer noch diese alte Kiste**
she's still driving that old banger

See also Section

53 ACCIDENTS.

27 DIE NATUR
NATURE

die Landschaft	landscape
das Land	countryside
ein Feld *(n)*	field
eine Wiese	meadow
ein Wald *(m)*	forest, wood
ein Obstgarten *(m)*	orchard
ein Gebirge *(n)*	mountains
die Heide	heath
das Moor	moor
ein Sumpf *(m)*	marsh
ein Tal *(n)*	valley
eine Wüste	desert
der Dschungel	jungle
Pflanzen	plants
wachsen	to grow
blühen	to flower, to bloom
verdorren	to wither
sterben	to die
eine Pflanze	plant
ein Baum *(m)*	tree
ein Strauch *(m)*	shrub
ein Busch *(m)*	bush
die Wurzel	root
der Stamm	trunk
ein Ast *(m)*	branch
ein Zweig *(m)*	twig
eine Knospe	bud
eine Blume	flower

eine Blüte	blossom
ein Blatt *(n)*	leaf
die Rinde	bark
der Wipfel	treetop
ein Tannenzapfen *(m)*	fir cone
eine Kastanie	horse chestnut
eine Eichel	acorn
eine Beere	berry
ein Pilz *(m)*	mushroom
ein Giftpilz *(m)*	poisonous mushroom
Algen *(pl)*	seaweed
das Heidekraut	heather
ein Pilz *(m)*	mushroom
der Farn	ferns
das Gras	grass
die Mistel	mistletoe
die Stechpalme	holly
der Efeu	ivy
das Unkraut	weeds
das Moos	moss
der Rhododendron	rhododendron
das Schilf	reeds
der Klee	clover
der Weinstock	vine

Bäume trees

ein Laubbaum *(m)*	deciduous tree
ein immergrüner Baum *(m)*	evergreen
ein Nadelbaum *(m)*	conifer
ein Ahorn *(m)*	maple tree
eine Birke	birch
eine Buche	beech
eine Eibe	yew tree
eine Eiche	oak tree
eine Kastanie	chestnut tree

eine Kiefer	pine tree
eine Pappel	poplar
eine Rosskastanie	horse chestnut tree
eine Tanne	fir tree
eine Trauerweide	weeping willow
eine Ulme	elm

Obstbäume

fruit trees

ein Apfelbaum *(m)*	apple tree
ein Aprikosenbaum *(m)*	apricot tree
ein Birnbaum *(m)*	pear tree
ein Brombeerstrauch *(m)*	blackberry bush
eine Erdbeerpflanze	strawberry plant
ein Himbeerstrauch *(m)*	raspberry bush
ein Kirschbaum *(m)*	cherry tree
ein Olivenbaum *(m)*	olive tree
ein Pflaumenbaum *(m)*	plum tree
ein Roter Johannisbeerstrauch *(m)*	redcurrant bush
ein Schwarzer Johannisbeerstrauch *(m)*	blackcurrant bush
ein Stachelbeerstrauch *(m)*	gooseberry bush

Blumen

flowers

der Stiel	stem
die Blüte	blossom
ein Blütenblatt *(n)*	petal
der Pollen	pollen
eine Butterblume	buttercup
eine Chrysantheme	chrysanthemum
der Flieder	lilac
ein Gänseblümchen *(n)*	daisy
das Geißblatt	honeysuckle
eine Geranie	geranium
eine Hyazinthe	hyacinth
die Iris	iris
der Jasmin	jasmine

eine Kornblume	cornflower
ein Krokus *(m)*	crocus
der Löwenzahn	dandelion
das Maiglöckchen	lily of the valley
eine Mohnblume	poppy
eine Nelke	carnation
eine Orchidee	orchid
eine Osterglocke	daffodil
eine Petunie	petunia
eine Primel	primrose
eine Rose	rose
ein Schneeglöckchen *(n)*	snowdrop
ein Stiefmütterchen *(n)*	pansy
eine Tulpe	tulip
ein Veilchen *(n)*	violet
ein Vergissmeinnicht *(n)*	forget-me-not
der Weißdorn	hawthorn

---

die Rosen fangen gerade an zu blühen
the roses are just coming into blossom

die Kirschbäume stehen in voller Blüte
the cherry trees are in full bloom

komm, wir gehen Pilze sammeln
let's go and pick some
mushrooms

wir pflückten Gänseblümchen
we went to pick daisies

See also Sections

**15 FOOD, 28 ANIMALS, 29 THE ENVIRONMENT, 47 AT THE
SEASIDE** *and* **48 GEOGRAPHICAL TERMS.**

28 TIERE

ANIMALS

bellen	to bark
miauen	to miaow
schnurren	to purr
knurren	to growl
grunzen	to grunt
muhen	to moo
wiehern	to neigh
blöken	to bleat
quieken	to squeak
zwitschern	to twitter
gackern	to cluck
krähen	to crow
fressen	to eat *(subj: animal)*
das Futter	food *(for animals)*
der Lebensraum	habitat
ein Nest *(n)*	nest
ein Bau *(m)*	burrow
ein Loch *(n)*	hole
ein Zwinger *(m)*	kennel
ein Käfig *(m)*	cage
ein Stall *(m)*	hutch
ein Becken *(n)*	tank

Haustiere — pets

ein Tier *(n)*	animal
ein Haustier *(n)*	pet
eine Katze	cat
ein Kater *(m)*	tom cat

ein Hund *(m)*	dog
ein Kaninchen *(n)*	rabbit
ein Meerschweinchen *(n)*	guinea pig
ein Hamster *(m)*	hamster
eine Rennmaus	gerbil
ein Goldfisch *(m)*	goldfish
Tropenfische *(pl)*	tropical fish
ein Wellensittich *(m)*	budgie

Tiere auf dem Bauernhof — farm animals

das Vieh	cattle
eine Kuh	cow
ein Bulle *(m)*	bull
ein Ochse *(m)*	ox
ein Kalb *(n)*	calf
ein Schaf *(n)*	sheep
ein Schafbock *(m)*	ram
ein Lamm *(n)*	lamb
eine Ziege	nanny goat
ein Ziegenbock *(m)*	billy goat
ein Schwein *(n)*	pig
ein Pferd *(n)*	horse
ein Esel *(m)*	donkey
ein Maultier *(n)*	mule
ein Hahn *(m)*	cockerel
ein Huhn *(n)*	chicken, hen
ein Küken *(n)*	chick
eine Ente	duck
eine Gans	goose
ein Truthahn *(m)*	turkey

wilde Tiere — wild animals

ein Säugetier *(m)*	mammal
ein Fisch *(m)*	fish
Reptilien *(pl)*	reptiles
ein Fleischfresser *(m)*	carnivore

ein Pflanzenfresser *(m)*	herbivore
ein Allesfresser *(m)*	omnivore
ein Wirbeltier *(n)*	vertebrate
ein Wirbelloser *(m)*	invertebrate
ein Bein *(n)*	leg
ein Huf *(n)*	hoof
eine Pfote	paw
das Maul	mouth
der Schwanz	tail
eine Mähne	mane
der Rüssel	trunk
die Schnauze	muzzle, snout
Krallen *(pl)*	claws
Hörner *(pl)*	horns
das Fell	skin, fur
der Pelz	fur
ein Zoo *(m)*	zoo
ein Tierpark *(m)*	zoo
ein Affe *(m)*	monkey
eine Antilope	antelope
ein Bär *(m)*	bear
ein Biber *(m)*	beaver
ein Büffel *(m)*	buffalo
ein Delfin *(m)*	dolphin
ein Eber *(m)*	boar
ein Eichhörnchen *(n)*	squirrel
ein Eisbär *(m)*	polar bear
ein Elefant *(m)*	elephant
ein Fuchs *(m)*	fox
eine Giraffe	giraffe
ein Gorilla *(m)*	gorilla
ein Hai *(m)*	shark
ein Hase *(m)*	hare
ein Hirsch *(m)*	stag, deer
ein Igel *(m)*	hedgehog

ein Kamel *(n)*	camel
ein Känguru *(n)*	kangaroo
ein Koalabär *(m)*	koala
ein Leopard *(m)*	leopard
ein Löwe, eine Löwin	lion
ein Maulwurf *(m)*	mole
eine Maus	mouse
ein Nashorn *(n)*	rhinoceros
ein Nilpferd *(n)*	hippopotamus
ein Orang-Utan *(m)*	orang-utan
eine Ratte	rat
eine Robbe	seal
ein Schimpanse *(m)*	chimpanzee
ein Tiger *(m)*	tiger
ein Tintenfisch *(m)*	octopus
ein Wal *(m)*	whale
ein Wiesel *(n)*	weasel
ein Wolf, eine Wölfin	wolf
ein Zebra *(n)*	zebra

Reptilien — reptiles

ein Krokodil *(n)*	crocodile
ein Alligator *(m)*	alligator
eine Schildkröte	tortoise
eine Wasserschildkröte	turtle
ein Frosch *(m)*	frog
eine Kröte	toad
eine Kaulquappe	tadpole
eine Schlange	snake
eine Klapperschlange	rattlesnake
eine Ringelnatter	grass snake
eine Otter	adder
eine Kobra	cobra
eine Boa	boa
ein Wurm *(m)*	worm
ein Aal *(m)*	eel

eine Eidechse	lizard
ein Dinosaurier *(m)*	dinosaur

Vögel — birds

ein Vogel *(m)*	bird
ein Raubvogel *(m)*	bird of prey
der Fuß	foot
Krallen *(pl)*	claws
Klauen *(pl)*	claws
der Flügel	wing
der Schnabel	beak
eine Feder	feather
ein Adler *(m)*	eagle
eine Amsel	blackbird
eine Blaumeise	bluetit
eine Drossel	thrush
eine Elster	magpie
eine Eule	owl
ein Falke *(m)*	falcon
ein Fasan *(m)*	pheasant
ein Flamingo *(m)*	flamingo
ein Geier *(m)*	vulture
ein Kanarienvogel *(m)*	canary
eine Krähe	crow
ein Kuckuck *(m)*	cuckoo
eine Lerche	lark
eine Möwe	seagull
eine Nachtigall	nightingale
ein Papagei *(m)*	parrot
ein Pfau *(m)*	peacock
ein Pinguin *(m)*	penguin
ein Reiher *(m)*	heron
ein Rotkehlchen *(n)*	robin
eine Schwalbe	swallow
ein Schwan *(m)*	swan
ein Spatz *(m)*	sparrow

ein Star *(m)*	starling
ein Storch *(m)*	stork
ein Strauß *(m)*	ostrich
eine Taube	dove; pigeon
ein Uhu *(m)*	owl

Insekten · insects

eine Ameise	ant
eine Biene	bee
eine Fliege	fly
ein Floh *(m)*	flea
eine Heuschrecke	grasshopper
eine Hornisse	hornet
eine Küchenschabe	cockroach
ein Marienkäfer *(m)*	ladybird
ein Moskito *(m)*	mosquito
eine Motte	moth
eine Mücke	midge
eine Raupe	caterpillar
ein Schmetterling *(m)*	butterfly
eine Schnake	daddy-long-legs
eine Spinne	spider
ein Tausendfüßler *(m)*	centipede
eine Wespe	wasp

See also Sections

27 NATURE *and* **29 THE ENVIRONMENT.**

29 DIE UMWELT
THE ENVIRONMENT

verschmutzen	to pollute
zerstören	to destroy
fällen	to chop down
schmilzen	to melt
verbrennen	to burn
recyceln	to recycle
wiederverwenden	to reuse
grün sein	to be green
wegwerfen	to throw away
den Müll sortieren	to sort one's rubbish
ein Regenwald *(m)*	rainforest
die Eisdecke	ice cap
das Ökosystem	ecosystem
die Ozonschicht	ozone layer
ein(e) Umweltschützer(in)	conservationist
ein(e) Umweltaktivist(in)	environmental campaigner
eine Pressure-Group	pressure group
ein(e) Aktivist(in)	activist
ein Grüner, eine Grüne	Green
ein(e) Ökokrieger(in)	ecowarrior
umweltfreundlich	environmentally friendly

Probleme
problems

die Umweltverschmutzung	pollution
eine Umweltkatastrophe	environmental disaster
ein vom Aussterben bedrohte Art *(n)*	endangered species

der saure Regen	acid rain
eine Ölkatastrophe	oil spill
der Smog	smog
die Entwaldung	deforestation
ein Waldbrand *(m)*	forest fire
die Erderwärmung	global warming
der Klimawechsel	climate change
der Treibhauseffekt	greenhouse effect
Treibhausgase *(pl)*	greenhouse gases
der Kohlendioxidausstoß	carbon emissions
fossile Brennstoffe *(pl)*	fossil fuels
die Atomenergie	nuclear power
eine Mülldeponie	landfill site
das Aerosol	aerosol
der FCKW	CFC
ein Pestizid *(n)*	pesticide

Lösungen solutions

das Recycling	recycling
ein Altglascontainer *(m)*	bottle bank
eine erneuerbare Energiequelle	renewable energy
das unverbleite Benzin	unleaded petrol
der Umweltschutz	conservation
der ökologische Anbau	organic farming
eine Windfarm	wind farm
die Sonnenenergie	solar power
Sonnenkollektoren *(pl)*	solar panels

---

ich interessiere mich sehr für Umweltthemen
I'm very interested in green issues

wir müssen den Kohlendioxidausstoß verringern
we need to cut carbon emissions

der Mensch zerstört die Erde
Man is destroying the planet

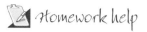 *Homework help*

Many people are concerned about... **Viele machen sich Sorgen über...**	climate change. **den Klimawandel.**
	the greenhouse effect. **den Treibhauseffekt.**
	the destruction of the rainforests. **die Zerstörung der Regenwälder.**
	pollution. **die Umweltverschmutzung.**
	nuclear power. **die Atomkraft.**
We need to... **Wir müssen**	save the planet. **die Erde retten.**
	save energy. **Energie sparen.**
	protect wildlife. **die Tierwelt schützen.**
	cut pollution. **die Umweltverschmutzung verringern.**
People should... **Die Menschen sollten...**	sort their rubbish. **ihren Müll sortieren.**
	recycle more. **mehr recyceln.**
	turn out the lights to save energy. **das Licht ausmachen, um Energie zu sparen.**
	drive smaller cars. **kleinere Autos fahren.**

	take fewer flights. **weniger fliegen.**
	eat organic food. **Biokost essen.**
Otherwise... **Sonst...**	we will run out of fuel. **geht uns der Brennstoff aus.**
	animals will become extinct. **werden Tiere aussterben.**
	there will be floods/droughts. **gibt es Überschwemmungen/ Dürrekatastrophen.**
	people will get ill/die. **werden die Menschen krank werden/sterben.**

See also Sections

27 NATURE, 28 ANIMALS, 34 TOPICAL ISSUES *and*
48 GEOGRAPHICAL TERMS.

30 WIE IST DAS WETTER?
WHAT'S THE WEATHER LIKE?

das Wetter	the weather
regnen	to rain
in Strömen regnen	to be pouring with rain
nieseln	to drizzle
schneien	to snow
hageln	to hail
frieren	to be freezing
tauen	to thaw
wehen	to blow
scheinen	to shine
schmelzen	to melt
sich verschlechtern	to get worse
sich verbessern	to improve
sich ändern	to change
bedeckt	overcast
wolkig	cloudy
klar	clear
sonnig	sunny
heiter	fine
regnerisch	rainy
neblig	misty, foggy
trüb	dull
stürmisch	stormy
schwül	muggy
trocken	dry
warm	warm
heiß	hot
kalt	cold
eisig	icy

mild	mild
angenehm	pleasant
furchtbar	awful
veränderlich	changeable
in der Sonne	in the sun
im Schatten	in the shade
die Temperatur	temperature
die Wettervorhersage	weather forecast
der Wetterbericht	weather report
der Wettermann/die Wetterfrau	weather man/girl
das Klima	climate
die Atmosphäre	atmosphere
die Luft	air
der Hochdruck/Tiefdruck	high/low pressure
der Himmel	sky
eine Verbesserung	improvement
eine Veränderung	change
das Thermometer	thermometer
ein Grad *(n)*	degree
das Barometer	barometer

Regen · rain

die Feuchtigkeit	humidity, dampness
ein Regentropfen *(m)*	raindrop
eine Pfütze	puddle
eine Wolke	cloud
ein Schauer *(m)*	shower
der Tau	dew
der Nieselregen	drizzle
der Nebel	fog, mist
der Hagel	hail
ein Hagelkorn *(n)*	hailstone
ein Wolkenbruch *(m)*	downpour
ein Dauerregen *(m)*	continuous rainfall

eine Überschwemmung	flood
ein Gewitter *(n)*	thunderstorm
der Donner	thunder
der Blitz	(flash of) lightning
eine Aufheiterung	sunny interval
ein Regenbogen *(m)*	rainbow

Kälte — cold weather

der Schnee	snow
eine Schneeflocke	snowflake
der Schneefall	snowfall
ein Schneesturm *(m)*	snowstorm
eine Lawine	avalanche
ein Schneeball *(m)*	snowball
ein Schneemann *(m)*	snowman
der Schneeregen	sleet
der Frost	frost
das Tauwetter	thaw
der Raureif	(hoar) frost
das Eis	ice
das Glatteis	(black) ice
ein Eiszapfen *(m)*	icicle

schönes Wetter — good weather

die Sonne	sun
der Sonnenschein	sunshine
ein Sonnenstrahl *(m)*	ray of sunshine
die Hitze	heat
eine Hitzewelle	heatwave
die Dürre	drought

Wind — wind

ein Luftzug *(m)*	draught
eine Bö	gust of wind
eine Brise	breeze
ein Orkan *(m)*	hurricane

30 WIE IST DAS WETTER?

ein Tornado *(m)*	tornado
ein Wirbelsturm *(m)*	cyclone
ein Sturm *(m)*	storm

es ist gutes/schlechtes Wetter
the weather is good/bad

wir haben Glück mit dem Wetter
we're lucky with the weather

es ist minus zehn Grad
it's minus 10 degrees

es ist dreißig Grad im Schatten
it's 30 degrees in the shade

es regnet immer noch
it's still raining

es regnet (Bindfäden)
it's raining (cats and dogs)

es schüttet
it's pouring

Inf **es gießt wie aus Kübeln**
it's chucking it down

es ist sonnig/neblig/regnerisch
it's sunny/foggy/rainy

es schneit
it's snowing

mir ist eiskalt
I'm freezing cold

ich schwitze
I'm roasting

die Sonne scheint
the sun's shining

bei Regen
when it's raining

es donnert
it's thundering

es blitzt
there's lightning

morgen wird es regnen
it's going to rain tomorrow

es gab Schneeregen
it was sleeting

was für ein furchtbares Wetter!
what awful weather!

bei diesem Sauwetter
in this foul weather

was ist die Vorhersage für das Wochenende?
what's the forecast for the weekend?

31 FAMILIE UND BEKANNTENKREIS

FAMILY AND FRIENDS

verwandt sein (mit)	to be related (to)
sich verheiraten (mit)	to get married (to)
sich verloben (mit)	to get engaged (to)
Kinder haben	to have children
adoptieren	to adopt
adoptiert sein	to be adopted
eine Waise sein	to be an orphan
in Pflege sein	to be in care
kennen	to know
gut auskommen (mit)	to get on well (with)
sich duzen	to use the 'du' form
sich siezen	to use the 'Sie' form

die Familie — the family

ein Familienmitglied *(n)*	family member
Eltern *(pl)*	parents
die Mutter	mother
der Vater	father
die Mutti	mum
der Vati	dad
das Kind	child
das Baby	baby
die Tochter	daughter
der Sohn	son
die Adoptivsohn, die Adoptivtochter	adopted son/daughter
ein Pflegekind *(n)*	foster child
der Bruder	brother
die Schwester	sister

173

der Zwillingsbruder, die Zwillingsschwester	twin brother/sister
der Großvater, die Großmutter	grandfather/grandmother
die Oma	granny
der Opa	grandad
Großeltern *(pl)*	grandparents
Enkelkinder *(pl)*	grandchildren
der Enkel, die Enkelin	grandson/granddaughter
der Urgroßvater, die Urgroßmutter	great-grandmother/grandfather
die Frau	wife; woman
die Ehefrau	wife
der Mann	husband; man
ein Paar *(n)*	couple
ein Ehepaar *(n)*	married couple
die (die) Verlobte	fiancé(e)
ein(e) Partner(in)	partner
der Schwager, die Schwägerin	brother-/sister-in-law
der Schwiegervater, die Schwiegermutter	father-/mother-in-law
Schwiegereltern *(pl)*	in-laws
der Schwiegersohn, die Schwiegertochter	son-/daughter-in-law
die Tante	aunt
der Onkel	uncle
der Cousin, die Cousine	cousin
der Vetter	cousin *(male)*
die Nichte	niece
der Neffe	nephew
der Pate, die Patin	godfather/godmother
der Patensohn, die Patentochter	godson/goddaughter
der Stiefvater, die Stiefmutter	stepfather/stepmother
der Stiefsohn, die Stieftochter	stepson/stepdaughter

Freunde und Bekannte

	friends
Leute *(pl)*	people
der Freund	friend, boyfriend
die Freundin	friend, girlfriend
ein Bekannter, eine Bekannte	acquaintance, friend
der Nachbar, die Nachbarin	neighbour

hast du Geschwister?
have you got any brothers and sisters?

ich bin ein Einzelkind
I'm an only child

ich habe keine Geschwister
I don't have any brothers or sisters

ich bin der/die Älteste
I'm the oldest

mein großer Bruder ist 21
my big brother is 21

meine älteste Schwester ist Friseuse
my eldest sister is a hairdresser

ich kümmere mich um meine kleine Schwester
I'm looking after my little sister

mein jüngster Bruder lutscht am Daumen
my youngest brother sucks his thumb

meine Mutter erwartet ein Kind
my mother is expecting a baby

du bist mein bester Freund, Michael
you are my best friend, Michael

sie haben Verwandte in Kanada
they have relatives in Canada

er ist ein Freund von mir
he's a friend of mine

Monika ist meine beste Freundin
Monika is my best friend

ihre Kinder sind wirklich süß
their kids are really cute

Inf **meine Schwiegereltern machen mich verrückt!**
my in-laws are driving me nuts!

> ## Note
>
> There are two different words in German for 'to know': wissen, used for facts or information, and kennen, used for people and places in the sense of 'to be familiar with'. The verb kennenlernen means 'to get to know'.
>
> **kennen Sie meine Mutter?**   **was ist das? – ich weiß nicht**
> do you know my mother?   what's that? – I don't know
>
> **ich habe Mark auf einer Party** kennengelernt
> I met/got to know Mark at a party

See also Section

8 IDENTITY AND AGE.

32 SCHULE UND AUSBILDUNG

SCHOOL AND EDUCATION

zur Schule gehen	to go to school
die Namen aufrufen	to take the register
studieren	to study
lernen	to learn
auswendig lernen	to learn by heart
die Hausaufgaben machen	to do one's homework
fragen	to ask
antworten	to answer
prüfen	to examine
aufpassen	to pay attention
sich melden	to put one's hand up
aufzeigen	to put one's hand up
wissen	to know
eine Frage stellen	to ask a question
eine Prüfung machen	to sit an exam
seine Prüfung bestehen	to pass one's exams
seine Prüfung nicht bestehen	to fail one's exams
bei einer Prüfung durchfallen	to fail an exam
sitzen bleiben	to repeat a year, to stay down
die Schule schwänzen	to play truant
verweisen	to expel, to suspend
bestrafen	to punish
von der Schule verwiesen werden	to be expelled
vom Unterricht ausgeschlossen werden	to be suspended
nachsitzen müssen	to get detention

abwesend	absent
anwesend	present
gewissenhaft	conscientious
fleißig	hard-working
intelligent	intelligent
begabt	gifted
unaufmerksam	inattentive
undiszipliniert	undisciplined
ungezogen	naughty
beliebt	popular
der Kindergarten	nursery school
die Grundschule	primary school
die Hauptschule	secondary school *(age 10-14)*
das Gymnasium	secondary school *(age 10-18)*
die Realschule	secondary school *(age 10-16)*
eine Gesamtschule	comprehensive
die Handelsschule	business school
ein Internat *(n)*	boarding school
die Universität	university
die Uni	university
die technische Hochschule	polytechnic

in der Schule at school

eine Klasse	class
das Klassenzimmer	classroom
die Schulleitung	headteacher's office
das Lehrerzimmer	staffroom
die Bibliothek	library
das Labor	laboratory
das Sprachlabor	language lab
die Berufsberatung	careers centre
der Schulhof	playground
der Gang	corridor
die Aula	assembly hall
die Turnhalle	gym, sports hall

das Sanitätszimmer	infirmary
das Klassenzimmer	**the classroom**
ein Tisch *(m)*	desk, table
der Lehrertisch	teacher's desk
das Klassenbuch	class register
ein Stuhl *(m)*	chair
ein Schrank *(m)*	cupboard
die Tafel	blackboard
die Kreide	chalk
ein Schwamm *(m)*	sponge, duster
die Weißwandtafel	whiteboard
der Overheadprojektor	overhead projector
eine Overheadfolie	OHP slide
eine Schultasche	schoolbag
ein Heft *(n)*	exercise book
ein Buch *(n)*	book
ein Schulbuch *(n)*	school book
ein Lehrbuch *(n)*	textbook
ein Wörterbuch *(n)*	dictionary
ein Federmäppchen *(n)*	pencilcase
ein Kugelschreiber *(m)*	ballpoint pen, biro
ein Füller *(m)*	(fountain) pen
ein Bleistift *(m)*	pencil
ein Filzstift *(m)*	felt-tip pen
ein (Bleistift)spitzer *(m)*	pencil sharpener
ein Radiergummi *(n)*	rubber
ein Lineal *(n)*	ruler
ein Zirkel *(m)*	pair of compasses
ein Geodreieck® *(n)*	set-square
ein Winkelmesser *(m)*	protractor
ein Taschenrechner *(m)*	pocket calculator
ein Computer *(m)*	computer

Turnen	**PE**
das Turnzeug	gym kit
ein Sportplatz *(m)*	playing field
der Ball	ball
das Netz	net
das Seil	rope
das Pferd	horse
eine Matte	mat
Lehrer und Schüler	**teachers and pupils**
ein(e) Grundschullehrer(in)	primary-school teacher
der Lehrer, die Lehrerin	teacher
der Direktor, die Direktorin	headmaster/headmistress
der Rektor	headteacher *(in a primary school)*
der Klassenlehrer	class teacher
der Deutschlehrer	German teacher
der Englischlehrer	English teacher
ein(e) Aushilfslehrer(in)	supply teacher
ein(e) Nachhilfelehrer(in)	tutor
ein Schulrat, eine Schulrätin	inspector
ein Krankenpfleger, eine Krankenschwester	nurse
ein(e) Berater(in)	counsellor
ein(e) Berufsberater(in)	careers adviser
ein(e) Schulsekretär(in)	school secretary
ein(e) Schüler(in)	pupil
ein(e) Gymnasiast(in)	secondary school pupil
ein(e) Student(in)	student
der Klassensprecher	class spokesperson
ein(e) Schulfreund(in)	schoolfriend
Lehrers Liebling *(m)*	teacher's pet
ein(e) Mobber(in)	bully
der Unterricht	**teaching**
das Schuljahr	school year
der Stundenplan	timetable

ein Fach *(n)*	subject
ein Wahlfach *(n)*	option
ein Pflichtfach *(n)*	compulsory subject
eine Stunde	lesson, period
ein Kurs *(m)*	class; course
der Deutschunterricht	German class
der Mathematikunterricht	maths class
die Freistunde	free period
der Privatunterricht	private tuition
die Mathematik	mathematics
Mathe	maths
die Algebra	algebra
das Rechnen	arithmetic
die Geometrie	geometry
die Trigonometrie	trigonometry
eine Addition	sum
eine Subtraktion	subtraction
eine Multiplikation	multiplication
eine Division	division
eine Gleichung	equation
ein Kreis *(m)*	circle
ein Dreieck *(n)*	triangle
ein Quadrat *(n)*	square
ein Rechteck *(n)*	rectangle
ein Winkel *(m)*	angle
ein rechter Winkel	right angle
die Oberfläche	surface
das Volumen	volume
der Durchmesser	diameter
der Umfang	circumference
die Geschichte	history
die Erdkunde	geography
die Naturwissenschaft	science
die Biologie	biology

die Chemie	chemistry
die Physik	physics
die Philosophie	philosophy
die Psychologie	psychology
die Soziologie	sociology
die Wirtschaftslehre	business studies
das Recht	law
die Informatik	IT
(neuere) Sprachen *(pl)*	(modern) languages
Deutsch	German
das Latein	Latin
die Vokabeln *(pl)*	vocabulary
die Grammatik	grammar
die Rechtschreibung	spelling
das Schreiben	writing
das Lesen	reading
ein Aufsatz *(m)*	essay
eine Übersetzung	translation
die Literatur	literature
ein Roman *(m)*	novel
eine Kurzgeschichte	short story
ein Drama *(n)*	play
ein Gedicht *(n)*	poem
die Musik	music
der Schauspielunterricht	drama
die Kunst	art
das Zeichnen	drawing
die Arbeitslehre	CDT, crafts
das Werken	woodwork, DIY
der Sportunterricht	physical education, PE
Hausaufgaben *(pl)*	homework
eine Aufgabe	exercise
ein Projekt	project

eine Präsentation	presentation
eine Frage	question
die Antwort	answer
die Kursarbeit	coursework
eine schriftliche Prüfung	written test
eine mündliche Prüfung	oral test
eine Klassenarbeit	test
ein Examen *(n)*	exam(ination)
ein Fehler *(m)*	mistake
ein Zeugnis *(n)*	report
eine gute Note	good mark
eine schlechte Note	bad mark
sehr gut	very good
gut	good
befriedigend	fair
ausreichend	satisfactory
mangelhaft	poor
ungenügend	unsatisfactory
das Ergebnis	result
das Zeugnis	report
ein Preis *(m)*	prize
das (Abschluss)zeugnis	(school-leaving) certificate
ein Diplom *(n)*	diploma
das Abitur	A levels
die mittlere Reife	GCSEs
die Disziplin	discipline
eine Strafe	punishment
eine Strafarbeit	punishment, lines
das Nachsitzen	detention
die Klingel	bell
die Pause	break
das Mittagessen	lunch
der Schulschluss	hometime

das Nachmittagsprogramm	after-school activities
die Schulferien *(pl)*	school holidays
die Sommerferien *(pl)*	summer holidays
die großen Ferien *(pl)*	summer holidays
die Osterferien *(pl)*	Easter holidays
die Weihnachtsferien *(pl)*	Christmas holidays
eine Klassenfahrt	school trip
ein Austauschbesuch *(m)*	exchange visit

die Universität — university

ein(e) Student(in)	student
ein Graduierter, eine Graduierte	postgraduate
ein(e) Hochschulabsolvent(in)	graduate
ein(e) Dozent(in)	lecturer
ein(e) Professor(in)	professor
ein(e) Tutor(in)	tutor
ein Fachbereich *(m)*	department
eine Vorlesung	lecture
ein Kolloquium *(n)*	tutorial
ein Seminar *(n)*	seminar
ein Hörsaal *(m)*	lecture theatre
ein Wohnheim *(n)*	hall of residence
ein Studentenbund *(m)*	students' union
eine Dissertation	dissertation
eine Diplomarbeit	thesis
ein Abschluss *(m)*	degree
ein Magisterabschluss *(m)*	masters
eine Promotion	PhD
ein Diplom *(n)*	diploma
ein alternierender Ausbildungslehrgang *(m)*	sandwich course
ein freiwiliges Jahr *(n)*	gap year
die Abschlussfeier	graduation

einen Schüler nachsitzen lassen
to give a pupil detention

er musste nachsitzen
he was kept in

es hat geklingelt
the bell has gone

wir haben heute schulfrei
we've got no school today

was hast du heute auf?
what have you got for homework today?

heute haben wir eine Doppelstunde Mathe
we have double maths today

er studiert Jura an der Universität
he's studying law at university

ich habe einen Hochschulabschluss in Medienwissenschaft
I've got a degree in media studies

Inf **ich habe mich in der Geschichtsstunde zu Tode gelangweilt**
I was bored stiff in that history class

Inf **wir haben Physik geschwänzt**
we bunked off physics

Inf **meine Schwester ist auf der Uni**
my sister's at uni

Note

False friend: the German word das Gymnasium means 'high school'. The word for a gymnasium or sports hall is die Turnhalle.

 Homework help

My favourite subject is...
Mein Lieblingsfach ist...

My least favourite subject is...
Das Fach, das ich am wenigsten mag, ist...

When I finish school I want to... **Nach der Schule möchte ich...**	go to university. **zur Universität gehen.**
	study to be a doctor/lawyer. **studieren, um Arzt/Rechtsanwalt zu werden.**
	train as a hairdresser/childminder. **eine Ausbildung als Friseuse/ Tagesmutter machen.**
	get a good job. **einen guten Job bekommen.**
	go travelling. **auf Reisen gehen.**
I think... **Ich denke,...**	it's important to study languages/ history/maths. **es ist wichtig, Sprachen/ Geschichte/Mathematik zu studieren.**
	we have too much homework/too many exams. **wir haben zu viele Hausaufgaben/ Prüfungen.**
	we should do more... at school. **wir sollten in der Schule mehr ... machen.**
	we do too much... at school. **wir machen in der Schule zu viel ...**
	we should have nicer/healthier school dinners. **wir sollten besseres/gesünderes Schulessen haben.**
	we need to stop bullying in schools. **wir müssen das Mobbing in der Schule stoppen.**

| However,... | going to university is expensive. |
| **Aber...** | **Studieren ist teuer.** |

some people find studying boring/
  difficult.
**manche finden Studieren
  langweilig/schwer.**

it will be useful in the future.
**es wird für die Zukunft nützlich
  sein.**

See also Section

9 JOBS AND WORK.

33 DAS GELD

MONEY

kaufen	to buy
verkaufen	to sell
ausgeben	to spend
(ver)leihen	to lend
(be)zahlen	to pay
bar zahlen	to pay cash
mit Scheck bezahlen	to pay by cheque
einen Scheck einlösen	to cash a cheque
in Raten bezahlen	to pay in instalments
Geld überweisen	to transfer money
zurückzahlen	to pay back
Schulden abbezahlen	to pay off debts
wechseln	to change
Geld abheben	to withdraw money
Geld einzahlen	to pay in money
Geld einwerfen	to insert money
sparen	to save money
abrechnen	to do one's accounts
Geld auf dem Konto haben	to be in credit
Schulden haben	to have debts
das Konto überzogen haben	to be overdrawn
Bankrott machen	to go bankrupt
reich	rich
arm	poor
stinkreich	loaded
pleite	broke
ein(e) Millionär(in)	millionaire

das Taschengeld	pocket money
das Bargeld	cash
das Kleingeld	small change
ein Geldschein *(m)*	banknote
eine Münze	coin
ein Portemonnaie *(n)*	purse
eine Brieftasche	wallet
eine Zahlung	payment
Ausgaben *(pl)*	expenses
Ersparnisse *(pl)*	savings
eine Bank	bank
das Bankwesen	banking
das Onlinebanking	online banking
eine Sparkasse	savings bank
ein Postamt *(n)*	post office
eine Wechselstube	bureau de change
der Wechselkurs	exchange rate
die Kasse	till, cashdesk
der Schalter	counter
ein Geldautomat *(m)*	cash dispenser
ein Bankkonto *(n)*	bank account
ein Girokonto *(n)*	current account
ein Sparkonto *(n)*	savings account
eine Abhebung	withdrawal
eine Überweisung	transfer
eine Kreditkarte	credit card
eine Kundenkarte	debit card
ein Scheckheft *(n)*	chequebook
ein Scheck *(m)*	cheque
ein Formular *(n)*	form
eine Postanweisung	postal order
ein Kredit *(m)*	credit
Schulden *(pl)*	debts

die Kontoüberziehung	overdraft
ein Darlehen *(n)*	loan
eine Hypothek	mortgage
die Währung	currency *(of a country)*
die Börse	Stock Exchange
eine Aktie	share
die Inflation	inflation
die Lebenshaltungskosten	cost of living
der Etat	budget
ein Euro *(m)*	euro
ein Cent *(m)*	cent
eine 2-Euro-Münze	a 2-euro coin
ein Zehneuroschein *(m)*	a 10-euro note
ein Schweizerfranken *(m)*	Swiss franc
ein Pfund *(n)* (Sterling)	pound sterling
ein Dollar *(m)*	dollar

---

ich möchte gern 500 Euro in Pfund umtauschen
I'd like to change 500 euros into pounds

ich habe das Geld auf mein Konto überwiesen
I transferred the money to my bank account

ich habe mir 100 Euro von meinem Vater geliehen
I borrowed 100 euros from my father

ich spare für ein Motorrad
I'm saving up for a motorbike

ich komme nur schwer mit dem Geld aus
I find it hard to make ends meet

mein Konto ist überzogen　　　　**ich habe 1000 Euro Schulden**
I'm overdrawn　　　　　　　　　　　I'm 1000 euros in debt

Inf **ich bin pleite**　　　　　　　*Inf* **was für ein Nepp!**
I'm broke　　　　　　　　　　　　　what a rip-off!

Inf **sie verpulvert ihr ganzes Geld für Schuhe**
she blows all her money on shoes

Inf **ihre Wohnung kostet ein Vermögen**
their flat cost an arm and a leg

Inf **er ist ein fürchterlicher Geizkragen**
he's such a tightwad

Note

★ The German words der Euro and der Cent have no plural forms:

ich habe 1000 Euro Schulden	**5 Euro und 20 Cent**
I have a debt of 1000 euros	5 euros and 20 cents

★ Note the following expressions, which are the equivalent of 'to be in the red' (in debt) and 'to be in the black' (to be in credit):

die Firma schreibt rote Zahlen/schwarze Zahlen
the company is in the red/in the black
(lit. 'the company is writing red figures/black figures')

 Homework help

These days...	people buy too much on credit cards.
Heutzutage...	**kaufen die Leute zu viel auf Kreditkarten.**
	too many people get into debt.
	machen zu viele Menschen Schulden.

	most people manage their accounts online. **führen die meisten ihr Konto online.**
I'm worried about... **Ich habe Angst davor,...**	getting into debt. **in Schulden zu geraten.**
	not having enough money. **nicht genug Geld zu haben.**
	my bank details being stolen. **dass meine Bankangaben gestohlen werden.**
It annoys me that... **Es ärgert mich, dass...**	I can't afford the things I want. **ich mir die Sachen, die ich will, nicht leisten kann.**
	I don't get enough pocket money. **ich nicht genug Taschengeld bekomme.**
	clothes/video games are so expensive. **Kleider/Videospiele so teuer sind.**
I need to... **Ich muss...**	get a weekend job. **mir einen Wochenendjob besorgen.**
	find a well-paid job. **einen gut bezahlten Job finden.**
	save money. **Geld sparen.**
	learn how to budget. **lernen, meine Finanzen zu planen.**

See also Sections

9 JOBS AND WORK *and* **18 SHOPPING.**

34 AKTUELLE THEMEN

TOPICAL ISSUES

diskutieren	to discuss
debattieren	to debate
sich streiten	to argue
verteidigen	to defend
denken	to think
glauben	to believe
vorschlagen	to suggest
auf etwas bestehen	to insist on something
überzeugen	to persuade
seine Meinung ändern	to change one's mind
für	for, in favour of
gegen	against, opposed to
intolerant	intolerant
tolerant	broad-minded
ein Thema *(n)*	topic
ein Problem *(n)*	problem
ein Argument *(n)*	argument
eine Demonstration	demonstration
eine Versammlung	rally
ein Aufruhr *(m)*	riot
die Gesellschaft	society
ein Vorurteil *(n)*	prejudice
die Moral	morals
die Haltung	attitude
die Überzeugung	belief

der Krieg	war
die Abrüstung	disarmament
Alliierte *(pl)*	allies
der Frieden	peace
der Friedensprozess	peace process
Europa *(n)*	Europe
die EU	EU
die Erweiterung der EU	EU enlargement
der Euro	euro
eine Supermacht	superpower
der Nahe Osten	Middle East
der Terrorismus	terrorism
ein(e) Terrorist(in)	terrorist
ein terroristischer Anschlag *(m)*	terrorist attack
ein Bombenattentat *(n)*	bombing
ein Selbstmordattentat *(n)*	suicide bombing
der Extremismus	extremism
ein(e) Fanatiker(in)	fanatic
die Globalisierung	globalization
die Armut	poverty
die Not	destitution
die Wohlfahrt	charity
die Arbeitslosigkeit	unemployment
die Obdachlosigkeit	homelessness
die Sozialhilfe	benefits
ein sozial benachteiligtes Gebiet *(n)*	deprived area
eine Sozialsiedlung	council estate
die Kriminalität	crime
die Gewalt	violence
die häusliche Gewalt	domestic violence
ein Angriff *(m)*	assault
die sexuelle Belästigung	sexual harassment
die Kindesmisshandlung	child abuse
der sexuelle Missbrauch	sexual abuse

ein Pädophiler, eine Pädophile	paedophile
die Teenagerschwangerschaft	teenage pregnancy
die Abtreibung	abortion
die Empfängnisverhütung	contraception
Aids	AIDS
der Gruppenzwang	peer pressure
das Mobbing	bullying
die Gleichheit	equality
die Gleichberechtigung	equal rights
die Diskriminierung	discrimination
der Sexismus	sexism
ein(e) Sexist(in)	sexist
ein Chauvinist *(m)*	male chauvinist
der Feminismus	feminism
ein(e) Feminist(in)	feminist
die Homosexualität	homosexuality
ein Homosexueller *(m)*	gay man
eine Lesbierin	lesbian
die Schwulenbewegung	gay rights movement
eine Lebenspartnerschaft	civil partnership
eine Behinderung	disability
der Rassismus	racism
ein(e) Rassist(in)	racist
ein Schwarzer, eine Schwarze	black person
ein(e) Ausländer(in)	foreigner
ein(e) Gastarbeiter(in)	foreign worker
ein Einwanderer, eine Einwanderin	immigrant
die Einwanderung	immigration
ein Getto *(n)*	ghetto
die Integration	integration
ein politischer Flüchtling	political refugee *(male and female)*
das politische Asyl	political asylum
ein Flüchtling *(m)*	refugee *(male and female)*
ein Flüchtlingslager *(n)*	refugee camp
Menschenrechte *(pl)*	human rights

die Folter	torture
die Verfolgung	persecution
die Todesstrafe	death penalty
eine Diktatur	dictatorship
der Menschenhandel	people trafficking
die Prostitution	prostitution
die Sklaverei	slave labour
die Kinderarbeit	child labour
ein Ausbeuterbetrieb *(m)*	sweatshop
der Waffenhandel	arms trade
Konfliktdiamanten *(pl)*	conflict diamonds
der faire Handel	fair trade
der Alkohol	alcohol
ein(e) Alkoholiker(in)	alcoholic
das Kampftrinken	binge drinking
das Rauchen	smoking
das Passivrauchen	passive smoking
Drogen *(pl)*	drugs
harte/weiche Drogen *(pl)*	hard/soft drugs
der Drogenmissbrauch	drug abuse
eine Überdosis	overdose
die Sucht	addiction
das Haschisch	hashish
das Kokain	cocaine
das Heroin	heroin
der Drogenhandel	drug trafficking
ein Dealer *(m)*	dealer
die Umwelt	environment
die Umweltverschmutzung	pollution
ein Gen *(n)*	gene
genmanipulierte Nahrungsmittel *(pl)*	genetically-modified food
eine Transplantation	transplant
ein Embryo *(m)*	embryo
eine Stammzelle	stem cell

Tierrechte *(pl)*	animal rights
Tierversuche *(pl)*	animal testing
der Vegetarismus	vegetarianism
die Euthanasie	euthanasia

---

ich stimme nicht mit dir überein
I don't agree (with you)

sie sind sich einig
they agree

sie ist rauschgiftsüchtig
she's a drug addict

wie stehst du zur Abtreibung?
what's your opinion on abortion?

er interessiert sich sehr für Tierrechte
he's very interested in animal rights issues

wir sollten mehr für die Obdachlosen tun
we should do more to help the homeless

Behinderte werden oft diskriminiert
disabled people are often discriminated against

Inf **das ist Quatsch!**
that's rubbish!

 Homework help

I'm for/against...
Ich bin für/gegen...

I approve/disapprove of...
Ich bin für/gegen...

I (don't) believe in...
Ich glaube (nicht) an...

It's important to...
Es ist wichtig, zu...

We need to do more to fight...
Wir müssen mehr tun, um ... zu bekämpfen.

We need to stop/reduce...
Wir müssen ... stoppen/reduzieren.

We need to improve/increase...
Wir müssen ... verbessern/erhöhen.

People could... **Die Menschen könnten...**	The government should... **Die Regierung sollte...**
I think it's shocking that... **Ich finde es schockierend, dass...**	people have to sleep on the streets. **Menschen auf der Straße schlafen müssen.**
	racism still exists. **es immer noch Rassismus gibt.**
	gay people are discriminated against. **Homosexuelle diskriminiert werden.**
I'm worried about... **Ich habe Angst davor,...**	being mugged. **überfallen zu werden.**
	dying in a terrorist attack. **bei einem Terroranschlag zu sterben.**
	the spread of AIDS. **dass Aids sich weiter ausbreitet.**
It would be better if... **Es ware besser, wenn...**	drugs were legalised. **Drogen legalisiert wären.**
	cloning was banned. **Klonen verboten ware.**
	we joined the euro. **wir den Euro einführen würden.**
	there were tighter immigration controls. **es strengere Einwanderungskontrollen gäbe.**

See also Sections

16 SMOKING *and* **29 THE ENVIRONMENT.**

35 DIE POLITIK
POLITICS

regieren	to govern
herrschen	to rule
unterdrücken	to repress
abschaffen	to abolish, to do away with
auferlegen	to impose
verstaatlichen	to nationalize
entstaatlichen	to privatize
importieren	to import
exportieren	to export
wählen	to elect, to vote
stimmen für/gegen	to vote for/against
organisieren	to organize
demonstrieren	to demonstrate
national	national
international	international
politisch	political
demokratisch	democratic
konservativ	conservative
sozialistisch	socialist
sozialdemokratisch	social-democratic
liberal	liberal
grün	green
kommunistisch	communist
faschistisch	fascist
anarchistisch	anarchic
kapitalistisch	capitalist
extremistisch	extremist
radikal	radical
gemäßigt	moderate

links	left-wing
rechts	right-wing
eine Mitte-Links-Regierung	centre-left government
eine Mitte-Rechts-Regierung	centre-right government
eine Nation	nation
ein Land *(n)*	country
ein Staat *(m)*	state
eine Republik	republic
die Bundesrepublik Deutschland (BRD)	Federal Republic of Germany (FRG)
eine Monarchie	monarchy
die Regierung	government
das Parlament	parliament
das Kabinett	Cabinet
die Verfassung	constitution
das Staatsoberhaupt	Head of State
der Regierungschef	head of government
der Bundeskanzler	German/Austrian Chancellor
der Bundespräsident	Federal German/Austrian President
der Premierminister, die Premierministerin	Prime Minister
ein(e) Minister(in)	minister
der Außenminister	foreign minister
ein Abgeordneter, eine Abgeordnete	MP
ein Europaabgeordneter, eine Europaabgeordnete	Euro-MP, MEP
ein(e) Politiker(in)	politician
ein(e) Bürgermeister(in)	mayor(ess)
eine Politik	policy
Wahlen *(pl)*	elections
eine Partei	political party
die Rechte	right
die Linke	left

das Wahlrecht	right to vote
ein Wahlkreis *(m)*	constituency
die Wahlurne	ballot box
ein(e) Kandidat(in)	candidate
der Wahlkampf	election campaign
eine Meinungsumfrage	opinion poll
ein(e) Imageberater(in)	spin doctor
ein(e) Bürger(in)	citizen
Verhandlungen *(pl)*	negotiations
eine Debatte	debate
ein Gesetz *(n)*	law
eine Krise	crisis
ein Skandal *(m)*	scandal
die Korruption	corruption
ein Staatsstreich *(m)*	coup
eine Revolution	revolution
die Diktatur	dictatorship
die Demokratie	democracy
der Sozialismus	socialism
der Kommunismus	communism
der Faschismus	fascism
der Kapitalismus	capitalism
der Pazifismus	pacifism
die Freiheit	freedom
die öffentliche Meinung	public opinion
das Volk	the people
die Aristokratie	aristocracy
die Oberschicht	upper class
der Mittelstand	middle classes
die Arbeiterklasse	working class
der König, die Königin	king/queen
ein(e) Kaiser(in)	emperor/empress
ein Prinz, eine Prinzessin	prince/princess

die UNO	UN
die Vereinten Nationen *(pl)*	United Nations
die EU (Europäische Union)	EU (European Union)
die NATO	NATO
die Welthandelsorganisation	World Trade Organization (WTO)

> **die Türkei hat sich um EU-Mitgliedschaft beworben**
> Turkey has applied to join the EU
>
> **die Regierung hält ein Referendum über den Euro ab**
> the government are holding a referendum on the euro
>
> **die Partei hat bei den Wahlen fünf Sitze gewonnen**
> the party gained five seats in the election

 Homework help

If I were the Prime Minister I would...
Wenn ich der Premierminister wäre, würde ich...

Young people...	aren't interested in politics.
Junge Leute...	**interessieren sich nicht für Politik.**
	don't understand politics.
	verstehen nichts von Politik.
	think politicians don't listen to them.
	glauben, dass die Politiker ihnen nicht zuhören.
	don't trust politicians.
	trauen den Politikern nicht.
I think...	it's important to vote.
Ich denke,...	**es ist wichtig, wählen zu gehen.**
	politicians should focus more on youth issues.
	die Politiker sollten sich mehr um Jugendthemen kümmern.

the government should do more to help poor people/asylum seekers.
die Regierung sollte mehr tun, um den Armen/Asylbewerbern zu helfen.

the voting age should be lowered/raised.
das Wahlalter sollte gesenkt/erhöht werden.

People should vote because...
Die Leute sollten wählen gehen, weil...

it's a chance to have your say.
man dadurch seine Meinung äußern kann.

we're lucky to live in a democracy.
wir das Glück haben, in einer Demokratie zu leben.

women fought very hard to get the vote.
die Frauen hart um das Wahlrecht gekämpft haben.

Some people don't vote because...
Manche gehen nicht wählen, weil...

they're too lazy.
sie zu faul sind.

they can't decide who to vote for.
sie sich nicht entscheiden können, für wen sie stimmen sollen.

they think all the parties are the same.
sie glauben, dass alle Parteien gleich sind.

See also Section

34 TOPICAL ISSUES.

36 DIE KOMMUNIKATION
COMMUNICATING

sagen	to say, to tell
sprechen	to talk, to speak
erzählen	to tell *(story)*
plaudern	to chat
wiederholen	to repeat
hinzufügen	to add
erklären	to declare, to state
ankündigen	to announce
ausdrücken	to express
behaupten	to claim
annehmen	to suppose
bezweifeln	to doubt
begreifen	to understand
kapieren	to understand, to get
sich unterhalten mit	to speak with
sich streiten	to argue
informieren	to inform
erwähnen	to mention
versprechen	to promise
meinen	to think, to believe
glauben	to believe
rufen	to shout
schreien	to yell, to shriek
flüstern	to whisper
murmeln	to murmur, to mumble
stottern	to stammer
sich aufregen	to get worked up

antworten	to reply, to answer
entgegnen	to reply, to retort
recht haben	to be right
unrecht haben	to be wrong
überreden	to persuade
überzeugen	to convince
beeinflussen	to influence
zustimmen	to agree
ablehnen	to decline
widersprechen	to contradict
bestreiten	to contest
einwenden	to object
übertreiben	to exaggerate
betonen	to emphasize
vorhersagen	to predict
bestreiten	to deny
zugeben	to admit
sich entschuldigen	to apologize
vorgeben	to pretend
täuschen	to deceive
schmeicheln	to flatter
kritisieren	to criticize
überzeugt	convinced
überzeugend	convincing
wahr	true
falsch	false
ein Gespräch *(n)*	conversation
eine Unterhaltung	talk
eine Diskussion	discussion
ein Streit *(m)*	argument
ein Dialog *(m)*	dialogue
eine Rede	speech
eine Vorlesung	lecture
eine Debatte	debate
eine Konferenz	conference

eine Erklärung	statement
das Gerede	gossip
ein Gerücht *(n)*	rumour
die Meinung	opinion
die Ansicht	view
eine Idee	idea
der Standpunkt	point of view
ein Argument *(n)*	argument
ein Missverständnis *(n)*	misunderstanding
die Kritik	criticism
ein Einwand *(m)*	objection
eine Erklärung	declaration, statement
offen	frankly
allgemein	generally
natürlich	naturally
selbstverständlich	of course
wirklich	really
völlig	entirely
zweifellos	undoubtedly
vielleicht	maybe, perhaps
aber	but
jedoch	however
oder	or
und	and
falls	if
weil	because
deshalb	therefore
also	therefore, so
dank *(+gen)*	thanks to
trotz *(+gen)*	despite
außer *(+dat)*	except
über	about, on
mit *(+dat)*	with
ohne	without
fast	almost

nicht wahr?
isn't it?/don't you?/aren't they? *etc*

du magst ihn nicht, oder? - doch
you don't like him, do you? - yes, I do

es ist mir egal	**er war sehr böse – wirklich?**
I don't mind	he was quite angry – was he?

das ist ein sehr überzeugendes Argument, nicht wahr?/meinst du nicht?
it's a very convincing argument, isn't it?/don't you think?

sie hat sich für/gegen ... ausgesprochen
she argued for/against...

ich halte nichts von seinen Ideen
I don't approve of his ideas

wir sollten akzeptieren, dass wir verschiedener Meinung sind
let's just agree to disagree

See also Sections

34 TOPICAL ISSUES *and* **38 THE PHONE.**

37 DER BRIEFVERKEHR
LETTER WRITING

schreiben	to write
kritzeln	to scribble
notieren	to jot down
beschreiben	to describe
(auf der Maschine) schreiben	to type
ausfüllen	to fill out
unterschreiben	to sign
beantworten	to answer
antworten	to reply
senden	to send
schicken	to send
erhalten	to receive
kleben	to stick
zukleben	to seal
freimachen	to put a stamp on
wiegen	to weigh
absenden	to post
einwerfen	to post
zurücksenden	to send back
nachsenden	to forward
beilegen	to enclose
enthalten	to contain
lesbar	legible, readable
unleserlich	illegible
per Luftpost	by airmail
per Eilboten	by express delivery
per Einschreiben	by registered mail
per Kurier	by courier

Anlagen	enclosures
von	from *(person)*
aus	from *(country)*
ein Brief *(m)*	letter
eine E-Mail	e-mail
eine Postkarte	postcard
die Post	mail
ein Zettel *(m)*	note
das Datum	date
die Unterschrift	signature
ein (Brief)umschlag *(m)*	envelope
die Adresse	address
die Anschrift	address
der Empfänger, die Empfängerin	addressee
der Absender, die Absenderin	sender
ein(e) Brieffreund(in)	penfriend
die Postleitzahl	postcode
der Ort	town
die Straße	street
eine Briefmarke	stamp
das Postwertzeichen	postmark
ein Briefkasten *(m)*	postbox
die Leerung	collection
die Post	post office
das Postamt	post office
der Schalter	counter
das Porto	postage
ein Paket *(n)*	parcel
ein Päckchen *(n)*	small parcel
die Empfangsbestätigung	acknowledgement of receipt
ein Formular *(n)*	form
eine Geldanweisung	postal order
der Inhalt	contents
der Briefträger	postman

die Handschrift	handwriting
ein Kugelschreiber *(m)*	biro®
ein Kuli *(m)*	biro®
ein Bleistift *(m)*	pencil
ein Füller *(m)*	fountain pen
der Computer	computer
der Text	text
die Seite	page
ein Paragraf *(m)*	paragraph
ein Absatz *(m)*	paragraph
eine Linie	line
ein Wort *(n)*	word
ein Zitat *(n)*	quotation
der Titel	title
der Rand	margin
eine Geburtstagskarte	birthday card
eine Weihnachtskarte	Christmas card
eine Einladung	invitation
ein Dankschreiben *(n)*	thank-you letter
ein Liebesbrief *(m)*	love letter
eine Beschwerde	complaint

---

drei Briefmarken für Großbritannien, bitte
I'd like three stamps for the UK please

ich sende eine Bestätigung per Fax **ich schicke dir morgen eine E-Mail**
I'll confirm all the details by fax   I'll e-mail you tomorrow

ihre Handschrift ist furchtbar!
her handwriting is appalling!

 Homework help

Starting the letter

Dear Mum and Dad,	Dear Sir/Madam,
Liebe Mutti, lieber Vati,	**Sehr geehrte Damen und Herren,**
Dear Jack/Susie,	Hi Julie!
Lieber Jack/Liebe Susie,	**Hallo Julie!**
How are you?	I hope you are well.
Wie geht es Dir?	**Ich hoffe, es geht Dir gut.**
Thank you for your letter.	It was great to hear from you.
Danke für Deinen Brief	**Es war schön, von Dir zu hören.**

Purpose of the letter

I'm writing to...	ask you for...
Ich schreibe, um...	**Dich um ... zu bitten.**
	thank you for...
	Dir für ... zu danken.
	wish you...
	Dir ... zu wünschen.
	tell you...
	Dir zu sagen, dass...
	invite you to...
	Dich zu ... einzuladen.
Could you...	please send me...
Könnten Sie...	**mir bitte ... schicken.**
	please tell me...
	mir bitte sagen...
	confirm that...
	bestätigen, dass...
Please find enclosed...	Please find attached...
In der Anlage finden Sie...	**Als Anhang finden Sie...**

Finishing the letter

Please do not hesitate to contact me.
Bei Fragen stehe ich Ihnen gern zur Verfügung.

I look forward to hearing from you.
Ich würde mich freuen, von Ihnen zu hören.

Write back soon!
Schreib mir bald!

Give my love to Alex.
Grüße Alex von mir.

Yours faithfully/sincerely,
Mit freundlichen Grüßen

Kind regards,
Beste Grüße,

All the best,
Alles Gute,

Love,
herzliche Grüße,

Lots of love from...
Viele liebe Grüße von...

See also Section

39 COMPUTERS AND THE INTERNET.

anrufen	to call, to phone
telefonieren	to phone, to make a phone call
wählen	to dial
sich melden	to answer
auflegen	to hang up
zurückrufen	to call back
eine Nachricht hinterlassen	to leave a message
texten	to text
eine SMS(-Nachricht) schicken/ senden	to send a text message
sich verwählen	to dial a wrong number
den Hörer abnehmen	to lift the receiver
das Telefon	phone
der Fernsprecher	telephone
der Hörer	receiver
ein drahtloses Telefon	cordless phone
das Amtszeichen	dialling tone
die Wählscheibe	dial
die Taste	button, key
die Stern-/Raute-Taste	star/hash key
das Telefonbuch	phone book
die Gelben Seiten®	Yellow Pages®
eine Telefonzelle	phone box
die Telefonkarte	phonecard
ein Ferngespräch (n)	long distance call
ein Ortsgespräch (n)	local call
ein R-Gespräch (n)	reverse charge call
eine gebührenfreie Rufnummer	Freefone® number
eine Mehrwert nummer	premium-rate number

die Vorwahl	dialling code
die Rufnummer	number
eine falsche Nummer	wrong number
die Auskunft	enquiries
die Vermittlung	operator
der Notruf	emergency
die Kurzwahl	speed dial
ein Handy (n)	mobile (phone)
ein Mobiltelefon (n)	mobile phone
eine SMS	text message
eine MMS	picture message
ein Klingelton (m)	ringtone
die Texterkennung	predictive text
ein Kamerahandy (n)	camera phone
ein Videohandy (n)	video phone
ein Netz (n)	network
ein Vertrag (m)	contract
ein Gesprächsguthaben (n)	credit
eine Prepaidkarte	top-up card
ein Signal (n)	signal
ein Ladegerät (n)	charger
besetzt	engaged
außer Betrieb	out of order

das Telefon klingelt
the phone's ringing

wer spricht bitte?
who's speaking?

hallo, hier (ist) Karl-Heinz
hello, this is Karl-Heinz

am Apparat
speaking

ich möchte gern mit Martin sprechen
I'd like to speak to Martin

bleiben Sie am Apparat
hang on

tut mir leid, er ist nicht da
I'm sorry, he's not here

es ist besetzt
it's engaged

es meldet sich niemand
there's no answer

möchten Sie eine Nachricht hinterlassen?
would you like to leave a message?

können Sie ihr ausrichten, dass ich angerufen habe?
can you tell her I called?

einen Moment, ich verbinde Sie mit ihm
one moment, I'll just hand you over to him

entschuldigen Sie, ich habe mich verwählt
sorry, I've got the wrong number

meine Nummer ist zweiundzwanzig, einundvierzig, null zwo
my number is two two four one zero two

ich muss jetzt Schluss machen
I have to go now

wir sind unterbrochen worden
we got cut off

mein Gesprächsguthaben ist aufgebraucht
I've run out of credit

ich bekomme hier kein Signal
I can't get a signal here

ich texte dir meine Adresse
I'll text you my address

schick mir heute Abend eine SMS
text me tonight

auf Wiederhören
goodbye

Note

★ Germans always introduce themselves by name on the phone:

hallo, hier (ist) Karl-Heinz
hello, it's Karl-Heinz here

★ When ending a phone call in German, remember to say auf Wiederhören (lit. 'hear you later') rather than auf Wiedersehen (lit. 'see you later'), which is used when speaking to someone in person.

★ When reading out phone numbers, Germans often pronounce the number 2 as zwo rather than zwei, to prevent it being mistaken for drei:

meine Nummer ist zwo, zwo, vier, eins, null, zwo, drei, acht
my number is two two four one, oh two three eight

'0' is pronounced null (never 'oh' as in English).

See also Section

39 COMPUTERS AND THE INTERNET.

39 COMPUTER UND DAS INTERNET

COMPUTERS AND THE INTERNET

speichern	to save
löschen	to delete
klicken	to click
(aus)drucken	print (out)
scannen	to scan
zippen	to zip
komprimieren	to zip
dekomprimieren	to unzip
abstürzen	to crash
einfrieren	to freeze
mailen	to e-mail *(document)*
eine E-Mail schicken	to e-mail *(person)*
antworten	to reply
weiterleiten	to forward
chatten	to chat
im Web surfen	to surf the Net
suchen nach	to search for
laden	to download
heraufladen	to upload
hacken in	to hack into

der Computer

the computer

ein Laptop *(m)*	laptop
ein Monitor *(m)*	monitor
ein Bildschirm *(m)*	screen
ein Drucker *(m)*	printer
ein Scanner *(m)*	scanner
eine Maus	mouse

ein Mauspad *(n)*	mouse mat
ein Laufwerk *(n)*	drive
die Hardware	hardware
eine Festplatte	hard disk
die Software	software
ein Softwarepaket *(n)*	software (package)
eine CD-ROM	CD-ROM
eine Diskette	(floppy) disk
ein Memorystick® *(m)*	memory stick
ein Programm *(n)*	program
eine Datei	file
ein Ordner	folder
der Papierkorb	recycle bin
eine Tabellenkalkulation	spreadsheet
eine Tabelle	table
eine Rechtschreibprüfung	spellcheck
der Cursor	cursor
eine Taste	key
ein Keyboard *(n)*	keyboard
eine Tastatur	keyboard
die Leertaste	space bar
die Enter-Taste	enter

E-mail und das Internet e-mail and the Internet

eine E-Mail	e-mail
eine E-Mail-Adresse	e-mail address
ein E-Mail-Konto *(n)*	e-mail account
ein Benutzername *(m)*	username
ein Passwort *(n)*	password
das At-Zeichen	at-sign
der Klammeraffe	at-sign
ein Punkt *(m)*	dot
ein Unterstrich *(m)*	underscore
der Eingang	inbox
der Ausgang	outbox
ein Anhang *(m)*	attachment
ein Attachment *(n)*	attachment

ein Modem *(n)*	modem
das Breitband	broadband
das Netz	the Net
das Web	the Web
eine Website	website
eine Webseite	web page
eine Homepage	homepage
ein(e) Internetbenutzer(in)	Internet user
ein Treffer *(m)*	hit
ein Hyperlink *(n)*	hyperlink
Serviceprovider *(m)*	service provider
eine Suchmaschine	search engine
ein Browser *(m)*	browser
ein Bookmark *(n)*	bookmark
ein Lesezeichen *(n)*	bookmark
ein Chatraum *(m)*	chatroom
ein Forum *(n)*	forum
ein Schwarzes Brett *(n)*	message board
ein Diskussionsforum *(n)*	discussion board
das Instant Messaging	instant messaging
eine Webcam	webcam
ein Computerspiel *(n)*	computer game
eine Spielkonsole	games console
ein(e) Gamer(in)	gamer
das Onlinegaming	online gaming
der Spam	spam
ein Spammer *(m)*	spammer
ein Virus *(n)*	virus
ein(e) Hacker(in)	hacker
online	online
offline	offline
drahtlos	wireless

Drucken aus dem Datei-Menü auswählen
select Print from the File menu

hast du zu Hause Breitband?
have you got broadband at home?

was ist deine E-Mail-Adresse? – M Punkt Schneider at mail Punkt DE
what's your e-mail address? – it's <u>m.schneider@mail.de</u>

ich muss gerade mal meine E-Mail checken
I just need to check my e-mail

kannst du mir eine Kopie der E-Mail schicken?
can you copy me in to the e-mail?

er hat den Witz an die ganze Klasse weitergeleitet
he forwarded the joke to the whole class

Inf **er ist ein echter Computerfreak**
he's a real computer geek

40 GRUSS- UND HÖFLICHKEITSFORMEN

GREETINGS AND POLITE PHRASES

grüßen	to greet
begrüßen	to welcome
vorstellen	to introduce
danken *(+dat)*	to thank
gratulieren	to congratulate
wünschen	to wish
sich verabschieden	to say goodbye
sich entschuldigen	to apologize
ein Kompliment *(n)*	compliment
guten Tag!	hello, good morning/afternoon
guten Morgen!	good morning
guten Abend!	good evening
hallo!	hi
grüß Gott!	hello, (good)bye *(southern Germany)*
tschüs!	cheerio
auf Wiedersehen!	(good)bye
gute Nacht!	good night, sleep well
freut mich!	pleased to meet you
wie geht es dir/Ihnen?	how are you?
wie geht's?	how are things?
bis bald!	see you soon
bis gleich!	see you soon
bis später!	see you later
bis nachher!	see you later
bis morgen!	see you tomorrow
guten Appetit!	enjoy your meal!

viel Glück!	good luck!
viel Spaß/Vergnügen!	have fun!
alles Gute!	all the best
gute Reise/Fahrt!	have a good trip, safe journey
willkommen	welcome
Entschuldigung!	sorry!, excuse me!
Verzeihung!	sorry!
(wie) bitte?	sorry? *(didn't hear)*, pardon?
tut mir leid	I'm sorry
ja	yes
nein	no
nein danke	no thanks
ja bitte	yes please
mit Vergnügen	with pleasure
bitte	please
bitte (schön/sehr)	you're welcome, here you are
danke (schön/sehr)	thank you
vielen Dank	thank you very much
keine Ursache	not at all
gern geschehen	you're welcome
auf dein/Ihr Wohl	good health!
zum Wohl!	cheers!
prost!	cheers!
Gesundheit!	bless you *(after sneezing)*
in Ordnung	OK
okay	OK
macht nichts	never mind

Festlichkeiten   festivities

fröhliche Weihnachten!	merry Christmas!
frohes neues Jahr!	happy New Year!
viele Grüße!	best wishes!
frohe Ostern!	happy Easter!
viel Glück zum Geburtstag!	happy birthday!
herzlichen Glückwunsch!	congratulations!
bravo!	well done!

darf ich Ihnen Gerd Müller vorstellen?
may I introduce Gerd Müller?

ich möchte Ihnen mein Beileid aussprechen
please accept my sympathy

bitte nehmen Sie Platz!
please take a seat

es geht
it's all right

das macht mir nichts aus
I don't mind

das kommt darauf an
it depends

viel Glück! - danke gleichfalls!
good luck! - thanks, same to you

ich bin Ihnen sehr dankbar
I'm very grateful to you

nichts zu danken
you're welcome/don't mention it

das tut mir (sehr) leid
I'm (terribly) sorry

wie schade
what a pity

tut mir leid, Sie zu stören
I'm sorry to bother you

stört es Sie, wenn ich rauche?
do you mind if I smoke?

grüßen Sie Ihre Mutter von mir
give my regards to your mother

können Sie mir Ihren Kugelschreiber leihen? - bitte
can you lend me your biro®? - here you are

entschuldigen Sie, können Sie mir sagen ...?
excuse me please, could you tell me ...?

41 IN URLAUB FAHREN
GOING ON HOLIDAY

in Urlaub fahren	to go on holiday
im Urlaub sein	to be on holiday
buchen	to book
online buchen	to book online
reisen	to travel
eine Tour machen	to go on a tour
besuchen	to visit
mieten	to rent
bestätigen	to confirm
rückgängig machen	to cancel
sich informieren (über)	to get information (about)
(ein)packen	to pack
die Koffer packen	to pack one's suitcases
mitnehmen	to take
vergessen	to forget
durchsuchen	to search
auspacken	to unpack
verzollen	to declare
schmuggeln	to smuggle
kontrollieren	to check
eine Versicherung abschließen	to take out insurance
seinen Reisepass verlängern lassen	to renew one's passport
sich impfen lassen	to be vaccinated
sich beschweren	to complain
die Reservierung	booking, reservation
eine Onlinebuchung	online booking
eine Anzahlung	deposit

der (Reise)pass	passport
der Personalausweis	identity card
die grüne Karte	green card *(insurance)*
das Visum	visa
die Fahrkarte	ticket
ein Reisescheck *(m)*	traveller's cheque
eine Reiseversicherung	travel insurance
eine Liste	list
das Gepäck	luggage
ein Koffer *(m)*	suitcase
eine Reisetasche	travel bag
ein Rucksack *(m)*	rucksack
eine Reisetasche	holdall
ein Etikett *(n)*	label
ein Kulturbeutel *(m)*	toilet bag

der Zoll	customs
der Zollbeamte	customs officer
die Grenze	border
die Passkontrolle	passport control
die Zollkontrolle	customs
im Urlaub	on holiday
berühmt	famous
malerisch	picturesque
zollfrei	duty-free

der Tourismus — tourism

der Urlaub	holiday(s) *(trip)*
die Ferien *(pl)*	holidays
eine Fernreise	long-haul trip
eine Weltreise	round-the-world trip
ein Kurzurlaub *(m)*	short break
ein Wochenendurlaub *(m)*	weekend break
ein Abenteuerurlaub *(m)*	adventure holiday
ein Sommerurlaub *(m)*	summer holiday
ein Wintersporturlaub *(m)*	winter sports holiday
Flitterwochen *(pl)*	honeymoon
eine Rundfahrt	tour

ein Reisebüro *(n)*	travel agent's
ein Prospekt *(m)*	leaflet, brochure
eine Broschüre	brochure
eine Pauschalreise	package tour
die Saison	season
ein(e) Tourist(in)	tourist
ein(e) Ausländer(in)	foreigner
die Gruppe	group, party
eine Touristen-Informationsstelle	tourist information centre
ein Reiseführer *(m)*	guide(book)
ein Sprachführer *(m)*	phrasebook
eine Karte	map
der Reiseleiter	holiday rep
ein(e) Führer(in)	guide *(person)*
ein Urlaubsort *(m)*	resort
Sehenswürdigkeiten *(pl)*	sights
Attraktionen *(pl)*	attractions
ein Besuch *(m)*	visit
eine Führung	guided tour
eine Fahrt	journey, trip
ein Tagesausflug *(m)*	day trip
ein Ausflug *(m)*	excursion, outing
eine Busreise	coach trip
ein Spaziergang	walk
der Aufenthalt	stay
die Gastfreundschaft	hospitality
das Konsulat	consulate
die Botschaft	embassy
Besonderheiten *(pl)*	specialities
das Kunstgewerbe	crafts
ein Souvenir *(n)*	souvenir
ein Andenken *(n)*	souvenir

Deutschland — Germany

der Bundesadler	German eagle
die Nationalhymne	national anthem

das Brandenburger Tor	Brandenburg Gate
der Kölner Dom	Cologne Cathedral
die Mauer	the (Berlin) Wall
die Wende	the fall of the Berlin Wall
die Grenze	the border
die Bundeshauptstadt	Federal capital of Germany

Bräuche — *customs*

die Lebensart	way of life
die Kultur	culture
die Küche	cooking
ein Gasthaus *(n)*	restaurant, inn
ein Gasthof *(m)*	restaurant, inn
der Weinbau	wine growing
das Oktoberfest	Munich beer festival
der Karneval	carnival

---

ich freue mich auf meinen Urlaub
I'm looking forward to going on holiday

nichts zu verzollen
nothing to declare

Inf **wir hatten einen Superurlaub**
we had a fab time on holiday

 Homework help

During my holidays I...
Im Urlaub habe ich...

We went to...
Wir sind nach ... gefahren.

I went on holiday with...
Ich bin mit ... in Urlaub gefahren.

We went by car/train/coach.
Wir sind mit dem Auto/Zug/Bus gefahren.

We stayed in a hotel/an apartment/a villa.
Wir haben in einem Hotel/einem Appartement/einer Villa gewohnt.

We visited...	I met...
Wir haben ... besucht.	**Ich habe ... getroffen.**

I went surfing/scuba diving.
Ich bin surfen/sporttauchen gegangen.

The hotel was lovely/a bit noisy.
Das Hotel war sehr nett/ein bisschen laut.

The food was really nice/not very good/unusual.
Das Essen war sehr gut/nicht besonders/ungewöhnlich.

The weather was lovely/OK/awful.
Das Wetter war schön/okay/furchtbar.

The people were friendly/rude.
Die Leute waren freundlich/unhöflich.

The best/worst bit was...
Das Beste/Schlimmste war...

I would/wouldn't go back there because...
Ich würde nicht wieder dorthin fahren, weil...

I would/wouldn't recommend it because...
Ich würde es empfehlen/nicht empfehlen, weil...

See also Sections

**16 FOOD, 25 THE CITY, 42 RAILWAYS, 43 FLYING, 44 PUBLIC
TRANSPORT, 45 AT THE HOTEL, 46 CAMPING, CARAVANNING
AND YOUTH HOSTELS, 47 AT THE SEASIDE** *and* **48 GEOGRAPHICAL
TERMS.**

42 EISENBAHN
RAILWAYS

eine Fahrkarte lösen	to buy a ticket
reservieren	to reserve, to book
umsteigen	to change
einsteigen	to get on/in
aussteigen	to get off
Verspätung haben	to be late
verunglücken	to crash
entgleisen	to be derailed
pünktlich	on time
verspätet	late
reserviert	reserved
besetzt	taken, occupied
frei	free
Nichtraucher	non-smoking

der Bahnhof
the station

der Bahnhof	station
die Eisenbahn	railways
die Deutsche Bahn	German railway system
der Fahrkartenschalter	ticket office
der Fahrkartenautomat	ticket vending machine
die Auskunft	information
die Abfahrts-/Ankunftstafel	departures/arrivals board
der Bahnhofsimbiss	station buffet
das Gepäck	luggage
ein Kofferkuli *(m)*	luggage trolley
die Gepäckannahme	left luggage
die Gepäckaufbewahrung	left luggage
Schließfächer *(pl)*	left luggage lockers

der Zug	**the train**
ein Nahverkehrszug *(m)*	local train
ein Eilzug *(m)*	fast train
ein Pendlerzug *(m)*	commuter train
ein Nachtzug *(m)*	night train
ein Schnellzug *(m)*	express train
ein IC *(m)* (Intercityzug)	Intercity train
ein ICE *(m)* (Intercityexpresszug)	Intercity express train
die Lok(omotive)	engine
eine Dampflok	steam engine
der Speisewagen	dining car
ein Wagen *(m)*	coach
ein Waggon *(m)*	coach, carriage
das Abteil	compartment
ein Liegewagen *(m)*	sleeper carriage
ein Schlafwagen *(m)*	sleeper carriage
ein Schlafplatz *(m)*	sleeping berth
der Gepäckwagen	luggage van
die Toilette	toilet
die Tür	door
das Fenster	window
der Sitz(platz)	seat
die Gepäckablage	luggage rack
das Gepäcknetz	luggage rack
die Notbremse	communication cord
das Alarmsignal	alarm
der Schaffner	guard, ticket collector
ein Reisender, eine Reisende	passenger

die Reise	**the journey**
das Gleis	platform; track
der Bahnsteig	platform
Geleise *(pl)*	tracks
die Bahnlinie	line
das Streckennetz	network
ein Bahnübergang *(m)*	level crossing

ein Tunnel *(m)*	tunnel
die Abfahrt	departure
die Ankunft	arrival
eine Haltestelle	stop
die Verbindung	connection

Fahrkarten   tickets

die Fahrkarte	ticket
der Fahrausweis	ticket
der Fahrschein	ticket
der ermäßigte Fahrpreis	reduced rate
ein Erwachsener, eine Erwachsene	adult
ein Kind *(n)*	child
eine Einzelfahrkarte	single (ticket)
eine Rückfahrkarte	return (ticket)
die erste/zweite Klasse	first/second class
eine Reservierung	reservation
der Fahrplan	timetable
Wochentage *(pl)*	weekdays
Sonn- und Feiertage	Sundays and public holidays
werktags	on weekdays (and Saturdays)
sonntags	on Sundays
in der Spitzenzeit	at peak time
außerhalb der Spitzenzeit	off-peak

---

per Bahn   **ich bin im Zug**
by rail/train   I'm on the train

ich bin mit dem Zug nach München gefahren
I went to Munich by train

eine einfache Fahrkarte/eine Rückfahrkarte nach Köln, bitte
a single/return to Cologne, please

wann fährt der nächste/letzte Zug nach Mannheim?
when is the next/last train to Mannheim?

---

der Zug aus Hamburg hat zwanzig Minuten Verspätung
the train arriving from Hamburg is 20 minutes late

der Zug ist pünktlich
the train is running on time

der Zug fährt über Essen
the train goes via Essen

die Fahrkarten bitte
tickets please

ich kam gerade noch rechtzeitig an
I got there just in time

er hat mich vom Bahnhof abgeholt
he came and picked me up at the station

ist dieser Platz besetzt?
is this seat taken?

Sie müssen in Leipzig umsteigen
you have to change at Leipzig

dieser Zug hält in...
this train calls at...

von den Türen zurücktreten
stand clear of the doors

gute Reise!
have a good journey!

43 FLIEGEN
FLYING

abfliegen	to leave
abheben	to take off
landen	to land
fliegen	to fly
einchecken	to check in
online einchecken	to check in online
durch die Sicherheitskontrolle gehen	to go through security

am Flughafen	**at the airport**
der Flughafen	airport
der Terminal	terminal
die Start- und Landebahn	runway
die Runway	runway
das Bodenpersonal	ground staff
die Flugleitung	air-traffic control
die Fluggesellschaft	airline
die Billigfluglinie	budget airline
die Abfertigung	check-in
ein Check-in-Automat *(m)*	self check-in
ein E-Ticket *(n)*	e-ticket
die Bordkarte	boarding pass
das Übergepäck	excess baggage
ein Zuschlag *(m)*	supplement
das Handgepäck	hand luggage
die Sicherheitskontrolle	security control
die Passkontrolle	passport control
der Duty-free-Laden	duty-free shop
zollfreie Waren *(pl)*	duty-free (goods)
die Abflughalle	departure lounge

eine Business Lounge	business lounge
der Flugsteig	gate
eine Ankunftshalle	arrivals hall
die Gepäckausgabe	baggage reclaim
ein Gepäckband *(n)*	baggage carousel
eine Autovermietung	car hire

an Bord

ein Flugzeug *(n)*	plane
ein Jumbojet *(m)*	jumbo jet
ein Hubschrauber *(m)*	helicopter
der Flügel	wing
der Propeller	propeller
die Nase	nose
der Schwanz	tail
ein Sitz *(m)*	seat
der Sicherheitsgurt	seat belt
das Fenster	window
der Gang	aisle
Gepäckfächer *(pl)*	overhead lockers
die Economy-/Businessklasse	economy/business class
der Notausstieg	emergency exit
eine Sauerstoffmaske	oxygen mask
eine Schwimmweste	life jacket
Sicherheitsmaßnahmen *(pl)*	safety procedures
der Flug	flight
ein Direktflug *(m)*	direct flight
ein Inlandsflug *(m)*	domestic flight
ein Auslandsflug *(m)*	international flight
ein Langstreckenflug *(m)*	long-haul flight
ein Kurzstreckenflug *(m)*	short-haul flight
ein Bordmagazin *(n)*	inflight magazine
die Höhe	altitude
die Geschwindigkeit	speed
der Abflug	departure
der Start	take-off
die Ankunft	arrival

die Landung	landing
eine Notlandung	emergency landing
eine Turbulenz	turbulence
eine Zwischenlandung	stop-over
eine Verzögerung	delay

die Besatzung	crew
der Pilot	pilot
ein(e) Steward(ess)	flight attendant, steward(ess)
ein Passagier *(m)*	passenger *(male and female)*
der Luftpirat	hijacker

| gestrichen | cancelled |
| verzögert | delayed |

---

möchten Sie einen Fenster- oder Gangplatz?
would you like a window or an aisle seat?

haben Sie alle Koffer selbst gepackt?
did you pack all your bags yourself?

das Einsteigen beginnt um 2.45 Uhr
boarding starts at 2.45

Ihr Gepäck hat 10 Kilo Übergewicht
your luggage is 10kg overweight

Passagiere des Fluges BA209 bitte zum Flugsteig 17
flight BA209 now boarding at gate number 17

letzter Aufruf für Flug AB222 nach Manchester
last call for flight AB222 to Manchester

bitte anschnallen   **mein Koffer ist nicht angekommen**
fasten your seat belts   my suitcase hasn't arrived

wir haben einen Billigflug im Internet gefunden
we found a cheap flight online

44 ÖFFENTLICHER NAHVERKEHR

PUBLIC TRANSPORT

einsteigen	to get on
aussteigen	to get off
warten (auf + *acc*)	to wait (for)
abfahren	to leave
ankommen	to arrive
umsteigen	to change
anhalten	to stop
verpassen	to miss
seinen Fahrschein entwerten	to punch one's ticket
schwarzfahren	to dodge the fare
ein Bus *(m)*	bus
ein Autobus *(m)*	bus
ein Gelenkbus *(m)*	bendy bus
ein Doppeldeckerbus *(m)*	double-decker bus
ein Shuttle *(m)*	shuttle
ein (Reise)bus *(m)*	coach
die Straßenbahn	tram
die U-Bahn	underground
die S-Bahn	local train
ein Taxi *(n)*	taxi
der Fahrer	driver
der Schaffner	inspector, conductor
ein Passagier *(m)*	passenger *(male and female)*
ein Fahrgast *(m)*	passenger *(male and female)*
ein(e) Schwarzfahrer(in)	fare dodger

der Busbahnhof	bus station
der Bahnhof	station
ein Wartehäuschen *(n)*	bus shelter
eine Bushaltestelle	bus stop
eine Straßenbahnhaltestelle	tram stop
der Fahrkartenschalter	booking office
ein Fahrkartenautomat *(m)*	ticket machine
der Ausgang	exit
ein Netz *(n)*	network
die Linie	line
der Einstieg	entrance
der Ausstieg	exit
die Abfahrt	departure
die Richtung	direction
die Ankunft	arrival
die Spitze	front
das Ende	back
der Sitz(platz)	seat
eine Fahrkarte	ticket
ein Fahrschein *(m)*	ticket
der Fahrpreis	fare
ein Fahrscheinheft *(n)*	book of tickets
eine Mehrfahrtenkarte	multi-journey ticket
eine Tageskarte	day ticket
eine Monatskarte	monthly ticket
eine Zeitkarte	season ticket
ein Buspass *(m)*	bus pass
ein Erwachsener, eine Erwachsene	adult
ein Kind *(n)*	child
der Tarif	fares
die Ermäßigung	reduction
ein Zuschlag *(m)*	excess fare
die Stoßzeit	rush hour

ich bin im Bus I'm on the bus	**steig in den Bus ein!** get on the bus!
ich fahre mit dem Bus zur Schule I go to school by bus	**ist dieser Fahrschein noch gültig?** is this ticket still valid?

mit welchem Bus kann ich zum Dom fahren?
what bus can I get to go to the Cathedral?

wo ist die nächste U-Bahn-Station?
where's the nearest underground station?

du musst am Rathaus aussteigen get off at the town hall	**es ist zwei Haltestellen von hier** it's two stops from here

Note

Note the use of mit with public transport:

mit dem Bus/dem Zug/der U-Bahn/der Fähre
by bus/train/underground/ferry

Remember that the preposition mit is always followed by the dative.

See also Sections

42 RAILWAYS *and* **43 FLYING.**

45 IM HOTEL

AT THE HOTEL

einchecken	to check in
auschecken	to check out
die Rechnung bezahlen	to pay one's bill
Zimmerservice bestellen	to order room service
sich beschweren	to complain
(voll) belegt	no vacancies
Zimmer frei	vacancies
geschlossen	closed
komfortabel	comfortable
inbegriffen	included
für Selbstversorger	self-catering
ein Hotel *(n)*	hotel
eine Pension	guest house
Fremdenzimmer *(pl)*	rooms to let
ein Motel *(n)*	motel
ein Appartement *(n)*	apartment
eine Villa	villa
ein Landhaus *(n)*	cottage
die Vollpension	full board
die Halbpension	half board
das Pauschalpreis	all-inclusive price
die Rechnung	bill
die Mehrwertsteuer	VAT
das Trinkgeld	tip
die Bedienung	service
eine Beschwerde	complaint
eine Reklamation	complaint
eine Reservierung	reservation

der Empfang	reception
das Foyer	lobby
das Restaurant	restaurant
der Speiseraum	dining room
die Bar	bar
ein Frühstücksbüfett *(n)*	breakfast buffet
das Mittagessen	lunch
das Abendessen	dinner
der Zimmerservice	room service
ein Weckruf *(m)*	wake-up call
ein Parkplatz *(m)*	car park
ein Aufzug *(m)*	lift

ein Gast *(m)*	guest *(male and female)*
der Direktor, die Direktorin	manager
der Empfangschef	receptionist *(male)*
die Empfangsdame	receptionist *(female)*
der Portier	porter
das Zimmermädchen	chambermaid

das Zimmer — the room

ein Einzelzimmer *(n)*	single room
ein Doppelzimmer *(n)*	double room
ein Zweibettzimmer *(n)*	twin room
ein Familienzimmer *(n)*	family room
ein Bett *(n)*	bed
ein Doppelbett *(n)*	double bed
ein Kinderbett *(n)*	cot
das Bettzeug	bedding
Handtücher *(pl)*	towels
ein Badezimmer *(n)*	bathroom
ein Bad *(n)*	bath
eine Dusche	shower
das warme Wasser	hot water
ein Waschbecken *(n)*	washbasin
die Toilette	toilet

die Klimaanlage	air conditioning
das Satelliten-/Kabelfernsehen	satellite/cable TV
der Internetzugang	Internet access
die Minibar	minibar
ein Schließfach *(n)*	safety deposit box
der Notausgang	emergency exit
eine Feuertreppe	fire escape
ein Balkon *(m)*	balcony
die Aussicht	view
der Schlüssel	key
eine Schlüsselkarte	keycard

Übernachtung mit Frühstück
bed and breakfast

ein Zwei-/Drei-Sterne-Hotel
a two/three star hotel

haben Sie Zimmer frei?
have you got any vacancies?

im zweiten Stock
on the second floor

ich möchte gern ein Einzelzimmer/ein Doppelzimmer
I'd like a single/double room

ich möchte ein Zimmer mit eigenem Bad
I'd like an ensuite room

ein Zimmer mit Blick auf die Berge
a room with a view of the mountains

für wie viel Nächte?
for how many nights?

wir sind voll belegt
we're full

das Bad ist gegenüber
the bathroom is just opposite

die Auscheckzeit ist 11 Uhr
check-out time is 11 o'clock

ist das einschließlich Frühstück?
is breakfast included?

den Schlüssel für Zimmer 12, bitte
the key for room 12, please

könnten Sie mich bitte um sieben Uhr wecken?
could you please wake me at seven a.m.?

könnten wir bitte noch eine Decke bekommen?
could we have an extra blanket, please?

'nicht stören'   **können wir bitte bezahlen?**
'do not disturb'   could we pay the bill, please?

kann ich meine Tasche irgendwo lassen?
is there somewhere I can leave my bag?

Inf **wir wohnten in einem Nobelhotel**
we stayed in a really posh hotel

Note

Double beds in Germany are often two single beds pushed
together. A traditional double bed is known as a 'French bed':

ich möchte ein Doppelzimmer mit französischem Bett
I'd like a double room with a double bed

46 CAMPING, WOHNWAGEN UND JUGENDHERBERGEN

CAMPING, CARAVANNING AND YOUTH HOSTELS

campen	to camp
zelten	to camp
Camping machen	to go camping
wild zelten	to camp in the wild
Ferien im Wohnwagen machen	to go caravanning
per Anhalter fahren	to hitch-hike
trampen	to hitch-hike
das Zelt aufbauen	to pitch the tent
das Zelt abbauen	to take down the tent
im Freien übernachten	to sleep out in the open
das Camping	camping
ein Campingplatz *(m)*	campsite
ein(e) Camper(in)	camper
ein Zelt *(n)*	tent
eine Luftmatratze	airbed
eine Bodenplane	ground sheet
ein Zeltpflock *(m)*	peg
ein Hering *(m)*	peg
ein Seil *(n)*	rope
ein Feuer *(n)*	fire
ein Lagerfeuer *(n)*	campfire
ein Campingkocher *(m)*	camping stove
das Campinggas®	Calorgas®
ein Barbecue *(n)*	barbecue

ein Taschenmesser *(n)*	penknife
eine Taschenlampe	torch
die sanitären Anlagen	showers and toilets
die Duschen *(pl)*	showers
die Toiletten *(pl)*	toilets
das Trinkwasser	drinking water
ein Abfalleimer *(m)*	rubbish bin
eine Stechmücke	midge, gnat
ein Spielbereich *(m)*	play area
ein Kinderklub *(m)*	kids' club
ein(e) Animateur(in)	activity leader
der Wohnwagenurlaub	caravanning
ein Wohnwagenplatz *(m)*	caravan site
ein Wohnwagen *(m)*	caravan
ein Campingbus *(m)*	camper (van)
ein Anhänger *(m)*	trailer
eine Herberge	hostel
eine Jugendherberge	youth hostel
ein Chalet *(n)*	chalet
eine Berghütte	mountain refuge
der Schlafraum	dormitory
ein Privatraum *(m)*	private room
ein(e) Mitbewohner(in)	roommate
ein Schlafsack *(m)*	sleeping bag
der Mitgliedsausweis	membership card
eine Kantine	canteen
eine Küche	kitchen
ein Spielezimmer *(n)*	games room
ein Ausgehverbot *(n)*	curfew
ein Rucksack *(m)*	rucksack
das Trampen	hitch-hiking
ein Wanderer, eine Wanderin	backpacker

dürfen wir hier zelten?
may we camp here?

'Zelten verboten'   **'Trinkwasser'**
'no camping'   'drinking water'

ich möchte einen Zeltplatz für zwei Tage
I'd like a space for a tent for two days

wo können wir unser Wohnmobil parken?
where can we park our camper van?

frische Bettlaken sind inbegriffen
clean sheets are included

Inf **die Jugendherberge war ein Dreckloch, aber ich hatte tolle Mitbewohner**
the youth hostel was a dump but my roommates were cool

Note

The German word der Hering can mean both 'herring' and 'tent peg'.

47 AM MEER

AT THE SEASIDE

schwimmen	to swim
baden	to bathe, to swim
treiben	to float, to drift
planschen	to splash about
tauchen	to dive
sporttauchen gehen	to go scuba diving
schnorcheln gehen	to go snorkelling
surfen gehen	to go surfing
windsurfen gehen	to go windsurfing
Wasserski fahren gehen	to go waterskiing
gleitschirmfliegen gehen	to go paragliding
ertrinken	to drown
sonnenbaden	to sunbathe
sich bräunen	to get a tan
einen Sonnenbrand bekommen	to get sunburnt
sich schälen	to peel
graben	to dig
segeln	to go sailing, to sail
seekrank sein	to be seasick
rudern	to row
sinken	to sink
kentern	to capsize
surfen	to surf
windsurfen	to windsurf
schattig	shady
sonnig	sunny
sonnengebräunt	tanned

im Schatten	in the shade
in der Sonne	in the sun
das Meer	sea
die See	sea
ein See *(m)*	lake
der Strand	beach
der Sand	sand
die Düne	sand dune
die Kieselsteine *(pl)*	pebbles, shingle
ein Fels(en) *(m)*	rock
eine Klippe	cliff
eine Welle	wave
die Flut	(high) tide
die Ebbe	low tide
die Strömung	current
die Küste	coast
das Deich	sea wall
ein Hafen *(m)*	harbour
der Kai	quay
der Jachthafen	marina
die Strandpromenade	esplanade
eine Kirmes	funfair
ein Leuchtturm *(m)*	lighthouse
eine Boje	buoy
der Horizont	horizon
die Überfahrt	crossing
ein Rettungsschwimmer *(m)*	lifeguard
ein(e) Schwimmer(in)	swimmer
ein(e) Surfer(in)	surfer
ein(e) Windsurfer(in)	windsurfer
der Meeresgrund	seabed
ein Fisch *(m)*	fish
eine Krabbe	crab

ein Krebs *(m)*	crab
eine Qualle	jellyfish
ein Seestern *(m)*	starfish
ein Seeigel *(m)*	sea urchin
eine Muschel	shell; mussel
ein Hai *(m)*	shark
ein Delfin *(m)*	dolphin
eine Möwe	seagull

Schiffe und Boote — boats

ein Schiff *(n)*	ship
ein Boot *(n)*	boat
ein Ruderboot *(n)*	rowing boat
ein Segelboot *(n)*	sailing boat
ein Motorboot *(n)*	motor boat
ein Segelschiff *(n)*	sailing ship
eine Jacht	yacht
ein Kreuzer *(m)*	cruise ship
eine Fähre	ferry
eine Autofähre	car ferry
ein Dingi *(n)*	dinghy
ein Gummiboot *(n)*	rubber dinghy
ein Tretboot *(n)*	pedalo
ein Ruder *(n)*	oar
das Segel	sail
ein Anker *(m)*	anchor
ein Wrack *(n)*	wreck
eine Bootsfahrt	boat trip

Strandzubehör — things for the beach

ein Badeanzug *(m)*	swimsuit
eine Badehose	trunks
ein Bikini *(m)*	bikini
Sandalen *(pl)*	flip flops
eine Badekappe	swimming cap
eine Taucherbrille	goggles

ein Schnorchel *(m)*	snorkel
Schwimmflossen *(pl)*	flippers
ein Surfbrett *(n)*	surfboard
ein Rettungsring *(m)*	lifebelt
eine Luftmatratze	Lilo®
ein Liegestuhl *(m)*	deckchair
eine Sonnenliege	sun lounger
ein Badetuch *(n)*	towel
ein Sonnenschirm *(m)*	parasol
ein Windschutz *(m)*	windbreak
ein Sonnenhut *(m)*	sunhat
eine Sonnenbrille	sunglasses
das Sonnenöl	suntan oil/lotion
die After-Sun-Creme	after-sun
ein Eimer *(m)*	bucket
ein Spaten *(m)*	spade
eine Sandburg	sand castle
eine Frisbee-Scheibe	frisbee
ein Ball *(m)*	ball
ein Picknick *(n)*	picnic
eine Strandbar	beach bar

---

ich kann nicht schwimmen
I can't swim

ich kann nicht mehr stehen
I can't touch the bottom

'Baden verboten'
'no bathing'

'Mann über Bord!'
'man overboard!'

au! mich hat eine Qualle gestochen
ouch! I've been stung by a jellyfish

kannst du meinen Rücken mit Sonnencreme einreiben?
can you put some suncream on my back?

sie ist rot wie ein Krebs
he's as red as a lobster

Inf **das ist vielleicht eine Bullenhitze!**
it's a real scorcher!

---

die Landkarte	map
der Kontinent	continent
der Erdteil	continent
ein Land *(n)*	country
ein Staat *(m)*	state
ein Entwicklungsland *(n)*	developing country
ein Gebiet *(n)*	area, region
ein Bundesland *(n)*	'Land' (or state) of the Federal Republic of Germany
der Bezirk	district
eine Stadt	town, city
ein Dorf *(n)*	village
die Hauptstadt	capital city
ein Gebirge *(n)*	mountains
ein Berg *(m)*	mountain, hill
eine Bergkette	mountain range
ein Hügel *(m)*	hill
eine Klippe	cliff
der Gipfel	summit
die Spitze	peak
der Pass	pass
die Schlucht	ravine
ein Tal *(n)*	valley
eine Ebene	plain
ein Plateau *(n)*	plateau
ein Gletscher *(m)*	glacier
ein Vulkan *(m)*	volcano
eine Höhle	cave
ein Stalaktit *(m)*	stalactite
ein Stalagmit *(m)*	stalagmite

das Meer	sea
die See	sea
der Ozean	ocean
der See	lake
der Fluss	river
der Strom	(large) river
der Bach	stream
der Kanal	canal
der Teich	pond
die Quelle	spring
die Küste	coast
eine Insel	island
eine Halbinsel	peninsula
das Kap	cape
die Bucht	bay
die Mündung	estuary
die Wüste	desert
der Wald	forest
der Regenwald	rainforest
der Dschungel	jungle
die Breite	latitude
die Länge	longitude
die Höhe	altitude
die Tiefe	depth
die Fläche	area
die Bevölkerung	population
die Welt	world
das Universum	universe
die Tropen *(pl)*	Tropics
der Nordpol	North Pole
der Südpol	South Pole
der Äquator	Equator

das **Sonnensystem**	solar system
die **Sonne**	sun
der **Mond**	moon
ein **Planet** *(m)*	planet
die **Erde**	Earth
der **Jupiter**	Jupiter
der **Mars**	Mars
der **Merkur**	Mercury
der **Neptun**	Neptune
der **Pluto**	Pluto
der **Saturn**	Saturn
der **Uranus**	Uranus
die **Venus**	Venus
ein **Stern** *(m)*	star
eine **Sternschnuppe**	shooting star
ein **Komet** *(n)*	comet
ein **Sternbild** *(n)*	constellation
die **Milchstraße**	Milky Way

---

welches ist der höchste Berg Europas?
what is the highest mountain in Europe?

Holland ist ein flaches Land   **die Erde bewegt sich um die Sonne**
the Netherlands is a flat country   the Earth moves around the Sun

---

See also Sections

49 COUNTRIES, CONTINENTS AND PLACE NAMES *and*
50 NATIONALITIES.

49 Länder, Erdteile und Ortsnamen

Countries, continents and place names

Länder	countries
Afghanistan	Afghanistan
Ägypten	Egypt
Argentinien	Argentina
Brasilien	Brazil
Belgien	Belgium
die Bundesrepublik Deutschland (BRD)	Federal Republic of Germany; West Germany *(historical)*
China	China
Dänemark	Denmark
die Deutsche Demokratische Republik (DDR)	GDR, East Germany *(historical)*
Deutschland	Germany
England	England
Finnland	Finland
Frankreich	France
Griechenland	Greece
Großbritannien	Great Britain
Holland	Holland
Hongkong	Hong Kong
Indien	India
Indonesien	Indonesia
(der) Iran	Iran
(der) Irak	Iraq

Irland	Ireland
Israel	Israel
Italien	Italy
Japan	Japan
Kanada	Canada
der Libanon	Lebanon
Libyen	Libya
Luxemburg	Luxembourg
Malta	Malta
Mexiko	Mexico
Marokko	Morocco
die Niederlande	Netherlands
Nordirland	Northern Ireland
Norwegen	Norway
Österreich	Austria
Pakistan	Pakistan
Polen	Poland
Portugal	Portugal
Russland	Russia
Saudi-Arabien	Saudi Arabia
Schottland	Scotland
Schweden	Sweden
die Schweiz	Switzerland
Singapur	Singapore
Spanien	Spain
Südafrika	South Africa
Syrien	Syria
Thailand	Thailand
Tschechien	Czech Republic
die Tschechische Republik	Czech Republic
die Türkei	Turkey
die Ukraine	Ukraine
Ungarn	Hungary
die USA	United States
das Vereinigte Königreich	United Kingdom
die Vereinigten Staaten	United States (of America)

Wales	Wales
Zypern	Cyprus

Erdteile — continents

Afrika	Africa
Amerika	America
die Antarktis	Antarctica
Asien	Asia
Australien	Australia
Europa	Europe
Nordamerika	North America
Südamerika	South America

Städte — cities

Amsterdam	Amsterdam
Athen	Athens
Belfast	Belfast
Berlin	Berlin
Bonn	Bonn
Brüssel	Brussels
Cardiff	Cardiff
Kopenhagen	Copenhagen
Edinburg	Edinburgh
Genf	Geneva
Helsinki	Helsinki
Kairo	Cairo
Köln	Cologne
Lissabon	Lisbon
London	London
Luxemburg	Luxembourg
Madrid	Madrid
Moskau	Moscow
München	Munich
Oslo	Oslo
Peking	Beijing
Prag	Prague

Rom	Rome
Schanghai	Shanghai
Stockholm	Stockholm
Tallinn	Tallinn
Tokio	Tokyo
Venedig	Venice
Warschau	Warsaw
Wien	Vienna

Gebiete / regions

die Dritte Welt	the Third World
West-/Ost-/Mitteleuropa	Western/Eastern/Central Europe
der Westen	the West
der Orient	East
der Osten	the East
der Nahe Osten	Middle East
der Ferne Osten	Far East
der Golf	the Gulf
Skandinavien	Scandinavia
Norddeutschland	North Germany
Süddeutschland	South Germany
Bayern	Bavaria
das Rheinland	Rhineland
der Balkan	Balkans
das schottische Hochland	Scottish Highlands

Meere, Flüsse und Gebirge / seas, rivers and mountains

das Mittelmeer	Mediterranean
die Nordsee	North Sea
die Ostsee	Baltic
der Atlantik	Atlantic
der Pazifik	Pacific
das Nordpolarmeer	Arctic Ocean
der Indische Ozean	Indian Ocean
der Kanal	English Channel

der Rhein	Rhine
die Elbe	Elbe
die Donau	Danube
die Mosel	Moselle
die Themse	Thames
der Bodensee	Lake Constance
die Alpen *(pl)*	Alps
die Anden *(pl)*	the Andes
der Himalaja	the Himalayas
die Pyrenäen *(pl)*	Pyrenees
die Rocky Mountains *(pl)*	the Rockies
die Sierra Nevada	the Sierra Nevada

Inseln / islands

die Antillen *(pl)*	West Indies
Barbados	Barbados
die Bahamas *(pl)*	the Bahamas
die Balearen *(pl)*	the Balearics
Bermuda	Bermuda
die Falklandinseln *(pl)*	the Falkland Islands
die Färöer *(pl)*	the Faroe Islands
Fidschi	Fiji
die Hebriden *(pl)*	Hebrides
der Iberische Halbinsel	Iberian Peninsula
Jamaika	Jamaica
die Jungferninseln *(pl)*	the Virgin Islands
die Kanalinseln *(pl)*	Channel Islands
die Kanaren *(pl)*	the Canaries
Korfu	Corfu
Korsika	Corsica
Kreta	Crete
Madagaskar	Madagascar
die Malediven *(pl)*	the Maldives
Mallorca	Majorca
Mauritius	Mauritius
die Nordfriesischen Inseln	North Friesian Islands *(pl)*

die Orkneys *(pl)*	the Orkneys
die Ostfriesischen Inseln *(pl)*	East Friesian Islands
der Peloponnes	Peloponnese
die Philippinen *(pl)*	the Philippines
Puerto Rico	Puerto Rico
Sardinien	Sardinia
die Seychellen *(pl)*	the Seychelles
die Shetlands *(pl)*	the Shetlands
Sizilien	Sicily
Trinidad und Tobago	Trinidad and Tobago
die Westindischen Inseln *(pl)*	the West Indies
das Mittelmeer	Mediterranean

---

ich komme aus England/aus der Türkei
I come from England/Turkey

ich wohne in Berlin   **ich fahre nach Wien**
I live in Berlin   I'm going to Vienna

ich habe meinen Urlaub in Spanien/in der Schweiz verbracht
I spent my holidays in Spain/Switzerland

Note

★ Most countries and regions in German do not need an
   article, but some always take one, eg die Turkei, die Schweiz,
   der Sudan, der Balkan (the Balkans):

   wir fahren in die Schweiz
   we're going to Switzerland

   Some countries can be found with or without an article, eg
   (der) Irak, (der) Iran, (der) Libanon. This means you can say
   either in Irak or im Irak.

Note—cont'd

★ The word See can be both masculine and feminine: der See means 'lake', whereas die See means 'sea'. The most common word for 'sea', though, is das Meer.

See also Section

50 NATIONALITIES.

50 NATIONALITÄTEN
NATIONALITIES

ausländisch	foreign
fremd	foreign
ein Afghane, eine Afghanin	Afghan
ein(e) Ägypter(in)	Egyptian
ein(e) Amerikaner(in)	American
ein(e) Australier(in)	Australian
ein(e) Belgier(in)	Belgian
ein Brite, eine Britin	Briton
ein Chinese, eine Chinesin	Chinese
ein Däne, eine Dänin	Dane
ein Deutscher, eine Deutsche	German
ein(e) Engländer(in)	Englishman/woman
ein Finne, eine Finnin	Finn
ein Franzose, eine Französin	Frenchman/woman
ein(e) Holländer(in)	Dutchman/woman
ein(e) Inder(in)	Indian
ein(e) Indonesier(in)	Indonesian
ein(e) Iraner(in)	Iranian
ein(e) Iraker(in)	Iraqi
ein Ire, eine Irin	Irishman/woman
ein(e) Israeli	Israeli
ein(e) Italiener(in)	Italian
ein(e) Japaner(in)	Japanese
ein(e) Kanadier(in)	Canadian
ein Kroate, eine Kroatin	Croat, Croatian
ein Libanese, eine Libanesin	Lebanese
ein(e) Luxemburger(in)	man/woman from Luxembourg
ein(e) Malteser(in)	Maltese
ein(e) Marokkaner(in)	Moroccan

ein(e) Niederländer(in)	man/woman from the Netherlands
ein(e) Norweger(in)	Norwegian
ein(e) Österreicher(in)	Austrian
ein(e) Pakistaner(in)	Pakistani
ein Pole, eine Polin	Pole
ein Portugiese, eine Portugiesin	Portuguese
ein Russe, eine Russin	Russian
ein(e) Saudi	Saudi
ein Schotte, eine Schottin	Scot
ein Schwede, eine Schwedin	Swede
ein(e) Schweizer(in)	Swiss
ein Serbe, eine Serbin	Serb, Serbian
ein Slowake, eine Slowakin	Slovak
ein(e) Spanier(in)	Spaniard
ein(e) Südafrikaner(in)	South African
ein(e) Thailänder(in)	Thai
ein Tscheche, eine Tschechin	Czech
ein Türke, eine Türkin	Turk
ein(e) Ukrainer(in)	Ukrainian
ein(e) Ungar(in)	Hungarian
ein(e) Waliser(in)	Welshman, Welsh woman
ein(e) Zyptiot(in)	Cypriot
afghanisch	Afghan
ägyptisch	Egyptian
amerikanisch	American
australisch	Australian
belgisch	Belgian
britisch	British
chinesisch	Chinese
dänisch	Danish
deutsch	German
englisch	English
finnisch	Finnish
französisch	French
holländisch	Dutch
indisch	Indian

indonesisch	Indonesian
iranisch	Iranian
irakisch	Iraqi
irisch	Irish
israelisch	Israeli
italienisch	Italian
japanisch	Japanese
kanadisch	Canadian
kroatisch	Croatian
libanesisch	Lebanese
luxemburgisch	Luxembourg
maltesisch	Maltese
marokkanisch	Moroccan
niederländisch	from the Netherlands
nordirisch	Northern Irish
norwegisch	Norwegian
österreichisch	Austrian
pakistanisch	Pakistani
polnisch	Polish
portugiesisch	Portuguese
russisch	Russian
saudi-arabisch	Saudi Arabian
schottisch	Scottish
schwedisch	Swedish
schweizerisch	Swiss
serbisch	Serbian
slowakisch	Slovakian
spanisch	Spanish
südafrikanisch	South African
thailändisch	Thai
tschechisch	Czech
türkisch	Turkish
ukrainisch	Ukrainian
ungarisch	Hungarian
walisisch	Welsh
zyptiotisch	Cypriot

orientalisch	Oriental
fernöstlich	Far Eastern
westlich	Western
östlich	Eastern
afrikanisch	African
asiatisch	Asian
europäisch	European
arabisch	Arabic
skandinavisch	Scandinavian
norddeutsch	North German
süddeutsch	South German
bayrisch	Bavarian
rheinisch	Rhenish, from the Rhineland
sächsisch	Saxon
schwäbisch	Swabian
Berliner	from Berlin
Münchner	from Munich
Londoner	from London

Ewan ist Schotte
Ewan is Scottish

Ewan hat schottische Eltern
Ewan has Scottish parents

eine Londoner Zeitung
a London newspaper

im In- und Ausland
at home and abroad

See also Section

51 LANGUAGES.

51 SPRACHEN
LANGUAGES

lernen	to learn
auswendig lernen	to learn by heart
studieren	to study
verstehen	to understand
schreiben	to write
lesen	to read
sprechen	to speak
wiederholen	to repeat
aussprechen	to pronounce
übersetzen	to translate
meinen	to mean
nachschlagen	to look up
(sich) verbessern	to improve
üben	to practise
sich einprägen	to memorise
zweisprachig sein	to be bilingual
Deutsch	German
Englisch	English
Französisch	French
Spanisch	Spanish
Italienisch	Italian
Griechisch	(modern) Greek
Altgriechisch	classical Greek
Lateinisch	Latin
Russisch	Russian
Arabisch	Arabic
Chinesisch	Chinese
Japanisch	Japanese
Gälisch	Gaelic

eine Sprache	language
die Muttersprache	native language, mother tongue
eine Fremdsprache	foreign language
neuere Sprachen *(pl)*	modern languages
der Dialekt	dialect
der Slang	slang
der Wortschatz	vocabulary
das Vokabular	vocabulary
die Grammatik	grammar
ein Akzent *(m)*	accent
die Aussprache	pronunciation
eine Übersetzung	translation
ein Wörterbuch *(n)*	dictionary
ein Synonymwörterbuch *(n)*	thesaurus
ein(e) Sprachlehrer(in)	language teacher
ein(e) Fremdsprachenassistent(in)	language assistant
ein Sprachlabor *(n)*	language laboratory

ich verstehe dich/Sie nicht
I don't understand

ich lerne gerade Deutsch
I'm learning German

sie spricht fließend Spanisch
she speaks fluent Spanish

Englisch ist seine Muttersprache
English is his mother tongue

Petra hat ein Talent für Sprachen
Petra is good at languages

sie hat Sprachgefühl
she has a feel for languages

**einen Satz ins Englische
  übersetzen**
to translate a sentence into English

auf Deutsch
in German

was bedeutet das?
what does that mean?

schlag es im Wörterbuch nach
look it up in the dictionary

könnten Sie bitte etwas langsamer sprechen?
could you speak more slowly, please?

könnten Sie das bitte noch einmal wiederholen?
could you repeat that, please?

Inf ich bringe keinen vernünftigen Satz zusammen!
I can hardly string two words together!

See also Section

50 NATIONALITIES.

52 ZWISCHENFÄLLE
INCIDENTS

geschehen	to happen
passieren	to happen
vorkommen	to occur
stattfinden	to take place
treffen	to meet
zusammentreffen	to coincide
vermissen	to miss
sich (wieder)finden	to find oneself
fehlen	to be missing
fallen lassen	to drop, to let go of
verschütten	to spill
umstoßen	to knock over
fallen	to fall
verderben	to spoil
beschädigen	to damage
brechen	to break
zerbrechen	to break
verursachen	to cause
vorsichtig sein	to be careful
bekommen	to get, to receive
kriegen	to (manage to) get
vergessen	to forget
liegen lassen	to leave
verlieren	to lose
suchen	to look for
versuchen	to try
erkennen	to recognize
finden	to find

wiederfinden	to find (again)
sich verirren	to get lost
sich verlaufen	to get lost
vom Weg abkommen	to lose one's way
zerstreut	absent-minded
ungeschickt	clumsy
nachlässig	careless
unerwartet	unexpected
zufällig	by chance
ungewollt	inadvertently
glücklicherweise	luckily, fortunately
unglücklicherweise	unfortunately
ein Zufall *(m)*	coincidence
der Zufall	chance
eine Überraschung	surprise
das Glück	luck, chance
das Pech	bad luck
ein Zusammentreffen *(n)*	meeting, encounter
eine Verabredung	date, meeting
der Schaden	damage
die Vergesslichkeit	forgetfulness
der Verlust	loss
das Fundbüro	lost-property office
eine Belohnung	reward

---

was ist los?
what's up?

er ist hingefallen
he fell over

ich bin die Treppe hinuntergefallen
I fell down the stairs

tut mir leid, ich habe es vergessen
sorry, it slipped my mind

Achtung!	**Vorsicht!**
watch out!	careful!
es hat geklappt/nicht geklappt	**ich habe eben immer Pech!**
it worked/didn't work	just my luck!
welch ein Zufall!	**wie schade!**
what a coincidence!	what a pity!
Inf **was für ein Pech!**	*Inf* **der Glückspilz!**
what rotten luck!	the lucky devil!

 Homework help

One day, I...	
Eines Tages ... ich...	
Once I was in town/at the beach and...	
Ich war einmal in der Stadt/am Strand und...	
Once when I was walking home/playing football...	
Als ich einmal auf dem Nachhauseweg/beim Fußballspielen war,...	
A few weeks/years ago...	Last year...
Vor ein paar Wochen/Jahren...	**Letztes Jahr...**
And then...	After that...
Und dann...	**Danach...**
Suddenly...	Soon...
Plötzlich...	**Bald...**
Later...	Finally...
Später...	**Schließlich...**
Afterwards...	It just so happened that...
Nachher...	**Zufällig...**

53 UNFÄLLE

ACCIDENTS

fahren	to drive, to go
die Vorfahrt nicht beachten	not to give way
ein Rotlicht *(n)* überfahren	to go through a red light
ein Stoppschild *(n)* überfahren	to ignore a stop sign
ins Schleudern geraten	to skid
platzen	to burst
die Kontrolle verlieren	to lose control
anfahren	to hit
fahren gegen	to run into
überfahren	to run over
sich überschlagen	to somersault
demolieren	to wreck, to demolish
beschädigen	to damage
zerstören	to wreck, to destroy
Feuer fangen	to catch fire
eingeschlossen sein	to be trapped
entkommen	to escape
retten	to rescue
den Notdienst rufen	to call the emergency services
unter Schock *(dat)* stehen	to be in shock
das Bewusstsein verlieren	to lose consciousness
das Bewusstsein wiedererlangen	to regain consciousness
im Koma liegen	to be in a coma
sterben	to die
umkommen	to die
ums Leben kommen	to be killed

Verkehrsunfälle — road accidents

ein Unfall *(m)*	accident
ein Verkehrsunfall *(m)*	road accident

ein Autounfall *(m)*	car accident
ein Motorradunfall *(m)*	motorbike accident
die Fahrerflucht	hit-and-run
ein Seitenstreifen *(m)*	hard shoulder
die Straßenverkehrsordnung	Highway Code
ein Zusammenstoß *(m)*	car crash
eine Massenkarambolage	pile-up
ein Wrack *(n)*	wreck
der Aufprall	impact
ein Airbag *(m)*	airbag
eine Explosion	explosion
eine Geschwindigkeits- überschreitung	speeding
eine Alkoholkontrolle	breath test
die Trunkenheit am Steuer	drink-driving
die schlechte Sicht	poor visibility
der Nebel	fog
der Regen	rain
das Glatteis	black ice
ein Abhang *(m)*	cliff, precipice
der Schaden	damage
betrunken	drunk
verletzt	injured
tot	dead
ernst	serious
tödlich	fatal
leicht	minor
versichert	insured

andere Unfälle   other accidents

entgleisen	to be derailed
ausrutschen	to slip
ertrinken	to drown
ersticken	to suffocate
fallen (von)	to fall (from)

aus dem Fenster stürzen	to fall out of the window
einen elektrischen Schlag bekommen	to get an electric shock
durch einen Stromschlag ums Leben kommen	to electrocute oneself
sich verbrennen	to burn oneself
sich verbrühen	to scald oneself
sich schneiden	to cut oneself
ein Arbeitsunfall *(m)*	industrial accident
ein Flugzeugabsturz *(m)*	plane crash
ein Bergunfall *(m)*	mountaineering accident
der Sturz	fall
das Ertrinken	drowning
ein Stromschlag *(m)*	electric shock

Verletzte und Unfallzeugen
injured persons and witnesses

ein Verletzter, eine Verletzte	injured person
ein Schwerverletzter, eine Schwerverletzte	seriously injured person
ein Toter, eine Tote	dead person
ein Opfer *(n)*	victim
ein Unfallopfer *(n)*	casualty
ein Überlebender, eine Überlebende	survivor
ein Zeuge, eine Zeugin	witness
eine Gehirnerschütterung	concussion
eine Verletzung	injury
eine Verbrennung	burn
der Blutverlust	loss of blood

Hilfe
help

Notdienste *(pl)*	emergency services
die Polizei	police
ein(e) Polizist(in)	police officer

ein Polizeiauto *(n)*	police car
die Feuerwehr	fire brigade
der Feuerwehrmann	firefighter
ein Feuerwehrauto *(n)*	fire engine
ein Feuerlöscher *(m)*	fire extinguisher
ein Schlauch *(m)*	hose
die Erste Hilfe	first aid
ein Notfall *(m)*	emergency
ein Krankenwagen *(m)*	ambulance
ein Arzt *(m)*	doctor
ein Krankenpfleger	(male) nurse
eine Krankenschwester	(female) nurse
ein(e) Sanitäter(in)	paramedic
die Sanitätsausrüstung	first-aid kit
eine Trage	stretcher
die künstliche Beatmung	artificial respiration
die Mund-zu-Mund-Beatmung	kiss of life
der Sauerstoff	oxygen
der Pannendienst	breakdown service
der Rettungsdienst	rescue services

die Folgen — **the consequences**

miterleben	to witness
untersuchen	to investigate
einen Bericht anfertigen	to draw up a report
entschädigen	to compensate
der Schaden	damage
eine Untersuchung	investigation
ein Gericht *(n)*	court
ein Bericht *(m)*	report
eine Geldstrafe	fine
der Führerscheinentzug	loss of driving licence
die Gerechtigkeit	justice
das Urteil	sentence
die Versicherung	insurance
die Verantwortung	responsibility

der Schadenersatz	damages
die Entschädigung	compensation

seine Bremsen haben versagt	**mein Auto hat Totalschaden**
his brakes failed	my car is a write-off
er ist mit ein paar Kratzern davongekommen	
he escaped with only a few scratches	
ihm ist der Führerschein entzogen worden	
he lost his driving licence	
hol Hilfe	**ruf einen Krankenwagen**
go and get help	call an ambulance
ich habe den Unfall gesehen	
I witnessed the accident	

See also Sections

6 HEALTH, ILLNESSES AND DISABILITIES, 26 CARS, 30 WHAT'S THE WEATHER LIKE? *and* **54 DISASTERS.**

54 KATASTROPHEN
DISASTERS

angreifen	to attack
verteidigen	to defend
zusammenbrechen	to collapse
verhungern	to starve
ausbrechen	to erupt
explodieren	to explode
zittern	to shake
ersticken	to suffocate; to choke
verbrennen	to burn
löschen	to extinguish
den Alarm auslösen	to raise the alarm
retten	to rescue
sinken	to sink
die Ordnung wiederherstellen	to restore order
die Ordnung wahren	to keep the peace

der Krieg	**war**
der Bürgerkrieg	civil war
die biologische Kriegführung	biological warfare
Waffen *(pl)*	weapons
Atomwaffen *(pl)*	nuclear weapons
chemische Waffen *(pl)*	chemical weapons
Massenvernichtungswaffen *(pl)*	weapons of mass destruction
ein Terroranschlag *(m)*	terrorist attack
das Schlachtfeld	battlefield
die Bombardierung	bombing
eine Bombe	bomb
eine Atombombe	atomic bomb
eine Granate	shell, grenade
eine Rakete	missile

ein Panzer *(m)*	tank
ein Gewehr *(n)*	gun
ein Maschinengewehr *(n)* (MG)	machine-gun
eine Mine	mine
die Armee	army
die Marine	navy
die Luftwaffe	air force
ein Soldat *(m)*	soldier
ein General *(m)*	general
ein Oberst *(m)*	colonel
ein Feldwebel *(m)*	sergeant
ein Kapitän *(m)*	captain
Marinetruppen *(pl)*	marines
Friedenstruppen *(pl)*	peacekeeing forces
der Feind	enemy
ein Verbündeter *(m)*	ally
Zivilisten *(pl)*	civilians
die Grausamkeit	cruelty
die Folter	torture
der Tod	death
eine Wunde	wound
eine Verwundung	wound
ein Opfer *(n)*	victim, casualty
der Krieg	war
ein Luftschutzbunker *(m)*	air-raid shelter
ein Waffenstillstand *(m)*	truce
ein Vertrag *(m)*	treaty
der Sieg	victory
die Niederlage	defeat
der Frieden	peace

Naturkatastrophen — natural disasters

eine Dürre	drought
eine Hungersnot	famine

die Unterernährung	malnutrition
der Mangel an *(+dat)*	lack of
eine Epidemie	epidemic
ein Tornado *(m)*	tornado
ein Wirbelsturm *(m)*	cyclone
ein Hurrikan *(m)*	hurricane
eine Überschwemmung	flood
eine Flutwelle	tidal wave
ein Tsunami *(m)*	tsunami
ein Erdbeben *(n)*	earthquake
ein Vulkan *(m)*	volcano
ein Vulkanausbruch *(m)*	volcanic eruption
die Lava	lava
eine Lawine	avalanche
eine Hilfsorganisation	aid agency
die humanitäre Hilfe	humanitarian aid
das Rote Kreuz	Red Cross
ein Freiwilliger, eine Freiwillige	volunteer
die Rettung	rescue
die Geldbeschaffung	fundraising
eine Unterkunft	shelter
das Trinkwasser	drinking water
ein Lebensmittelpaket *(n)*	food parcel
Decken *(pl)*	blankets
Medikamente *(pl)*	medication

Feuer

fires

ein Feuer *(n)*	fire
der Rauch	smoke
Flammen *(pl)*	flames
eine Explosion	explosion
die Feuerwehr	fire brigade
ein Feuerwehrmann *(m)*	firefighter
ein Feuerwehrauto *(n)*	fire engine

eine Leiter	ladder
ein Schlauch *(m)*	hose
der Notausgang	emergency exit
die Panik	panic
ein Krankenwagen *(m)*	ambulance
ein Notfall *(m)*	emergency
die Hilfe	help
die künstliche Beatmung	artificial respiration
ein Überlebender, eine Überlebende	survivor

Hilfe!   **Feuer!**
help!   fire!

in Sierra Leone herrscht Bürgerkrieg
there is a civil war going on in Sierra Leone

der Krieg zwischen Großbritannien und Deutschland begann 1939
Britain went to war with Germany in 1939

wir führen einen Krieg gegen den Terror
we are fighting a war on terror

in Japan ist ein Vulkan ausgebrochen
a volcano has erupted in Japan

die Feuerwehr hat den Brand unter Kontrolle gebracht
firemen brought the blaze under control

unser Haus war überflutet
our home was flooded

durch das Erdbeben sind Tausende von Menschen obdachlos
the earthquake has left thousands of people homeless

die Hungersnot kann Millionen Menschen das Leben kosten
the famine could claim millions of lives

 Homework help

The biggest problem in the world today is....
Das größte Problem in der heutigen Welt ist...

I think it's terrible that... **Ich denke es ist schrecklich, dass...**	people are dying of starvation. **Menschen vor Hunger sterben.**
	children can't go to school. **Kinder nicht zur Schule gehen können.**
	people have lost their homes. **Menschen ihr Zuhause verloren haben.**
	innocent people are being killed/tortured. **unschuldige Menschen getötet/gefoltert werden.**
The most important thing is... **Am wichtigsten ist es,...**	to rescue the victims. **die Opfer zu retten.**
	to feed the children. **den Kindern zu essen zu geben.**
	to educate people. **die Menschen aufzuklären.**
	to destroy the regime. **das Regime zu zerstören.**
	to establish peace. **Frieden zu schaffen.**
We can help by... **Wir können helfen, indem wir...**	donating money. **Geld spenden.**
	writing to our MPs. **an unsere Abgeordneten schreiben.**

volunteering in the community.
Freiwilligenarbeit leisten.

raising people's awareness.
**den Menschen die Probleme
bewusst machen.**

boycotting these products.
diese Produkte boykottieren.

See also Sections

34 TOPICAL ISSUES *and* **53 ACCIDENTS.**

stehlen	to steal
klauen	to nick
einbrechen	to burgle
einbrechen	to break in
überfallen	to mug
ermorden	to murder, to assassinate
töten	to kill
erstechen	to stab (to death)
erwürgen	to strangle (to death)
schießen	to shoot
erschießen	to shoot dead
vergiften	to poison
angreifen	to attack
zusammenschlagen	to beat up
vergewaltigen	to rape
bedrohen	to threaten
zwingen	to force
erpressen	to blackmail
betrügen	to swindle
unterschlagen	to embezzle
betrügen	to defraud
spionieren	to spy
sich prostituieren	to prostitute oneself
mit Drogen betäuben	to drug
entführen	to kidnap, to abduct
kidnappen	to kidnap
Geiseln nehmen	to take hostages
entführen	to hijack
in Brand setzen	to set fire to
in die Luft jagen	to blow up
beschädigen	to damage

festnehmen	to arrest
untersuchen	to investigate
befragen	to question, to interrogate
durchsuchen	to search
einsperren	to imprison
umzingeln	to surround
retten	to rescue
verteidigen	to defend
beschuldigen	to accuse
anklagen	to charge
vor Gericht *(acc)* stellen	to judge, to try
beweisen	to prove
verurteilen	to sentence, to convict
freisprechen	to acquit
freilassen	to release
in Untersuchungshaft sein	to be remanded in custody
auf Kaution entlassen werden	to be released on bail
schuldig	guilty
unschuldig	innocent
legal	legal
gesetzwidrig	illegal

Verbrechen — crime

ein Diebstahl *(m)*	theft
ein Raub *(m)*	robbery
ein bewaffneter Überfall *(m)*	armed robbery
ein Taschendiebstahl	pickpocketing
ein Einbruch *(m)*	burglary, break-in
ein Raubüberfall *(m)*	hold-up
ein Überfall *(m)*	attack
ein bewaffneter Überfall	armed robbery, armed attack
ein Mord *(m)*	murder
ein Straßenraub	mugging
ein Totschlag *(m)*	manslaughter

die Notzucht	sexual assault
eine Vergewaltigung	rape
der Missbrauch	abuse
die Grausamkeit	cruelty
die Vernachlässigung	neglect
ein Betrug *(m)*	fraud
ein Schwindel *(m)*	confidence trick
eine Erpressung	blackmail
eine Erpressung	extortion
ein Identitätsdiebstahl	identity theft
ein Kidnapping *(n)*	kidnap
eine Entführung	abduction
die Prostitution	prostitution
die Zuhälterei	procuring
der Drogenhandel	drug trafficking
der Schmuggel	smuggling
die Spionage	spying
der Vandalismus	vandalism
eine Störung der öffentlichen Ordnung	breach of the peace
das antisoziale Verhalten	antisocial behaviour
der Terrorismus	terrorism
eine Geisel	hostage
ein(e) Verbrecher(in)	criminal
ein(e) Mörder(in)	murderer
ein(e) Serienmörder(in)	serial killer
ein Vergewaltiger *(m)*	rapist
ein(e) Sexualtäter(in)	sex offender
ein(e) Straßenräuber(in)	mugger
ein(e) Dieb(in)	thief
ein Taschendieb *(m)*	pickpocket
ein(e) Einbrecher(in)	burglar
ein Brandstifter *(m)*	arsonist
ein Zuhälter *(m)*	pimp
ein(e) Menschenhändler(in)	people trafficker

ein Drogenhändler *(m)*	drug dealer
ein(e) Schmuggler(in)	smuggler
ein(e) Schwindler(in)	confidence trickster
ein(e) Erpresser(in)	blackmailer
ein(e) Kidnapper(in)	kidnapper
ein(e) Jugendstraftäter*(n)*	young offender
ein Minderjähriger, eine Minderjährige	minor

Waffen

weapons

eine Pistole	pistol
ein Revolver *(m)*	gun, revolver
ein Gewehr *(n)*	gun, rifle
ein Luftgewehr *(n)*	air rifle
ein Messer *(n)*	knife
ein Dolch *(m)*	dagger
das Gift	poison
ein Schlag *(m)*	punch
ein Tritt *(m)*	kick

die Polizei

police

ein(e) Polizist(in)	police officer
ein Polizeibeamter, eine Polizeibeamtin	police officer
ein(e) Polizist(in) in Zivil	plain-clothes police officer
ein(e) Detektiv(in)	detective
ein(e) Kommissar(in)	superintendent
die Bereitschaftspolizei	riot police
die Polizeiwache	police station
das Polizeipräsidium	police headquarters
ein Bericht *(m)*	report
Nachforschungen *(pl)*	investigations
eine Untersuchung	enquiry
ein Hinweis *(m)*	clue
eine Spur	lead

ein Überfall *(m)*	raid
ein Polizeihund *(m)*	police dog
ein Spürhund *(m)*	sniffer dog
ein(e) Informant(in)	informer
ein Gummiknüppel *(m)*	truncheon
Handschellen *(pl)*	handcuffs
ein Helm *(m)*	helmet
ein Schild *(m)*	shield
das Tränengas	tear gas
ein Polizeiauto *(n)*	police van
ein Streifenwagen *(m)*	patrol car
eine Sirene	siren
eine Zelle	cell

die Justiz — the judicial system

der Prozess	trial
ein Angeklagter, eine Angeklagte	accused, defendant
das Opfer	victim
ein Beweis *(m)*	proof
ein Zeuge, eine Zeugin	witness
ein Rechtsanwalt, eine Rechtsanwältin	lawyer
der Richter	judge
ein Schöffe, eine Schöffin	juror
die Verteidigung	defence
das Urteil	sentence
ein Strafaufschub *(m)*	reprieve
ein Urteil *(n)* mit Bewährung	suspended sentence
die Bewährung	probation
eine Geldstrafe	fine
der Sozialdienst	community service
das Gefängnis	imprisonment, prison
die lebenslängliche Freiheitsstrafe	life sentence
die Todesstrafe	death sentence
der elektrische Stuhl	electric chair

55 VERBRECHEN

der Tod durch den Strang	hanging
ein Justizirrtum *(m)*	miscarriage of justice
die Therapie	rehabilitation

er wurde zu zwanzig Jahren Gefängnis verurteilt
he was sentenced to 20 years' imprisonment

er hat sie um ihre gesamten Ersparnisse gebracht
he conned her out of all her savings

man sollte sie einsperren!   *Inf* **er ist im Knast**
they should be locked up!   he's in the slammer

Inf **mein Rad ist geklaut worden**
my bike got nicked

56 ABENTEUER UND TRÄUME

ADVENTURES AND DREAMS

spielen	to play
sich amüsieren	to have fun
sich *(dat)* vorstellen	to imagine
so tun, als ob	to pretend
sich verkleiden (als)	to dress up (as a)
geschehen	to happen
sich verstecken	to hide
Versteck spielen	to play hide-and-seek
weglaufen	to run off
entkommen	to escape
verfolgen	to chase
entdecken	to discover
erforschen	to explore
wagen	to dare
vorsichtig sein	to be careful
wahrsagen	to tell fortunes
vorhersagen	to foretell
träumen	to dream
einen Traum haben	to have a dream
einen Albtraum haben	to have a nightmare

Abenteuer

adventures

ein Abenteuer *(n)*	adventure
ein Spiel *(n)*	game
eine Reise	journey
eine Flucht	escape
eine Verkleidung	disguise
das Unbekannte	the unknown

ein Ereignis *(n)*	event
eine Entdeckung	discovery
der Zufall	chance
das Glück	luck
das Pech	bad luck
die Gefahr	danger
die Lebensgefahr	mortal danger
ein Risiko *(n)*	risk
ein Versteck *(n)*	hiding place
eine Höhle	cave
eine Insel	island
ein Schatz *(m)*	treasure
der Mut	courage
die Feigheit	cowardice

Märchen und Sagen

fairytales and legends

eine Prinzessin	princess
ein schöner Prinz *(m)*	handsome prince
die böse Stiefmutter	wicked stepmother
eine Hexe	witch
ein Zauberer *(m)*	wizard, magician
eine Fee	fairy
ein Hexenmeister *(m)*	sorcerer
ein Flaschengeist *(m)*	genie
ein Gnom *(m)*	gnome
ein Kobold *(m)*	imp, goblin
ein Zwerg *(m)*	dwarf
ein Riese *(m)*	giant
ein Geist *(m)*	ghost
ein Gespenst *(m)*	ghost
ein Skelett *(m)*	skeleton
ein(e) Pirat(in)	pirate
ein Vampir *(m)*	vampire
ein Drache *(m)*	dragon
ein Werwolf *(m)*	werewolf
ein Ungeheuer *(n)*	monster
ein außerirdisches Wesen *(n)*	alien

ein Raumschiff *(n)*	spaceship
ein UFO *(n)*	UFO
eine Eule	owl
eine Kröte	toad
eine schwarze Katze	black cat
ein Spukhaus *(n)*	haunted house
ein Friedhof *(m)*	cemetery
ein Wald *(m)*	forest
ein Happy End *(n)*	happy ending
die Magie	magic
ein Zauber *(m)*	spell
ein Zaubertrank *(m)*	magic potion
ein Zauberstab *(m)*	magic wand
ein fliegender Teppich	flying carpet
der Besenstiel	broomstick
ein Geheimnis *(n)*	secret
der Aberglaube	superstition
eine Glaskugel	crystal ball
das Tarock	tarot
Handlinien *(pl)*	lines of the hand
der Vollmond	full moon
die Astrologie	astrology
der Tierkreis	zodiac
das Sternzeichen	star sign
ein Horoskop *(n)*	horoscope
der Wassermann	Aquarius
Fische *(pl)*	Pisces
der Stier	Taurus
der Widder	Aries
Zwillinge *(pl)*	Gemini
der Krebs	Cancer
der Löwe	Leo
die Jungfrau	Virgo
die Waage	Libra
der Skorpion	Scorpio
der Schütze	Sagittarius
der Steinbock	Capricorn

Träume	**dreams**
ein Traum *(m)*	dream
ein Tagtraum *(m)*	daydream
ein Albtraum *(m)*	nightmare
die Einbildung	imagination
eine Halluzination	hallucination

ich hatte einen schönen Traum/einen furchtbaren Albtraum
I had a nice dream/horrible nightmare

du hast zu viel Fantasie!
you've got an overactive imagination!

eine Wahrsagerin hat mir aus der Hand gelesen
a fortune teller read my palm

glaubst du an Gespenster?   **sie tun so, als ob sie Piraten sind**
do you believe in ghosts?   they're pretending to be pirates

es war einmal eine Prinzessin...
once upon a time there was a princess...

und wenn sie nicht gestorben sind, dann leben sie noch heute
they all lived happily ever after

Note

Star signs do not need an article in German:

ich bin Stier
I'm (a) Taurus

Signs with plural names are expressed in the singular, again with no article:

ich bin Fisch/Zwilling
I'm (a) Pisces/(a) Gemini

klingeln	to ring
läuten	to chime
ticken	to tick
messen	to time
die Uhren vorstellen	to put the clocks forward
die Uhren zurückstellen	to put the clocks back
Jetlag haben	to have jetlag

Zeitmesser	**things that tell the time**
eine Uhr	watch; clock
eine Armbanduhr	wristwatch
eine Digitaluhr	digital clock/watch
Zeiger *(pl)*	hands *(of a clock/watch)*
der Stundenzeiger	hour hand
der Minutenzeiger	minute hand
der Sekundenzeiger	second hand
ein Wecker *(m)*	alarm clock
ein Radiowecker *(m)*	radio alarm clock
eine Stoppuhr	stopwatch
eine Standuhr	grandfather clock
die Zeitansage	speaking clock
eine Kuckucksuhr	cuckoo clock
die Sonnenuhr	sun dial
die Eieruhr	eggtimer
die Glocke	bell
das Klingeln	ringing

die Zeitzone	time zone
die westeuropäische Zeit	Greenwich Mean Time

57 DIE ZEIT

wie spät ist es?
ein Uhr
acht Uhr (morgens)

fünf nach acht
Viertel nach acht
halb elf
fünf nach halb elf
zwanzig vor elf
Viertel vor elf
drei viertel elf

zwei Uhr (nachmittags)

vierzehn Uhr
vierzehn Uhr dreißig
zehn Uhr (abends)
zweiundzwanzig Uhr

Zeiteinteilungen
die Zeit
ein Augenblick *(m)*
ein Moment *(m)*
eine Sekunde
eine Minute
eine Viertelstunde
eine halbe Stunde
eine Dreiviertelstunde
eine Stunde
eineinhalb Stunden

ein Tag *(m)*
der Sonnenaufgang
der Morgen
der Vormittag
der Mittag

what time is it?
one o'clock
eight am, eight o'clock in the morning

five (minutes) past eight
a quarter past eight
ten thirty, half past ten
twenty-five to eleven
twenty to eleven
a quarter to eleven
a quarter to eleven *(southern Germany)*

two pm, two o'clock in the afternoon

two pm
two thirty pm
ten pm, ten o'clock in the evening
ten pm

divisions of time
time
moment, instant
moment
second
minute
quarter of an hour
half an hour
three quarters of an hour
hour
an hour and a half

day
sunrise
morning
morning
noon

der Nachmittag	afternoon
der Abend	evening
der Sonnenuntergang	sunset
die Nacht	night
Mitternacht	midnight

pünktlich/zu spät kommen
being on time/late

zu früh kommen	to be (too) early
pünktlich sein	to be on time
pünktlich ankommen	to arrive on time
zu spät kommen	to be (too) late
Verspätung haben	to be late
rechtzeitig kommen	to arrive in time
es eilig haben	to be in a hurry
sich beeilen	to hurry (up)

wann?
when?

wann	when
seit	since
als	when
vor *(+dat)*	before
nach	after
während	during
früh	early
spät	late
später	later
schon	already
jetzt	now
im Moment	at the moment
sofort	immediately, straight away
sogleich	straight away
plötzlich	suddenly
zurzeit	at present
vor kurzem	a short while ago
bald	soon
dann	then *(next)*

damals	then *(at that time in the past)*
schließlich	finally
zu der Zeit	at that time
kürzlich	recently
währenddessen	meanwhile
lange Zeit	for a long time
vor langer Zeit	a long time ago
immer	always
nie(mals)	never
manchmal	sometimes
oft	often
von Zeit zu Zeit	from time to time
kaum jemals	rarely

wie viel Uhr ist es?
what time is it?

es ist zwei Uhr
it's two o'clock

können Sie mir die (genaue) Zeit sagen?
do you have the (exact) time?

es ist etwa zwei Uhr
it's about two o'clock

es ist genau neun Uhr
it's nine o'clock exactly

um wie viel Uhr fährt der Zug ab?
what time does the train leave?

es ist noch nicht so weit
it's not time yet

er kommt erst um halb sechs
he's not coming until half past five

meine Uhr geht vor/nach
my watch is fast/slow

ich habe meine Uhr gestellt
I've set my watch right

wir sind spät dran
we're late

komm nicht zu spät!
don't be late!

ich habe keine Zeit um auszugehen
I haven't got time to go out

die Uhren werden an diesem Wochenende zurückgestellt/vorgestellt
the clocks go back/forward this weekend

der Zeitunterschied ist sechs Stunden
there's a six-hour time difference

er ist den Marathon in Rekordzeit gelaufen
he ran the marathon in record time

Note

Remember that the half-hour is expressed in German as 'half *to* the hour', rather than 'half past'. So halb sechs is half past five ('half to six'), not half past six.

Montag	Monday
Dienstag	Tuesday
Mittwoch	Wednesday
Donnerstag	Thursday
Freitag	Friday
Samstag	Saturday
Sonnabend	Saturday
Sonntag	Sunday
der Tag *(m)*	day
die Woche	week
das Wochenende	weekend
acht Tage	a week
zwei Wochen	a fortnight
vierzehn Tage	a fortnight
heute	today
morgen	tomorrow
übermorgen	the day after tomorrow
gestern	yesterday
vorgestern	the day before yesterday
am Vortag	the day before
am nächsten Tag	the day after
am übernächsten Tag	two days later
diese Woche	this week
nächste Woche	next week
letzte Woche	last week
vorige Woche	last week
vergangene Woche	last week

letzten Montag	last Monday
vorigen Montag	last Monday
nächsten Montag	next Monday
montags	on Mondays
montags morgens	on Monday mornings
montags abends	on Monday evenings
heute in einer Woche	in a week's time, a week today
heute in vierzehn Tagen	in two weeks' time, two weeks today
Donnerstag in einer Woche	Thursday week
gestern Morgen	yesterday morning
gestern Abend	last night, yesterday evening
heute Abend	this evening, tonight
diese/heute Nacht	last night, tonight
morgen früh	tomorrow morning
morgen Abend	tomorrow evening
vor drei Tagen	three days ago

am Sonntag gehe ich zum Gottesdienst
on Sunday I go to church

donnerstags gehe ich ins Schwimmbad
on Thursdays I go to the swimming pool

er besucht mich jeden Tag
he comes to see me every day

bis morgen!
see you tomorrow!

bis nächste Woche!
see you next week!

innerhalb drei Tagen
(with)in three days

wir sehen uns am Montag
see you on Monday

ich habe ihn am Wochenende getroffen
I met him at the weekend

Note

Although days of the week are generally treated as nouns and thus written with a capital letter, they can also be used as adverbs, expressing when/how often something happens. In this case they are not capitalized:

samstags gehe ich in die Stadt
on Saturdays I go into town

59 DAS JAHR
THE YEAR

Monate	**months of the year**
Januar	January
Februar	February
März	March
April	April
Mai	May
Juni	June
Juli	July
August	August
September	September
Oktober	October
November	November
Dezember	December
ein Monat *(m)*	month
ein Jahr *(n)*	year
ein Schaltjahr *(n)*	leap year
ein Jahrzehnt *(n)*	decade
ein Jahrhundert *(n)*	century
ein Jahrtausend *(n)*	millenium

Jahreszeiten	**seasons**
die Jahreszeit	season
der Frühling	spring
der Sommer	summer
der Herbst	autumn
der Winter	winter

Feiertage	**festivals**
ein Feiertag *(m)*	holiday *(one day)*
der Geburtstag	birthday

der Namenstag	name day
Weihnachten	Christmas
Neujahr	New Year's Day
Silvester	New Year's Eve
der Valentinstag	St Valentine's Day
der erste April	April Fools' Day
Ostern	Easter
der Karfreitag	Good Friday
der Rosenmontag	Monday before Ash Wednesday
der Aschermittwoch	Ash Wednesday
Pfingsten	Whitsun
Allerheiligen	All Saints' Day
der Tag der Deutschen Einheit	Day of German Unity (national holiday, 3rd October)

ich habe im Februar Geburtstag
my birthday is in February

im März regnet es viel
it rains a lot in March

ich mag den Sommer am liebsten
summer is my favourite season

im Winter gehe ich Ski fahren
in winter I go skiing

60 DAS DATUM
THE DATE

zurückgehen auf *(+acc)*	to date from, to go back to
dauern	to last
die Vergangenheit	past
die Zukunft	future
die Gegenwart	present
die Geschichte	history
die Vorgeschichte	prehistory
die Antike	antiquity
das Mittelalter	Middle Ages
die industrielle Revolution	Industrial Revolution
das einundzwanzigste Jahrhundert	twenty-first century
das Jahr 2000	year 2000
das Datum	date
eine Generation	generation
aktuell	present, current
modern	modern
gegenwärtig	present
vergangen	past
zukünftig	future
jährlich	annual, yearly
monatlich	monthly
wöchentlich	weekly
täglich	daily
früher	in the past, formerly
in der Vergangenheit	in the past
damals	then, in those days
heutzutage	nowadays
in der Zukunft	in the future

60 DAS DATUM

lange Zeit	for a long time
niemals	never
immer	always
manchmal	sometimes
als	when
wenn	when
seit	since
noch	again, still
zu der Zeit	at that time
am Anfang/Ende des Jahrhunderts	at the beginning/end of the century
in der Mitte des Jahrhunderts	in the middle of the century
in den 60er-/90er-Jahren	in the 60s/90s
Mitte der Fünfzigerjahre	in the mid-fifties
vor Christus (v.Chr.)	BC
nach Christus (n.Chr.)	AD

---

welches Datum ist heute?
what's the date today?

den Wievielten haben wir heute?
what's the date today?

es ist der 1. Juni 2008/der erste Juni zweitausendacht
it's the first of June 2008

im Jahre 2001/zweitausendeins
in 2001

es ist der 15./fünfzehnte August
it's the fifteenth of August

Bonn, den 5. April 1986
Bonn, 5th of April 1986

er ist vor einem Jahr gegangen
he left a year ago

er kommt am 16. Juli zurück
he'll be back on the 16th of July

als er da war
when he was there

wenn er zurückkommt
when he comes back

seit ich hier wohne
since I've been living here

es war einmal ...
once upon a time, there was ...

See also Section

59 THE YEAR.

61 ZAHLEN
NUMBERS

null	zero
eins	one
zwei	two
drei	three
vier	four
fünf	five
sechs	six
sieben	seven
acht	eight
neun	nine
zehn	ten
elf	eleven
zwölf	twelve
dreizehn	thirteen
vierzehn	fourteen
fünfzehn	fifteen
sechzehn	sixteen
siebzehn	seventeen
achtzehn	eighteen
neunzehn	nineteen
zwanzig	twenty
einundzwanzig	twenty-one
zweiundzwanzig	twenty-two
dreißig	thirty
vierzig	forty
fünfzig	fifty
sechzig	sixty
siebzig	seventy
achtzig	eighty
neunzig	ninety

(ein)hundert	one hundred
(ein)hundert(und)eins	one hundred and one
(ein)hundert(und)zweiundsechzig	one hundred and sixty-two
zweihundert	two hundred
zweihundert(und)zwei	two hundred and two
(ein)tausend	one thousand
zweitausend	two thousand
zehntausend	ten thousand
hunderttausend	hundred thousand
eine Million	million
erste	first
letzte	last
zweite	second
dritte	third
vierte	fourth
fünfte	fifth
sechste	sixth
siebte	seventh
achte	eighth
neunte	ninth
zehnte	tenth
elfte	eleventh
zwölfte	twelfth
dreizehnte	thirteenth
vierzehnte	fourteenth
fünfzehnte	fifteenth
sechzehnte	sixteenth
siebzehnte	seventeenth
achtzehnte	eighteenth
neunzehnte	nineteenth
zwanzigste	twentieth
einundzwanzigste	twenty-first
zweiundzwanzigste	twenty-second
dreißigste	thirtieth
vierzigste	fortieth

fünfzigste	fiftieth
sechzigste	sixtieth
siebzigste	seventieth
achtzigste	eightieth
neunzigste	ninetieth
hundertste	hundredth
hundert(und)erste	hundred and first
hundertzwanzigste	hundred and twentieth
zweihundertste	two hundredth
tausendste	thousandth
zweitausendste	two thousandth
die Ziffer	figure
die Zahl	number
die Nummer	number *(telephone, house etc)*

---

hundert/tausend Euro
a/one hundred/thousand euros

eine Million Euro
one million euros

zwei Komma drei (2,3)
two point three (2.3)

eine große Zahl von Schülern
a large number of pupils

der/die/das Achte und der/die/das Elfte
the eighth and the eleventh

---

62 MENGEN
QUANTITIES

berechnen	to calculate
zählen	to count
wiegen	to weigh
messen	to measure
schätzen	to estimate
teilen	to divide
verteilen	to distribute, to share out
füllen	to fill
leeren	to empty
wegnehmen	to remove
vermindern	to lessen, to reduce
erhöhen	to increase
hinzufügen	to add
genügen	to be enough
nichts	nothing
alles	everything
aller/alle/alles ...	all the ..., the whole ...
jeder/jede/jedes ...	all the ..., every ...
etwas	something, some
einige	several, some
jeder	everybody
alle *(pl)*	everybody
ein bisschen	a little (bit of)
ein wenig	a little (bit of)
wenig	few
viel	a lot (of), much
viele	a lot of, many
kein(e) ...	no ..., not any ...
keine ... mehr	no more ...

mehr	more
weniger	less
der/die/das meiste	most
genug	enough
zu viel	too much
zu viele	too many
etwa	about
ungefähr	about
mehr oder weniger	more or less
kaum	scarcely
ungefähr	roughly
gerade	just
genau	exactly
völlig	absolutely
höchstens	at the most
wieder	again
nur	only
mindestens	at least
die Hälfte	half
ein Viertel *(n)*	a quarter (of)
ein Drittel *(n)*	a third
und ein halb	and-a-half
anderthalb	one-and-a-half
eineinhalb	one-and-a-half
zwei Drittel	two thirds
drei Viertel	three quarters
das Ganze	the whole
selten	rare
häufig	frequent
unzählig	innumerable
genug	enough
überflüssig	excessive
gleich	equal
ungleich	unequal
voll	full

leer	empty
einfach	single
zweifach	double
doppelt	double
dreifach	treble
eine Menge	lots (of)
ein Haufen *(m)*	a stack (of)
ein Stück *(n)*	a piece (of)
ein Glas *(n)*	a glass (of)
eine Flasche	a bottle (of)
eine Dose	a box/tin (of)
ein Bissen *(m)*	a mouthful (of) *(food)*
ein Schluck *(m)*	a mouthful (of) *(drink)*, a swallow
ein Löffel *(m)*	a spoonful (of)
eine Hand voll	a handful (of)
ein Paar *(n)*	a pair (of)
ein paar	a couple (of)
eine große Zahl von	a large number of
der (An)teil	share
ein Teil *(n)* (von)	part (of)
ein Dutzend *(n)*	dozen
Hunderte	hundreds
Tausende	thousands
die Übrigen	the rest/remainder
die Menge	quantity
die Zahl	number
der Durchschnitt	average
das Gewicht	weight

Maße und Gewichte

weights and measurements

ein Gramm *(n)*	gramme
ein Pfund *(n)*	pound (half kilo)
ein Kilo *(n)*	kilo
ein Zentner *(m)*	50 kilos

eine Tonne	tonne (1000 kg)
ein Liter *(m)*	litre
ein Millimeter *(m)*	millimetre
ein Zentimeter *(m)*	centimetre
ein Meter *(m)*	metre
ein Kilometer *(m)*	kilometre
eine Meile	mile

es ist nicht viel Geld übrig
there isn't much money left

es gab viele Verletzte
many people were injured

wir haben uns die meiste Zeit gestritten
we spent most of the time arguing

sie haben ein paar Gemälde
they have a few paintings

sie haben nur wenige Gemälde
they have few paintings

ich schätze, dass es etwa 300 Pfund kosten wird
I estimate it will cost about 300 pounds

Inf **ich habe massenhaft Hausaufgaben!**
I've got tons of homework!

Inf **sie hat unwahrscheinlich viele Freunde**
she has loads of friends

Inf **nimm ein Bonbon, ich habe jede Menge**
have a sweet, I've got loads

Note

Note that when talking about a certain quantity of something in German, the measuring unit is always singular:

ich hätte gern zwei Pfund Äpfel/zwei Glas Wein
I'd like two pounds of apples/two glasses of wine

See also Section

61 NUMBERS.

DESCRIBING THINGS

ein Ding *(n)*	thing
eine Art (von)	a kind of
die Größe	size
der Umfang	size
die Breite	width, breadth
die Höhe	height
die Tiefe	depth
die Form	shape
die Gestalt	shape
die Schönheit	beauty
die Hässlichkeit	ugliness
die Eigenschaft	quality
der Vorteil	advantage
der Nachteil	disadvantage
groß	tall, big, large
klein	small
riesig	enormous
winzig	tiny
breit	wide
schmal	narrow
eng	narrow, small
dick	thick, large, fat
dünn	thin, slim
flach	flat, shallow
tief	deep
lang	long

kurz	short
hoch	high
niedrig	low
steil	steep
von erstklassiger Qualität	of top quality
von schlechter Qualität	of poor quality
schön	lovely, beautiful
gut	good, well
besser	better
am besten	the best
wichtig	important
hauptsächlich	main
hübsch	pretty
wunderbar	marvellous
sehenswert	worth seeing
großartig	magnificent, superb
fantastisch	fantastic
prima	great
klasse	terrific
bemerkenswert	remarkable
überraschend	surprising
außergewöhnlich	exceptional
ausgezeichnet	excellent
perfekt	perfect
normal	normal
gewöhnlich	ordinary
außergewöhnlich	unusual
seltsam	strange
komisch	strange, funny
hässlich	ugly
schlecht	bad(ly)
schlechter	worse
am schlechtesten	the worst
furchtbar	abominable
entsetzlich	appalling

schrecklich	dreadful
grauenvoll	atrocious
unmöglich	impossible
leicht	light
schwer	heavy
hart	hard
fest	firm
solide	solid
stabil	sturdy
kaputt	broken
weich	soft
zart	tender
fein	fine, delicate
zerbrechlich	fragile
glatt	smooth
rau	rough
glänzend	shiny
funkelnd	sparkly
warm	warm
heiß	hot
kalt	cold
kühl	cool
lauwarm	lukewarm, tepid
trocken	dry
nass	wet
feucht	damp
flüssig	liquid, runny
einfach	simple
kompliziert	complicated
schwierig	difficult
leicht	easy
möglich	possible
unmöglich	impossible

praktisch	practical, handy
nützlich	useful
nutzlos	useless
alt	old
uralt	ancient
neu	new
modern	modern
veraltet	out of date
altmodisch	old-fashioned
frisch	fresh, cool
sauber	clean
schmutzig	dirty
dreckig	filthy
widerlich	disgusting
gebogen	curved
gerade	straight
rund	round, circular
oval	oval
rechteckig	rectangular
quadratisch	square
viereckig	square, rectangular, four-sided
dreieckig	triangular
länglich	oblong
sehr	very
zu	too
ziemlich	rather
ganz	quite

was ist das?
what's that?

wozu dient das?
what's it for?

das ist ja kinderleicht
it's child's play

es ist 10 Zentimeter breit/lang
it's 10 cm wide/long

die Wand ist 20 Zentimeter dick
the wall is 20 cm thick

das Wasser ist nur 60 Zentimeter tief
the water is only 60 cm deep

es ist eine Art Schrank   **was ist das Blaue da?**
it's a sort of cupboard   what's that blue thing?

Inf **wo ist dieses Schraubenschlüsselding?**
where's that spanner thingy gone?

See also Section

64 COLOURS.

64 FARBEN
COLOURS

die Farbe	colour
beige	beige
blau	blue
blond	blond
braun	brown
fleischfarben	flesh-coloured
gelb	yellow
golden	gold, golden
grau	grey
grün	green
himmelblau	sky blue
lila	purple
orange(farben)	orange
rosa	pink
rot	red
schwarz	black
silbern	silver
türkis	turquoise
violett	purple
weiß	white
lebhaft	bright, vivid
blass	pale
einfarbig	plain, all one colour
uni(farben)	plain, all one colour
mehrfarbig	multicoloured
bunt	colourful
hell	light
dunkel	dark

hellgrün	light green
dunkelgrün	dark green

was ist deine Lieblingsfarbe?
what's your favourite colour?

welche Farbe hat es?
what colour is it?

es ist hellblau
it's light blue

es ist rötlich/grünlich
it's reddish/greenish

ich habe ein knallgelbes T-Shirt gekauft
I bought a bright yellow t-shirt

Note

★ Colour nouns are formed from the adjective. When talking about the colour in general, the ending of the adjective does not change:

das Blau des Himmels
the blue of the sky

But when a colour is used as the name of a particular object, the adjective ending changes:

das Weiße seiner Augen
the whites of his eyes

das Gelbe vom Ei
the egg yolk
(lit. 'the egg yellow')

★ The word Ton (pl. Töne) refers to a shade of a particular colour:

die verschiedene Rottöne des Gemäldes
the different shades of red in the painting

65 STOFFE UND MATERIALIEN
MATERIALS

echt	real
unecht	fake
natürlich	natural
synthetisch	synthetic
künstlich	artificial
dehnbar	stretchy
steif	stiff
weich	soft
juckend	itchy
bequem	comfortable
unbequem	uncomfortable
die Erde	earth
das Wasser	water
die Luft	air
das Feuer	fire
das Material	material, substance
der Stein	stone
der Fels	rock
der Sandstein	sandstone
das Mineral	mineral
ein Edelstein *(m)*	precious stone
das Kristall	crystal
der Marmor	marble
der Granit	granite
der Diamant	diamond
der Ton	clay

das Öl	oil, petroleum
das Gas	gas
das Metall	metal
das Aluminium	aluminium
die Bronze	bronze
das Kupfer	copper
das Messing	brass
der Zinn	tin
das Eisen	iron
der Stahl	steel
das Blei	lead
das Gold	gold
das Silber	silver
das Platin	platinum
das Holz	wood
das Rohr	wicker
das Stroh	straw
der Bambus	bamboo
die Pappe	cardboard
das Papier	paper
der Beton	concrete
der Zement	cement
der Backstein	brick
der Gips	plaster
der Kitt	putty
der Leim	glue
das Glas	glass
der Ton	earthenware
das Porzellan	porcelain, china
das Plastik	plastic
das Gummi	rubber
das Wachs	wax

der Stoff	fabric, material
das Leder	leather
das Wildleder	suede
der Pelz	fur
das Acryl	acrylic
die Baumwolle	cotton
die Spitze	lace
die Wolle	wool
das Leinen	linen
der Jeansstoff	denim
das Nylon	nylon
das Polyester	polyester
die Seide	silk
das Schaffell	fleece
das Lycra®	Lycra®
die Leinwand	canvas
der Tweed	tweed
die Kaschmirwolle	cashmere
der Samt	velvet
der Velours	velours
der Kord	cord(uroy)
fest	solid
flüssig	liquid
kupfern	copper
eisern	iron
bleiern	lead
golden	gold, golden
silbern	silver
steinern	stone
tönern	clay, earthenware
hölzern	wooden
gläsern	glass
ledern	leather
seiden	silk
wollen	woollen

65 STOFFE UND MATERIALIEN

ein Holzlöffel
a wooden spoon

dieses Haus ist aus Holz
this house is made of wood

ich habe Vorhangstoff gekauft
I bought some curtain material

ein Jeansrock
a denim skirt

diese Jacke ist aus Kunstpelz
this jacket is fake fur

66 RICHTUNGEN
DIRECTIONS

sich verlaufen haben	to be lost
sich verlaufen	to get lost
den Weg kennen	to know the way
auf die Karte sehen	to look at the map
fragen	to ask
zeigen	to show
nehmen	to take, to follow
weitergehen/weiterfahren	to keep going
folgen	to follow
vorbeigehen/vorbeifahren an (+dat)	to go past
wenden	to turn
zurückgehen/zurückfahren	to go back
rückwärts fahren	to reverse
rechts abbiegen	to turn right
links abbiegen	to turn left

Richtungen

directions

links	(on the) left
rechts	(on the) right
nach links	to the left
nach rechts	to the right
geradeaus	straight ahead
wo ... hin	where ... to
wo ... her	where ... from

Himmelsrichtungen

the points of the compass

der Norden	north
der Süden	south
der Osten	east

der Westen	west
der Nordosten	north-east
der Südwesten	south-west
der Kompass	compass
ein Wegweiser *(m)*	signpost
wo	where
vor	in front of, before
hinter	behind
über	over
unter	under
neben	beside
gegenüber	opposite
mitten in *(+dat)*	in the middle of
entlang	along
am Ende	at the end
zwischen	between
irgendwo	somewhere
nach	to, after
hinter der Ampel	after the traffic lights
kurz vor *(+dat)*	just before
auf ... Meter	for ... metres
an der nächsten Kreuzung	at the next crossroads
die erste Straße rechts	first on the right
die zweite Straße links	second on the left

---

können Sie mir sagen, wie ich zum Bahnhof komme?
can you tell me how to get to the station?

fahren Sie geradeaus, biegen Sie dann links ab ...
go straight on, then turn left ...

ist es weit von hier?	**100 Meter entfernt**
is it far from here?	100 metres away
links vom Postamt	**südlich von Mainz**
to the left of the post office	south of Mainz

kannst du mir das auf der Karte zeigen?
can you show me on the map?

die Schweiz liegt südlich von Deutschland
Switzerland is to the south of Germany

München ist in Süddeutschland
Munich is in the south of Germany

ich habe keinen Orientierungssinn
I've got no sense of direction

wir haben uns total verlaufen
we're totally lost

GENITIVE AND PLURAL FORMS

Many German nouns have regular endings for the genitive and plural. For example, the word die Nation (the nation) has a genitive form (the form which corresponds to 'of the nation' or 'the nation's' in English) der Nation, and its plural form is die Nationen (the nations). All other feminine nouns ending in -ion (such as Million, Sensation etc) form their genitive and plural in the same way.

If the singular form as listed in the various sections of this book has one of the following endings, and if the gender of the word is as shown, then the genitive and plural endings will always be as given below:

Ending	Gender	Genitive	Plural
-chen	n	-chens	-chen
-heit	f	-heit	-heiten
-ie	f	-ie	-ien
-in	f	-in	-innen
-ion	f	-ion	-ionen
-keit	f	-keit	-keiten
-lein	n	-leins	-lein
-ung	f	-ung	-ungen

Some examples:

Nominative	Genitive	Plural
das Mädchen	des Mädchens	die Mädchen
die Industrie	der Industrie	die Industrien
die Engländerin	der Engländerin	die Engländerinnen
die Sendung	der Sendung	die Sendungen

The following list of around 1,500 German nouns gives you genitive and plural forms for all those nouns given in this book that don't come under these rules.

Compound nouns (nouns made up of two or more separate words) always take the genitive and plural ending of the last word in the compound. The other parts of the compound don't change. So, for example, if you want to check the plural of Apfelbaum, you should look under Baum. Here you will find the plural form Bäume. From this you now know that the plural of Apfelbaum is Apfelbäume.

Nominative	Genitive	Plural
der Abend	des Abends	die Abende
das Abenteuer	des Abenteuers	die Abenteuer
der Abhang	des Abhang(e)s	die Abhänge
die Ablage	der Ablage	die Ablagen
der Absatz	des Absatzes	die Absätze
der Absturz	des Absturzes	die Abstürze
der Abszess	des Abszesses	die Abszesse
das Abteil	des Abteils	die Abteile
die Ader	der Ader	die Adern
der Adler	des Adlers	die Adler
die Adresse	der Adresse	die Adressen
der Affe	des Affen	die Affen
der Afrikaner	des Afrikaners	die Afrikaner
die Agentur	der Agentur	die Agenturen
der Ägypter	des Ägypters	die Ägypter
der Ahorn	des Ahorns	die Ahorne
der Akzent	des Akzent(e)s	die Akzente
das Album	des Albums	die Alben
der Alkoholiker	des Alkoholikers	die Alkoholiker
die Allee	der Allee	die Alleen
der Alligator	des Alligators	die Alligatoren
der Amateur	des Amateurs	die Amateure
die Ameise	der Ameise	die Ameisen
der Amerikaner	des Amerikaners	die Amerikaner
die Ampel	der Ampel	die Ampeln
die Amsel	der Amsel	die Amseln

das Amt	des Amt(e)s	die Ämter
die Ananas	der Ananas	die Ananas
das Andenken	des Andenkens	die Andenken
die Anemone	der Anemone	die Anemonen
der Anfall	des Anfall(e)s	die Anfälle
der/die Angeklagte	des/der Angeklagten	die Angeklagten
die Angel	der Angel	die Angeln
der/die Angestellte	des/der Angestellten	die Angestellten
der Anhalter	des Anhalters	die Anhalter
der Anhänger	des Anhängers	die Anhänger
der Anker	des Ankers	die Anker
die Ankunft	der Ankunft	die Ankünfte
die Anlage	der Anlage	die Anlagen
der Anorak	des Anoraks	die Anoraks
die Anrichte	der Anrichte	die Anrichten
der Ansager	des Ansagers	die Ansager
die Anschrift	der Anschrift	die Anschriften
die Ansicht	der Ansicht	die Ansichten
der Anstreicher	des Anstreichers	die Anstreicher
die Antenne	der Antenne	die Antennen
die Antilope	der Antilope	die Antilopen
das Antiseptikum	des Antiseptikums	die Antiseptika
die Antwort	der Antwort	die Antworten
der Anwalt	des Anwalts	die Anwälte
die Anzeige	der Anzeige	die Anzeigen
der Anzeiger	des Anzeigers	die Anzeiger
der Anzug	des Anzugs	die Anzüge
das Apartment	des Apartments	die Apartments
der Aperitif	des Aperitifs	die Aperitifs
der Apfel	des Apfels	die Äpfel
die Apfelsine	der Apfelsine	die Apfelsinen
die Apotheke	der Apotheke	die Apotheken
der Apotheker	des Apothekers	die Apotheker
der Apparat	des Apparat(e)s	die Apparate
die Aprikose	der Aprikose	die Aprikosen
die Arbeit	der Arbeit	die Arbeiten
der Arbeiter	des Arbeiters	die Arbeiter
der Arbeitgeber	des Arbeitgebers	die Arbeitgeber
der Arbeitnehmer	des Arbeitnehmers	die Arbeitnehmer

der/die Arbeitslose	des/der Arbeitslosen	die Arbeitslosen
der/die Arbeitssuchende	des/der Arbeitssuchenden	die Arbeitssuchenden
der Architekt	des Architekten	die Architekten
das Argument	des Argument(e)s	die Argumente
der Arm	des Arm(e)s	die Arme
die Armee	der Armee	die Armeen
das Aroma	des Aromas	die Aromen
der Artikel	des Artikels	die Artikel
die Artischocke	der Artischocke	die Artischocken
der Arzt	des Arztes	die Ärzte
der Ast	des Astes	die Äste
der Astronaut	des Astronauten	die Astronauten
der Astronom	des Astronomen	die Astronomen
der Athlet	des Athleten	die Athleten
die Aubergine	der Aubergine	die Auberginen
der Aufenthalt	des Aufenthalt(e)s	die Aufenthalte
die Aufgabe	der Aufgabe	die Aufgaben
der Aufkleber	des Aufklebers	die Aufkleber
die Auflage	der Auflage	die Auflagen
der Auflauf	des Auflauf(e)s	die Aufläufe
die Aufnahme	der Aufnahme	die Aufnahmen
der Aufsatz	des Aufsatzes	die Aufsätze
der Aufzug	des Aufzug(e)s	die Aufzüge
das Auge	des Auges	die Augen
die Aula	der Aula	die Aulen
der Ausbilder	des Ausbilders	die Ausbilder
der Ausbruch	des Ausbruch(e)s	die Ausbrüche
der Ausflug	des Ausflug(e)s	die Ausflüge
der Ausgang	des Ausgang(e)s	die Ausgänge
der Ausländer	des Ausländers	die Ausländer
der Auspuff	des Auspuff(e)s	die Auspuffe
der Ausschlag	des Ausschlag(e)s	die Ausschläge
das Aussehen	des Aussehens	-
der Ausstieg	des Ausstieg(e)s	die Ausstiege
der Australier	des Australiers	die Australier
der Ausweis	des Ausweises	die Ausweise
der/die Auszubildende	des/der Auszubildenden	die Auszubildenden

das Auto	des Autos	die Autos
die Autobahn	der Autobahn	die Autobahnen
der Automat	des Automaten	die Automaten
das Baby	des Babys	die Babys
der Babysitter	des Babysitters	die Babysitter
der Bach	des Bach(e)s	die Bäche
die Backe	der Backe	die Backen
der Bäcker	des Bäckers	die Bäcker
die Bäckerei	der Bäckerei	die Bäckereien
das Bad	des Bades	die Bäder
die Bahn	der Bahn	die Bahnen
der Bahnsteig	des Bahnsteig(e)s	die Bahnsteige
der Balkon	des Balkons	die Balkons
der Ball	des Ball(e)s	die Bälle
das Ballett	des Ballett(e)s	die Ballette
die Banane	der Banane	die Bananen
das Band	des Band(e)s	die Bänder
die Bank	der Bank	die Banken
die Bar	der Bar	die Bars
der Bär	des Bären	die Bären
das Barometer	des Barometers	die Barometer
der Barren	des Barrens	die Barren
der Bart	des Bart(e)s	die Bärte
der Bau	des Bau(e)s	die Bauten
der Bauch	des Bauch(e)s	die Bäuche
der Bauer	des Bauern	die Bauern
der Baum	des Baum(e)s	die Bäume
der Beamte	des Beamten	die Beamten
der Becher	des Bechers	die Becher
das Becken	des Beckens	die Becken
das Bedürfnis	des Bedürfnisses	die Bedürfnisse
die Beere	der Beere	die Beeren
die Beilage	der Beilage	die Beilagen
das Bein	des Bein(e)s	die Beine
der/die Bekannte	des/der Bekannten	die Bekannten
der Belgier	des Belgiers	die Belgier
der Berater	des Beraters	die Berater
der Bereich	des Bereich(e)s	die Bereiche
der Berg	des Berg(e)s	die Berge

der Bergsteiger	des Bergsteigers	die Bergsteiger
der Bericht	des Bericht(e)s	die Berichte
der Beruf	des Beruf(e)s	die Berufe
die Beschwerde	der Beschwerde	die Beschwerden
der Besen	des Besens	die Besen
der Besuch	des Besuch(e)s	die Besuche
der Betrieb	des Betrieb(e)s	die Betriebe
der Betriebsrat	des Betriebsrat(e)s	die Betriebsräte
das Bett	des Bett(e)s	die Betten
der Beutel	des Beutels	die Beutel
der Beweis	des Beweises	die Beweise
der Bezirk	des Bezirks	die Bezirke
der BH	des BHs	die BHs
der Biber	des Bibers	die Biber
die Bibliothek	der Bibliothek	die Bibliotheken
das Bidet	des Bidets	die Bidets
die Biene	der Biene	die Bienen
das Bier	des Biers	die Biere
der Bikini	des Bikinis	die Bikinis
das Bild	des Bild(e)s	die Bilder
die Binde	der Binde	die Binden
die Birke	der Birke	die Birken
die Birne	der Birne	die Birnen
der Bissen	des Bissens	die Bissen
die Blase	der Blase	die Blasen
das Blatt	des Blatt(e)s	die Blätter
der Blick	des Blick(e)s	die Blicke
die Blindschleiche	der Blindschleiche	die Blindschleichen
der Blinker	des Blinkers	die Blinker
der Block	des Block(e)s	die Blöcke
das Blouson	des Blousons	die Blousons
die Blume	der Blume	die Blumen
die Bluse	der Bluse	die Blusen
die Blüte	der Blüte	die Blüten
die Bö	der Bö	die Böen
die Boa	der Boa	die Boas
der Bock	des Bock(e)s	die Böcke
der Boden	des Bodens	die Böden
der Bogen	des Bogens	die Bögen

der Bohrer	des Bohrers	die Bohrer
die Boje	der Boje	die Bojen
die Bombe	der Bombe	die Bomben
das Boot	des Boot(e)s	die Boote
die Botschaft	der Botschaft	die Botschaften
die Boutique	der Boutique	die Boutiquen
der Boxer	des Boxers	die Boxer
die Branche	der Branche	die Branchen
der Brand	des Brand(e)s	die Brände
der Brandstifter	des Brandstifters	die Brandstifter
der Braten	des Bratens	die Braten
die Braut	der Braut	die Bräute
der Bräutigam	des Bräutigams	die Bräutigame
die Bremse	der Bremse	die Bremsen
das Brett	des Brett(e)s	die Bretter
der Brief	des Brief(e)s	die Briefe
die Brille	der Brille	die Brillen
die Brise	der Brise	die Brisen
der Brite	des Briten	die Briten
die Brosche	der Brosche	die Broschen
die Broschüre	der Broschüre	die Broschüren
das Brot	des Brot(e)s	die Brote
der Bruch	des Bruch(e)s	die Brüche
die Brücke	der Brücke	die Brücken
der Bruder	des Bruders	die Brüder
der Brunnen	des Brunnens	die Brunnen
die Brust	der Brust	die Brüste
das Buch	des Buch(e)s	die Bücher
die Buche	der Buche	die Buchen
die Bücherei	der Bücherei	die Büchereien
der Buchhalter	des Buchhalters	die Buchhalter
die Büchse	der Büchse	die Büchsen
die Bucht	der Bucht	die Buchten
der Büffel	des Büffels	die Büffel
das Bügeleisen	des Bügeleisens	die Bügeleisen
die Bühne	der Bühne	die Bühnen
der Bulle	des Bullen	die Bullen
der Bungalow	des Bungalows	die Bungalows
der Bunker	des Bunkers	die Bunker

die Burg	der Burg	die Burgen
der Bürger	des Bürgers	die Bürger
der Bürgersteig	des Bürgersteig(e)s	die Bürgersteige
das Büro	des Büros	die Büros
die Bürste	der Bürste	die Bürsten
der Bus	des Busses	die Busse
der Busch	des Busches	die Büsche
der Busen	des Busens	die Busen
das Café	des Cafés	die Cafés
der Camper	des Campers	die Camper
der CD-Player	des CD-Players	die CD-Player
das Cello	des Cellos	die Cellos
der Cent	des Cents	die Cents
der Champignon	des Champignons	die Champignons
der Chauvinist	des Chauvinisten	die Chauvinisten
der Chef	des Chefs	die Chefs
der Chinese	des Chinesen	die Chinesen
der Chirurg	des Chirurgen	die Chirurgen
der Choke	des Chokes	die Chokes
der Chor	des Chor(e)s	die Chöre
die Chrysantheme	der Chrysantheme	die Chrysanthemen
der Comicstrip	des Comicstrips	die Comicstrips
die Compact Disc	der Compact Disc	die Compact Discs
der Computer	des Computers	die Computer
der Cousin	des Cousins	die Cousins
die Cousine	der Cousine	die Cousinen
die Creme	der Creme	die Cremes
das Dach	des Dach(e)s	die Dächer
die Dame	der Dame	die Damen
der Dampfer	des Dampfers	die Dampfer
der Däne	des Dänen	die Dänen
das Darlehen	des Darlehens	die Darlehen
die Datei	der Datei	die Dateien
das Datum	des Datums	die Daten
der Daumen	des Daumens	die Daumen
der Dealer	des Dealers	die Dealer
die Debatte	der Debatte	die Debatten
die Decke	der Decke	die Decken
der Delfin	des Delfins	die Delfine

das Denkmal	des Denkmals	die Denkmäler
das Deo	des Deos	die Deos
das Deodorant	des Deodorants	die Deodorants
der Detektiv	des Detektivs	die Detektive
der/die Deutsche	des/der Deutschen	die Deutschen
das Dia	des Dias	die Dias
der Dialog	des Dialog(e)s	die Dialoge
der Diamant	des Diamanten	die Diamanten
die Diät	der Diät	die Diäten
der Dieb	des Dieb(e)s	die Diebe
der Diebstahl	des Diebstahls	die Diebstähle
die Diele	der Diele	die Dielen
der Diener	des Dieners	die Diener
die Diktatur	der Diktatur	die Diktaturen
das Ding	des Ding(e)s	die Dinge
das Dingi	des Dingis	die Dingis
das Diplom	des Diploms	die Diplome
der Direktor	des Direktors	die Direktoren
die Diskette	der Diskette	die Disketten
der Discjockey	des Discjockeys	die Discjockeys
die Diskothek	der Diskothek	die Diskotheken
der Dolch	des Dolch(e)s	die Dolche
der Dollar	des Dollars	die Dollar
der Dolmetscher	des Dolmetschers	die Dometscher
der Dom	des Dom(e)s	die Dome
das Dorf	des Dorf(e)s	die Dörfer
die Dose	der Dose	die Dosen
der Dozent	des Dozenten	die Dozenten
der Drache	des Drachen	die Drachen
das Dreieck	des Dreiecks	die Dreiecke
der Dressman	des Dressman(s)	die Dressmen
der Drink	des Drinks	die Drinks
das Drittel	des Drittels	die Drittel
der Drogist	des Drogisten	die Drogisten
die Drossel	der Drossel	die Drosseln
der Druck	des Druck(e)s	die Drucke
der Drucker	des Druckers	die Drucker
der Duft	des Duft(e)s	die Düfte
der Durchmesser	des Durchmessers	die Durchmesser

die Dürre	der Dürre	die Dürren
die Dusche	der Dusche	die Duschen
das Dutzend	des Dutzends	die Dutzend(e)
die Ebene	der Ebene	die Ebenen
der Eber	des Ebers	die Eber
das Echo	des Echos	die Echos
die Ecke	der Ecke	die Ecken
das Ei	des Ei(e)s	die Eier
die Eibe	der Eibe	die Eiben
die Eiche	der Eiche	die Eichen
die Eichel	der Eichel	die Eicheln
die Eidechse	der Eidechse	die Eidechsen
der Eigentümer	des Eigentümers	die Eigentümer
der Eimer	des Eimers	die Eimer
der Einbrecher	des Einbrechers	die Einbrecher
der Einbruch	des Einbruch(e)s	die Einbrüche
der Einstieg	des Einstieg(e)s	die Einstiege
der Einwand	des Einwand(e)s	die Einwände
der Einwanderer	des Einwanderers	die Einwanderer
der Einwohner	des Einwohners	die Einwohner
der Eisenbahner	des Eisenbahners	die Eisenbahner
der Elefant	des Elefanten	die Elefanten
der Elektriker	des Elektrikers	die Elektriker
der Elektrorasierer	des Elektrorasierers	die Elektrorasierer
der Ell(en)bogen	des Ell(en)bogens	die Ell(en)bögen
die Elster	der Elster	die Elstern
die E-Mail	der E-Mail	die E-Mails
der Empfänger	des Empfängers	die Empfänger
das Ende	des Endes	die Enden
der Engländer	des Engländers	die Engländer
der Enkel	des Enkels	die Enkel
die Ente	der Ente	die Enten
der Entferner	des Entferners	die Entferner
das Erdbeben	des Erdbebens	die Erdbeben
das Ereignis	des Ereignisses	die Ereignisse
der Erfolg	des Erfolg(e)s	die Erfolge
das Ergebnis	des Ergebnisses	die Ergebnisse
der Erpresser	des Erpressers	die Erpresser
der/die Erwachsene	des/der Erwachsenen	die Erwachsenen

die Esche	der Esche	die Eschen
der Esel	des Esels	die Esel
die Etage	der Etage	die Etagen
die Etappe	der Etappe	die Etappen
der Etat	des Etats	die Etats
das Etikett	des Etikett(e)s	die Etiketten
die Eule	der Eule	die Eulen
der Euro	des Euros	die Euro
das Examen	des Examens	die Examen
die Fabrik	der Fabrik	die Fabriken
das Fabrikat	des Fabrikat(e)s	die Fabrikate
das Fach	des Fach(e)s	die Fächer
der Faden	des Fadens	die Fäden
die Fähre	der Fähre	die Fähren
der Fahrer	des Fahrers	die Fahrer
die Fahrt	der Fahrt	die Fahrten
das Fahrzeug	des Fahrzeugs	die Fahrzeuge
der Falke	des Falken	die Falken
der Fall	des Fall(e)s	die Fälle
der Fan	des Fans	die Fans
der Fanatiker	des Fanatikers	die Fanatiker
die Farbe	der Farbe	die Farben
der Fasan	des Fasans	die Fasane
die Faust	der Faust	die Fäuste
die Feder	der Feder	die Federn
die Fee	der Fee	die Feen
der Fehler	des Fehlers	die Fehler
die Feier	der Feier	die Feiern
der Feind	des Feindes	die Feinde
das Feld	des Feld(e)s	die Felder
der Feldwebel	des Feldwebels	die Feldwebel
der Fels	des Felsens	die Felsen
der Felsen	des Felsens	die Felsen
das Fenster	des Fensters	die Fenster
der Fernseher	des Fernsehers	die Fernseher
die Ferse	der Ferse	die Fersen
das Fest	des Fest(e)s	die Feste
die Fete	der Fete	die Feten
das Feuer	des Feuers	die Feuer

der Feuerlöscher	des Feuerlöschers	die Feuerlöscher
das Feuerwerk	des Feuerwerk(e)s	die Feuerwerke
der Film	des Film(e)s	die Filme
der Filmemacher	des Filmemachers	die Filmemacher
das Finale	des Finales	die Finale
der Finger	des Fingers	die Finger
der Fink	des Finken	die Finken
der Finne	des Finnen	die Finnen
die Firma	der Firma	die Firmen
der Fisch	des Fisch(e)s	die Fische
der Fischer	des Fischers	die Fischer
die Fläche	der Fläche	die Flächen
die Flagge	der Flagge	die Flaggen
der Flamingo	des Flamingos	die Flamingos
die Flasche	der Flasche	die Flaschen
der Fleck	des Flecks	die Flecken
das Fleisch	des Fleisch(e)s	-
der Fleischer	des Fleischers	die Fleischer
die Fleischerei	der Fleischerei	die Fleischereien
die Fliege	der Fliege	die Fliegen
die Flocke	der Flocke	die Flocken
die Flöte	der Flöte	die Flöten
der Flüchtling	des Flüchtlings	die Flüchtlinge
der Flug	des Fluges	die Flüge
der Flügel	des Flügels	die Flügel
der Flugsteig	des Flugsteig(e)s	die Flugsteige
das Flugzeug	des Flugzeug(e)s	die Flugzeuge
der Flur	des Flur(e)s	die Flure
der Fluss	des Flusses	die Flüsse
der Fön	des Föns	die Föne
die Forelle	der Forelle	die Forellen
die Form	der Form	die Formen
das Formular	des Formulars	die Formulare
das Foto	des Fotos	die Fotos
der Fotograf	des Fotografen	die Fotografen
die Frage	der Frage	die Fragen
der Franzose	des Franzosen	die Franzosen
die Frau	der Frau	die Frauen
der/die Freiwillige	des/der Freiwilligen	die Freiwilligen

der Freund	des Freund(e)s	die Freunde
der Friedhof	des Friedhof(e)s	die Friedhöfe
die Frikadelle	der Frikadelle	die Frikadellen
der Friseur	des Friseurs	die Friseure
die Friseuse	der Friseuse	die Friseusen
der Frosch	des Frosch(e)s	die Frösche
die Frucht	der Frucht	die Früchte
der Fuchs	des Fuchses	die Füchse
der Führer	des Führers	die Führer
der Füller	des Füllers	die Füller
der Fuß	des Fußes	die Füße
der Fußgänger	des Fußgängers	die Fußgänger
die Gabel	der Gabel	die Gabeln
der Gang	des Gang(e)s	die Gänge
die Gans	der Gans	die Gänse
die Garage	der Garage	die Garagen
die Garderobe	der Garderobe	die Garderoben
der Garten	des Gartens	die Gärten
der Gärtner	des Gärtners	die Gärtner
die Gasse	der Gasse	die Gassen
der Gast	des Gast(e)s	die Gäste
der Gastgeber	des Gastgebers	die Gastgeber
die Gaststätte	der Gaststätte	die Gaststätten
das Gebiet	des Gebiet(e)s	die Gebiete
das Gebirge	des Gebirges	die Gebirge
das Gebiss	des Gebisses	die Gebisse
die Gebühr	der Gebühr	die Gebühren
die Geburt	der Geburt	die Geburten
das Gedicht	des Gedicht(e)s	die Gedichte
die Gefahr	der Gefahr	die Gefahren
das Gefängnis	des Gefängnisses	die Gefängnisse
das Gehalt	des Gehalt(e)s	die Gehälter
das Gehirn	des Gehirns	die Gehirne
der Geier	des Geiers	die Geier
die Geige	der Geige	die Geigen
die Geisel	der Geisel	die Geiseln
der Geist	des Geistes	die Geister
der Geistliche	des Geistlichen	die Geistlichen
das Gel	des Gels	die Gele

das Geld	des Geld(e)s	die Gelder
die Geldbuße	der Geldbuße	die Geldbußen
das Gelenk	des Gelenk(e)s	die Gelenke
das Gemälde	des Gemäldes	die Gemälde
das Gemüse	des Gemüses	die Gemüse
der General	des Generals	die Generäle
das Gerät	des Gerät(e)s	die Geräte
das Geräusch	des Geräusch(e)s	die Geräusche
das Gericht	des Gericht(e)s	die Gerichte
das Gerücht	des Gerücht(e)s	die Gerüchte
das Gesäß	des Gesäßes	die Gesäße
das Geschäft	des Geschäft(e)s	die Geschäfte
das Geschenk	des Geschenk(e)s	die Geschenke
das Geschlecht	des Geschlecht(e)s	die Geschlechter
das Geschwür	des Geschwür(e)s	die Geschwüre
die Gesellschaft	der Gesellschaft	die Gesellschaften
das Gesetz	des Gesetzes	die Gesetze
das Gesicht	des Gesicht(e)s	die Gesichter
das Gespenst	des Gespenstes	die Gespenster
das Gespräch	des Gespräch(e)s	die Gespräche
die Gestalt	der Gestalt	die Gestalten
die Geste	der Geste	die Gesten
das Gewehr	des Gewehr(e)s	die Gewehre
die Gewerkschaft	der Gewerkschaft	die Gewerkschaften
der Gewerkschafter	des Gewerkschafters	die Gewerkschafter
das Gewicht	des Gewicht(e)s	die Gewichte
das Gewitter	des Gewitters	die Gewitter
der Gipfel	des Gipfels	die Gipfel
die Giraffe	der Giraffe	die Giraffen
die Gitarre	der Gitarre	die Gitarren
das Glas	des Glases	die Gläser
das Gleis	des Gleises	die Gleise
der Gletscher	des Gletschers	die Gletscher
das Glied	des Glied(e)s	die Glieder
die Glocke	der Glocke	die Glocken
der Gnom	des Gnomen	die Gnomen
das Gold	des Gold(e)s	-
der Gorilla	des Gorillas	die Gorillas
das Grad	des Grad(e)s	die Grade

GENITIVE AND PLURAL FORMS

das Gramm	des Gramms	die Gramm(e)
die Grammatik	der Grammatik	die Grammatiken
die Granate	der Granate	die Granaten
die Grenze	der Grenze	die Grenzen
die Grimasse	der Grimasse	die Grimassen
das Grinsen	des Grinsens	-
die Grippe	der Grippe	die Grippen
die Größe	der Größe	die Größen
die Gruppe	der Gruppe	die Gruppen
das Gummi	des Gummis	die Gummis
die Gurke	der Gurke	die Gurken
der Gurt	des Gurt(e)s	die Gurte
der Gürtel	des Gürtels	die Gürtel
der Gymnasiast	des Gymnasiasten	die Gymnasiasten
das Gymnasium	des Gymnasiums	die Gymnasien
das Haar	des Haar(e)s	die Haare
der Hacker	des Hackers	die Hacker
der Hafen	des Hafens	die Häfen
der Hahn	des Hahn(e)s	die Hähne
der Hai	des Hais	die Haie
die Hälfte	der Hälfte	die Hälften
die Halle	der Halle	die Hallen
der Hals	des Halses	die Hälse
der Halter	des Halters	die Halter
der Hamburger	des Hamburgers	die Hamburger
der Hammer	des Hammers	die Hämmer
der Hamster	des Hamsters	die Hamster
die Hand	der Hand	die Hände
der Handfeger	des Handfegers	die Handfeger
der Händler	des Händlers	die Händler
die Harke	der Harke	die Harken
der Hase	des Hasen	die Hasen
die Haube	der Haube	die Hauben
die Haut	der Haut	die Häute
der Hebel	des Hebels	die Hebel
das Heck	des Hecks	die Hecks
das Heft	des Heft(e)s	die Hefte
die Heide	der Heide	die Heiden
der Helm	des Helm(e)s	die Helme

das Hemd	des Hemd(e)s	die Hemden
die Herberge	der Herberge	die Herbergen
der Herd	des Herd(e)s	die Herde
der Hering	des Herings	die Heringe
der Herr	des Herrn	die Herren
das Herz	des Herzens	die Herzen
die Heuschrecke	der Heuschrecke	die Heuschrecken
die Hexe	der Hexe	die Hexen
die Hilfe	der Hilfe	die Hilfen
der Hintern	des Hinterns	die Hintern
der Hirsch	des Hirsch(e)s	die Hirsche
die Hitparade	der Hitparade	die Hitparaden
das Hobby	des Hobbys	die Hobbys
die Hochzeit	der Hochzeit	die Hochzeiten
der Hocker	des Hockers	die Hocker
der Hof	des Hof(e)s	die Höfe
die Höhe	der Höhe	die Höhen
die Höhle	der Höhle	die Höhlen
der Holländer	des Holländers	die Holländer
der Homosexuelle	des Homosexuellen	die Homosexuellen
der Hörer	des Hörers	die Hörer
das Horn	des Horn(e)s	die Hörner
die Hose	der Hose	die Hosen
das Hotel	des Hotels	die Hotels
der Hubschrauber	des Hubschraubers	die Hubschrauber
die Hüfte	der Hüfte	die Hüften
der Hügel	des Hügels	die Hügel
das Huhn	des Huhn(e)s	die Hühner
die Hummel	der Hummel	die Hummeln
der Hummer	des Hummers	die Hummer
der Hund	des Hundes	die Hunde
die Hungersnot	der Hungersnot	die Hungersnöte
die Hupe	der Hupe	die Hupen
der Hut	des Hut(e)s	die Hüte
die Hyazinthe	der Hyazinthe	die Hyazinthen
die Hymne	der Hymne	die Hymnen
die Hypothek	der Hypothek	die Hypotheken
die Idee	der Idee	die Ideen
die Identität	der Identität	die Identitäten

GENITIVE AND PLURAL FORMS

der Igel	des Igels	die Igel
die Illustrierte	der Illustrierten	die Illustrierten
der Imbiss	des Imbisses	die Imbisse
der Inder	des Inders	die Inder
der Infarkt	des Infarkt(e)s	die Infarkte
der Informant	des Informanten	die Informanten
der Ingenieur	des Ingenieurs	die Ingenieure
der Inhaber	des Inhabers	die Inhaber
der Innenausstatter	des Innenausstatters	die Innenausstatter
die Insel	der Insel	die Inseln
der Installateur	des Installateurs	die Installateure
der Instinkt	des Instinkt(e)s	die Instinkte
das Interesse	des Interesses	die Interessen
das Internat	des Internat(e)s	die Internate
das Interview	des Interviews	die Interviews
der Ire	des Iren	die Iren
der Irrtum	des Irrtums	die Irrtümer
der Israeli	des Israelis	die Israelis
der Italiener	des Italieners	die Italiener
die Jacht	der Jacht	die Jachten
die Jacke	der Jacke	die Jacken
das Jahr	des Jahres	die Jahre
das Jahrhundert	des Jahrhunderts	die Jahrhunderte
das Jarhtausend	des Jahrtausends	die Jahrtausende
das Jahrzehnt	des Jahrzehnt(e)s	die Jahrzehnte
der Japaner	des Japaners	die Japaner
die Jeans	der Jeans	die Jeans
der Jet	des Jets	die Jets
der Job	des Jobs	die Jobs
der Joghurt	des Joghurts	die Joghurts
der Journalist	des Journalisten	die Journalisten
das Jucken	des Juckens	-
der/die Jugendliche	des/der Jugendlichen	die Jugendlichen
der Junge	des Jungen	die Jungen
der Junggeselle	des Junggesellen	die Junggesellen
das Juwel	des Juwels	die Juwelen
der Juwelier	des Juweliers	die Juweliere
das Kabinett	des Kabinetts	die Kabinette
das Kabriolett	des Kabrioletts	die Kabrioletts

der Käfer	des Käfers	die Käfer
der Käfig	des Käfigs	die Käfige
der Kai	des Kais	die Kais
der Kaiser	des Kaisers	die Kaiser
das Kalb	des Kalb(e)s	die Kälber
das Kamel	des Kamels	die Kamele
die Kamera	der Kamera	die Kameras
der Kamin	des Kamins	die Kamine
der Kamm	des Kamm(e)s	die Kämme
der Kanadier	des Kanadiers	die Kanadier
der Kanal	des Kanals	die Kanäle
der Kandidat	des Kandidaten	die Kandidaten
das Känguru	des Kängurus	die Kängurus
die Kanne	der Kanne	die Kannen
das Kanu	des Kanus	die Kanus
das Kap	des Kaps	die Kaps
der Kapitän	des Kapitäns	die Kapitäne
die Kappe	der Kappe	die Kappen
die Karambolage	der Karambolage	die Karambolagen
die Karte	der Karte	die Karten
die Kartoffel	der Kartoffel	die Kartoffeln
der Käse	des Käses	die Käse
die Kaserne	der Kaserne	die Kasernen
die Kasse	der Kasse	die Kassen
die Kasserolle	der Kasserolle	die Kasserollen
die Kassette	der Kassette	die Kassetten
der Kasten	des Kastens	die Kästen
der Kater	des Katers	die Kater
die Kathedrale	der Kathedrale	die Kathedralen
die Katze	der Katze	die Katzen
die Kaulquappe	der Kaulquappe	die Kaulquappen
die Kehle	der Kehle	die Kehlen
das Kehrblech	des Kehrblech(e)s	die Kehrbleche
der Keller	des Kellers	die Keller
der Kellner	des Kellners	die Kellner
die Kerze	der Kerze	die Kerzen
der Kessel	des Kessels	die Kessel
die Kette	der Kette	die Ketten
der Kiefer	des Kiefers	die Kiefer

die Kiefer	der Kiefer	die Kiefern
das Kilo	des Kilos	die Kilo(s)
das Kind	des Kind(e)s	die Kinder
das Kinn	des Kinn(e)s	die Kinne
das Kino	des Kinos	die Kinos
der Kiosk	des Kiosks	die Kioske
die Kirche	der Kirche	die Kirchen
die Kirsche	der Kirsche	die Kirschen
das Kissen	des Kissens	die Kissen
die Kiste	der Kiste	die Kisten
die Klarinette	der Klarinette	die Klarinetten
die Klasse	der Klasse	die Klassen
das Klavier	des Klaviers	die Klaviere
das Kleid	des Kleid(e)s	die Kleider
der Klempner	des Klempners	die Klempner
die Klinge	der Klinge	die Klingen
die Klingel	der Klingel	die Klingeln
die Klinik	der Klinik	die Kliniken
die Klinke	der Klinke	die Klinken
die Klippe	der Klippe	die Klippen
das Klo	des Klos	die Klos
der Klub	des Klubs	die Klubs
die Kneipe	der Kneipe	die Kneipen
das Knie	des Knies	die Knie
der Knöchel	des Knöchels	die Knöchel
der Knochen	des Knochens	die Knochen
der Knödel	des Knödels	die Knödel
der Knopf	des Knopf(e)s	die Knöpfe
die Knospe	der Knospe	die Knospen
der Knüppel	des Knüppels	die Knüppel
der Kobold	des Kobold(e)s	die Kobolde
die Kobra	der Kobra	die Kobras
der Koch	des Koch(e)s	die Köche
der Koffer	des Koffers	die Koffer
der Kollege	des Kollegen	die Kollegen
das Kollier	des Kolliers	die Kolliers
der Kommissar	des Kommissars	die Kommissare
die Kommode	der Kommode	die Kommoden
der Kompass	des Kompasses	die Kompasse

der Konditor	des Konditors	die Konditoren
die Konditorei	der Konditorei	die Konditoreien
die Konferenz	der Konferenz	die Konferenzen
die Konfitüre	der Konfitüre	die Konfitüren
der König	des Königs	die Könige
das Konsulat	des Konsulat(e)s	die Konsulate
der Kontinent	des Kontinents	die Kontinente
das Konto	des Kontos	die Konten
der Kontrast	des Kontrast(e)s	die Kontraste
die Kontrolle	der Kontrolle	die Kontrollen
das Konzert	des Konzert(e)s	die Konzerte
der Kopf	des Kopf(e)s	die Köpfe
das Kopfweh	des Kopfwehs	-
der Korb	des Korb(e)s	die Körbe
der Korkenzieher	des Korkenziehers	die Korkenzieher
das Korn	des Korn(e)s	die Körner
der Körper	des Körpers	die Körper
das Kostüm	des Kostüms	die Kostüme
das Kotelett	des Koteletts	die Koteletts
die Kraft	der Kraft	die Kräfte
der Kragen	des Kragens	die Kragen
die Krähe	der Krähe	die Krähen
der Kratzer	des Kratzers	die Kratzer
die Krawatte	der Krawatte	die Krawatten
der Kredit	des Kredit(e)s	die Kredite
der Kreis	des Kreises	die Kreise
das Kreuz	des Kreuzes	die Kreuze
das Krieg	des Krieg(e)s	die Kriege
der Krimi	des Krimis	die Krimis
die Krise	der Krise	die Krisen
der Kroate	des Kroaten	die Kroaten
das Krokodil	des Krokodils	die Krokodile
der Krokus	des Krokusses	die Krokusse
die Kröte	der Kröte	die Kröten
die Küche	der Küche	die Küchen
der Kuchen	des Kuchens	die Kuchen
die Küchenschabe	der Küchenschabe	die Küchenschaben
der Kuckuck	des Kuckucks	die Kuckucke
die Kugel	der Kugel	die Kugeln

der Kugelschreiber	des Kugelschreibers	die Kugelschreiber
die Kuh	der Kuh	die Kühe
der Kühler	des Kühlers	die Kühler
das Küken	des Kükens	die Küken
der Kuli	des Kulis	die Kulis
der Kunde	des Kunden	die Kunden
der Künstler	des Künstlers	die Künstler
die Kur	der Kur	die Kuren
der Kurs	des Kurses	die Kurse
die Kurve	der Kurve	die Kurven
die Kusine	der Kusine	die Kusinen
die Küste	der Küste	die Küsten
das Labor	des Labors	die Labors
das Lächeln	des Lächelns	-
der Lachs	des Lachses	die Lachse
der Lack	des Lack(e)s	die Lacke
der Laden	des Ladens	die Läden
das Laken	des Lakens	die Laken
das Lamm	des Lamm(e)s	die Lämmer
die Lampe	der Lampe	die Lampen
das Land	des Landes	die Länder
der Lappen	des Lappens	die Lappen
der Laptop	des Laptops	die Laptops
der Lauf	des Lauf(e)s	die Läufe
der Läufer	des Läufers	die Läufer
die Laune	der Laune	die Launen
die Lawine	der Lawine	die Lawinen
das Leben	des Lebens	die Leben
die Leber	der Leber	die Lebern
der Lehrer	des Lehrers	die Lehrer
der Lehrling	des Lehrlings	die Lehrlinge
das Leiden	des Leidens	die Leiden
der Leiter	des Leiters	die Leiter
die Leiter	der Leiter	die Leitern
der Leopard	des Leoparden	die Leoparden
die Lerche	der Lerche	die Lerchen
der Libero	des Liberos	die Liberos
das Licht	des Licht(e)s	die Lichter
das Lied	des Lied(e)s	die Lieder

der Lieferant	des Lieferanten	die Lieferanten
die Liege	der Liege	die Liegen
der Lift	des Lift(e)s	die Lifte
der Likör	des Likörs	die Liköre
die Limousine	der Limousine	die Limousinen
das Lineal	des Lineals	die Lineale
die Liste	der Liste	die Listen
der Liter	des Liters	die Liter
der Lkw	des Lkws	die Lkws
das Loch	des Loch(e)s	die Löcher
die Locke	der Locke	die Locken
der Lockenwickler	des Lockenwicklers	die Lockenwickler
der Löffel	des Löffels	die Löffel
die Loge	der Loge	die Logen
der Lohn	des Lohn(e)s	die Löhne
die Lok	der Lok	die Loks
das Lokal	des Lokals	die Lokale
der Lotse	des Lotsen	die Lotsen
der Löwe	des Löwen	die Löwen
die Luft	der Luft	die Lüfte
die Lunge	der Lunge	die Lungen
die Lupe	der Lupe	die Lupen
der Luxemburger	des Luxe mburgers	die Luxemburger
das Magazin	des Magazins	die Magazine
der Magen	des Magens	die Mägen
die Mahlzeit	der Mahlzeit	die Mahlzeiten
der Maler	des Malers	die Maler
der Manager	des Managers	die Manager
die Mandarine	der Mandarine	die Mandarinen
der Mann	des Mann(e)s	die Männer
das Mannequin	des Mannequins	die Mannequins
die Mannschaft	der Mannschaft	die Mannschaften
der Mantel	des Mantels	die Mäntel
die Mappe	der Mappe	die Mappen
die Marke	der Marke	die Marken
der Markt	des Markt(e)s	die Märkte
die Marmelade	der Marmelade	die Marmeladen
der Marokkaner	des Marokkaners	die Marokkaner
die Maschine	der Maschine	die Maschinen

das Material	des Materials	die Materialien
die Matratze	der Matratze	die Matratzen
der Matrose	des Matrosen	die Matrosen
die Matte	der Matte	die Matten
die Mauer	der Mauer	die Mauern
das Maul	des Maul(e)s	die Mäuler
die Maus	der Maus	die Mäuse
der Mechaniker	des Mechanikers	die Mechaniker
die Medaille	der Medaille	die Medaillen
das Medikament	des Medikament(e)s	die Medikamente
das Meer	des Meer(e)s	die Meere
die Meile	der Meile	die Meilen
die Meise	der Meise	die Meisen
der Meister	des Meisters	die Meister
die Meisterschaft	der Meisterschaft	die Meisterschaften
die Melone	der Melone	die Melonen
die Menge	der Menge	die Mengen
das Menü	des Menüs	die Menüs
das Messer	des Messers	die Messer
der Meter	des Meters	die Meter
der Metzger	des Metzgers	die Metzger
die Metzgerei	der Metzgerei	die Metzgereien
das MG	des MGs	die MGs
die Miete	der Miete	die Mieten
der Mieter	des Mieters	die Mieter
das Mikroskop	des Mikroskops	die Mikroskope
die Mine	der Mine	die Minen
der Minister	des Ministers	die Minister
die Minute	der Minute	die Minuten
das Missgeschick	des Missgeschicks	die Missgeschicke
das Missverständnis	des Missverständnisses	die Missverständnisse
die Mistel	der Mistel	die Misteln
das Mitglied	des Mitglied(e)s	die Mitglieder
das Mittel	des Mittels	die Mittel
der Mixer	des Mixers	die Mixer
der Möbelpacker	des Möbelpackers	die Möbelpacker
die Mode	der Mode	die Moden
das Modell	des Modells	die Modelle
die Modenschau	der Modenschau	die Modenschauen

der Moderator	des Moderators	die Moderatoren
der Modeschöpfer	des Modeschöpfers	die Modeschöpfer
das Mofa	des Mofas	die Mofas
die Möhre	der Möhre	die Möhren
der Mönch	des Mönch(e)s	die Mönche
der Monolog	des Monolog(e)s	die Monologe
das Moor	des Moor(e)s	die Moore
das Moped	des Mopeds	die Mopeds
der Mord	des Mord(e)s	die Morde
der Mörder	des Mörders	die Mörder
der Moskito	des Moskitos	die Moskitos
der Motor	des Motors	die Motoren
die Motte	der Motte	die Motten
die Möwe	der Möwe	die Möwen
die Mücke	der Mücke	die Mücken
die Mühle	der Mühle	die Mühlen
der Mund	des Mund(e)s	die Münder
die Münze	der Münze	die Münzern
die Muschel	der Muschel	die Muscheln
das Museum	des Museums	die Museen
das Musical	des Musicals	die Musicals
der Muskel	des Muskels	die Muskeln
die Mutter	der Mutter	die Mütter
die Mütze	der Mütze	die Mützen
der Nachbar	des Nachbarn	die Nachbarn
die Nachricht	der Nachricht	die Nachrichten
die Nacht	der Nacht	die Nächte
der Nachteil	des Nachteils	die Nachteile
die Nachtigall	der Nachtigall	die Nachtigallen
der Nacken	des Nackens	die Nacken
die Nadel	der Nadel	die Nadeln
der Nagel	des Nagels	die Nägel
der Name	des Namens	die Namen
die Narbe	der Narbe	die Narben
die Narkose	der Narkose	die Narkosen
die Nase	der Nase	die Nasen
die Natter	der Natter	die Nattern
der Neffe	des Neffen	die Neffen
die Nelke	der Nelke	die Nelken

das Netz	des Netzes	die Netze
die Nichte	der Nichte	die Nichten
die Niederlage	der Niederlage	die Niederlagen
der Niederländer	des Niederländers	die Niederländer
die Nische	der Nische	die Nischen
die Nonne	der Nonne	die Nonnen
der Norweger	des Norwegers	die Norweger
die Note	der Note	die Noten
die Notiz	der Notiz	die Notizen
die Nudel	der Nudel	die Nudeln
die Nummer	der Nummer	die Nummern
der Ober	des Obers	die Ober
das Oberhaupt	des Oberhaupt(e)s	die Oberhäupter
der Oberst	des Obersten	die Oberste
der Ochse	des Ochsen	die Ochsen
der Ofen	des Ofens	die Öfen
der Offizier	des Offiziers	die Offiziere
der Öffner	des Öffners	die Öffner
das Ohr	des Ohr(e)s	die Ohren
die Oma	der Oma	die Omas
das Omelett	des Omeletts	die Omeletts
der Onkel	des Onkels	die Onkel
der Opa	des Opas	die Opas
die Oper	der Oper	die Opern
die Operette	der Operette	die Operetten
das Opfer	des Opfers	die Opfer
der Optiker	des Optikers	die Optiker
die Orange	der Orange	die Orangen
das Orchester	des Orchesters	die Orchester
die Orchidee	der Orchidee	die Orchideen
das Organ	des Organs	die Organe
der Orkan	des Orkan(e)s	die Orkane
der Ort	des Ort(e)s	die Orte
der Österreicher	des Österreichers	die Österreicher
die Otter	der Otter	die Ottern
der Ozean	des Ozeans	die Ozeane
das Paar	des Paar(e)s	die Paare
das Paket	des Paket(e)s	die Pakete
die Palme	der Palme	die Palmen

die Pampelmuse	der Pampelmuse	die Pampelmusen
die Panne	der Panne	die Pannen
der Panzer	des Panzers	die Panzer
der Papagei	des Papageis	die Papageien
die Pappel	der Pappel	die Pappeln
der Paragraf	des Paragrafen	die Paragrafen
das Parfüm	des Parfüms	die Parfüms
der Park	des Parks	die Parks
das Parlament	des Parlament(e)s	die Parlamente
die Partei	der Partei	die Parteien
die Party	der Party	die Partys
der Pass	des Passes	die Pässe
der Passagier	des Passagiers	die Passagiere
der Passant	des Passanten	die Passanten
die Pastete	der Pastete	die Pasteten
der Pastor	des Pastors	die Pastoren
der Pate	des Paten	die Paten
der Patient	des Patienten	die Patienten
die Pause	der Pause	die Pausen
das Pedal	des Pedals	die Pedale
die Perle	der Perle	die Perlen
die Perücke	der Perücke	die Perücken
die Pfanne	der Pfanne	die Pfannen
der Pfau	des Pfau(e)s	die Pfaue
die Pfeife	der Pfeife	die Pfeifen
das Pferd	des Pferd(e)s	die Pferde
der Pfirsich	des Pfirsichs	die Pfirsiche
die Pflanze	der Pflanze	die Pflanzen
das Pflaster	des Pflasters	die Pflaster
die Pflaume	der Pflaume	die Pflaumen
der Pfleger	des Pflegers	die Pfleger
der Pflock	des Pflock(e)s	die Pflöcke
der Pflug	des Pflug(e)s	die Pflüge
die Pfote	der Pfote	die Pfoten
das Pfund	des Pfund(e)s	die Pfunde
die Pfütze	der Pfütze	die Pfützen
der Physiker	des Physikers	die Physiker
der Pickel	des Pickels	die Pickel
das Picknick	des Picknicks	die Picknicks

GENITIVE AND PLURAL FORMS

die Pille	der Pille	die Pillen
der Pilot	des Piloten	die Piloten
der Pilz	des Pilzes	die Pilze
der Pinguin	des Pinguins	die Pinguine
der Pinsel	des Pinsels	die Pinsel
der Pirat	des Piraten	die Piraten
die Piste	der Piste	die Pisten
die Pistole	der Pistole	die Pistolen
die Pizzeria	der Pizzeria	die Pizzerien
der Pkw	des Pkws	die Pkws
der Plan	des Plan(e)s	die Pläne
die Plane	der Plane	die Planen
der Planet	des Planeten	die Planeten
das Plateau	des Plateaus	die Plateaus
die Platte	der Platte	die Platten
der Platz	des Platzes	die Plätze
die Plombe	der Plombe	die Plomben
der Pokal	des Pokals	die Pokale
der Pol	des Pol(e)s	die Pole
der Pole	des Polen	die Polen
die Police	der Police	die Policen
der Politiker	des Politikers	die Politiker
der Polizist	des Polizisten	die Polizisten
der Pony	des Ponys	die Ponys
das Portemonnaie	des Portemonnaies	die Portemonnaies
der Portier	des Portiers	die Portiers
der Portugiese	des Portugiesen	die Portugiesen
der Postbote	des Postboten	die Postboten
das Poster	des Posters	die Poster
der Preis	des Preises	die Preise
die Presse	der Presse	die Pressen
der Priester	des Priesters	die Priester
die Primel	der Primel	die Primeln
der Prinz	des Prinzen	die Prinzen
das Problem	des Problems	die Probleme
das Produkt	des Produkt(e)s	die Produkte
der Profi	des Profis	die Profis
das Programm	des Programmes	die Programme
der Projektor	des Projektors	die Projektoren

die Promenade	der Promenade	die Promenaden
der Propeller	des Propellers	die Propeller
der Prospekt	des Prospekt(e)s	die Prospekte
der Prozess	des Prozesses	die Prozesse
der Psychiater	des Psychiaters	die Psychiater
der Psychologe	des Psychologen	die Psychologen
der Pudding	des Puddings	die Puddings
das Puder	des Puders	die Puder
der Pulli	des Pullis	die Pullis
der Pullover	des Pullovers	die Pullover
das Pult	des Pult(e)s	die Pulte
das Pulver	des Pulvers	die Pulver
der Punkt	des Punkt(e)s	die Punkte
die Pupille	der Pupille	die Pupillen
die Puppe	der Puppe	die Puppen
das Püree	des Pürees	die Pürees
das Puzzle	des Puzzles	die Puzzles
der Pyjama	des Pyjamas	die Pyjamas
das Quadrat	des Quadrat(e)s	die Quadrate
die Qualle	der Qualle	die Quallen
das Quiz	des Quiz	die Quiz
das Rad	des Rades	die Räder
das Radio	des Radios	die Radios
der Radler	des Radlers	die Radler
das Ragout	des Ragouts	die Ragouts
der Rahmen	des Rahmens	die Rahmen
die Rakete	der Rakete	die Raketen
der Rand	des Rand(e)s	die Ränder
der Rasen	des Rasens	die Rasen
der Rasenmäher	des Rasenmähers	die Rasenmäher
die Ratte	der Ratte	die Ratten
der Raub	des Raubes	die Raube
der Raureif	des Raureif(e)s	-
der Raum	des Raum(e)s	die Räume
die Raupe	der Raupe	die Raupen
der Rausschmeißer	des Rausschmeißers	die Rausschmeißer
der Rechner	des Rechners	die Rechner
das Reck	des Recks	die Recks
der Redakteur	des Redakteurs	die Redakteure

die Rede	der Rede	die Reden
das Regal	des Regal(e)s	die Regale
die Regel	der Regel	die Regeln
das Reh	des Reh(e)s	die Rehe
der Reifen	des Reifens	die Reifen
die Reihe	der Reihe	die Reihen
der Reiher	des Reihers	die Reiher
die Reise	der Reise	die Reisen
der/die Reisende	des/der Reisenden	die Reisenden
der Rekord	des Rekord(e)s	die Rekorde
der Rekorder	des Rekorders	die Rekorder
der Rektor	des Rektors	die Rektoren
das Rennen	des Rennens	die Rennen
die Rente	der Rente	die Renten
der Rentner	des Rentners	die Rentner
die Reparatur	der Reparatur	die Reparaturen
die Reportage	der Reportage	die Reportagen
der Reporter	des Reporters	die Reporter
die Republik	der Republik	die Republiken
das Restaurant	des Restaurants	die Restaurants
der Rettich	des Rettichs	die Rettiche
der Revolver	des Revolvers	die Revolver
das Rezept	des Rezept(e)s	die Rezepte
der Richter	des Richters	die Richter
der Riegel	des Riegels	die Reigel
der Riemen	des Riemens	die Riemen
der Riese	des Riesen	die Riesen
die Rinde	der Rinde	die Rinden
der Ring	des Ring(e)s	die Ringe
die Rippe	der Rippe	die Rippen
das Risiko	des Risikos	die Risiken
die Robbe	der Robbe	die Robben
der Rock	des Rock(e)s	die Röcke
die Rolle	der Rolle	die Rollen
der Roller	des Rollers	die Roller
der Roman	des Romans	die Romane
die Rose	der Rose	die Rosen
der Rowdy	des Rowdys	die Rowdys
der Rubin	des Rubins	die Rubine

die Rubrik	der Rubrik	die Rubriken
der Rücken	des Rückens	die Rücken
das Rückgrat	des Rückgrat(e)s	die Rückgrate
das Ruder	des Ruders	die Ruder
die Runway	der Runway	die Runways
der Russe	des Russen	die Russen
der Rüssel	des Rüssels	die Rüssel
die Rute	der Rute	die Ruten
der Saal	des Saal(e)s	die Säle
der Sack	des Sack(e)s	die Säcke
der Saft	des Saft(e)s	die Säfte
die Säge	der Säge	die Sägen
das Sakko	des Sakkos	die Sakkos
der Salat	des Salat(e)s	die Salate
die Salbe	der Salbe	die Salben
der Salon	des Salons	die Salons
der Sänger	des Sängers	die Sänger
der Sanitäter	des Sanitäters	die Sanitäter
der Saphir	des Saphirs	die Saphire
der Sattel	des Sattels	die Sättel
der Sattelschlepper	des Sattelschleppers	die Sattelschlepper
die Säule	der Säule	die Säulen
die Schachtel	der Schachtel	die Schachteln
der Schädel	des Schädels	die Schädel
der Schaden	des Schadens	die Schäden
das Schaf	des Schaf(e)s	die Schafe
der Schäfer	des Schäfers	die Schäfer
der Schaffner	des Schaffners	die Schaffner
der Schal	des Schals	die Schals
die Schale	der Schale	die Schalen
der Schalter	des Schalters	die Schalter
der Schatten	des Schattens	die Schatten
der Schatz	des Schatzes	die Schätze
der Schauer	des Schauers	die Schauer
der Schauspieler	des Schauspielers	die Schauspieler
der Scheck	des Schecks	die Schecks
die Scheibe	der Scheibe	die Scheiben
der Schein	des Schein(e)s	die Scheine
der Scheitel	des Scheitels	die Scheitel

der Schenkel	des Schenkels	die Schenkel
die Schicht	der Schicht	die Schichten
das Schiff	des Schiff(e)s	die Schiffe
das Schild	des Schild(e)s	die Schilder
der Schinken	des Schinkens	die Schinken
der Schirm	des Schirm(e)s	die Schirme
die Schläfe	der Schläfe	die Schläfen
der Schlag	des Schlag(e)s	die Schläge
der Schlager	des Schlagers	die Schlager
der Schläger	des Schlägers	die Schläger
die Schlange	der Schlange	die Schlangen
der Schlauch	des Schlauch(e)s	die Schläuche
die Schleuder	der Schleuder	die Schleudern
der Schlips	des Schlipses	die Schlipse
der Schlitz	des Schlitzes	die Schlitze
das Schloss	des Schlosses	die Schlösser
die Schlucht	der Schlucht	die Schluchten
der Schluck	des Schluck(e)s	die Schlucke
der Schlüssel	des Schlüssels	die Schlüssel
der Schmerz	des Schmerzes	die Schmerzen
der Schmetterling	des Schmetterlings	die Schmetterlinge
der Schnabel	des Schnabels	die Schnäbel
die Schnake	der Schnake	die Schnaken
der Schnaps	des Schnapses	die Schnäpse
die Schnauze	der Schnauze	die Schnauzen
der Schneider	des Schneiders	die Schneider
der Schnitt	des Schnitt(e)s	die Schnitte
das Schnitzel	des Schnitzels	die Schnitzel
der Schnorchel	des Schnorchels	die Schnorchel
der Schöffe	des Schöffen	die Schöffen
die Scholle	der Scholle	die Schollen
der Schöpfer	des Schöpfers	die Schöpfer
der Schornsteinfeger	des Schornsteinfegers	die Schornsteinfeger
die Schote	der Schote	die Schoten
der Schotte	des Schotten	die Schotten
der Schrank	des Schrank(e)s	die Schränke
die Schraube	der Schraube	die Schrauben
der Schraubenzieher	des Schraubenziehers	die Schraubenzieher
die Schrift	der Schrift	die Schriften

der Schriftsteller	des Schriftstellers	die Schriftsteller
der Schuh	des Schuh(e)s	die Schuhe
der Schuhmacher	des Schuhmachers	die Schuhmacher
die Schule	der Schule	die Schulen
der Schüler	des Schülers	die Schüler
die Schulter	der Schulter	die Schultern
die Schüssel	der Schüssel	die Schüsseln
der Schwager	des Schwagers	die Schwäger
die Schwalbe	der Schwalbe	die Schwalben
der Schwamm	des Schwamm(e)s	die Schwämme
der Schwan	des Schwan(e)s	die Schwäne
der Schwanz	des Schwanzes	die Schwänze
der/die Schwarze	des/der Schwarzen	die Schwarzen
der Schwede	des Schweden	die Schweden
das Schwein	des Schwein(e)s	die Schweine
der Schweizer	des Schweizers	die Schweizer
die Schwester	der Schwester	die Schwestern
der Schwimmer	des Schwimmers	die Schwimmer
der See	des Sees	die Seen
die See	der See	die Seen
der Seemann	des Seemanns	die Seeleute
das Segel	des Segels	die Segel
die Seife	der Seife	die Seifen
das Seil	des Seil(e)s	die Seile
die Seite	der Seite	die Seiten
die Sekunde	der Sekunde	die Sekunden
der Sender	des Senders	die Sender
der Serbe	des Serben	die Serben
der Sessel	des Sessels	die Sessel
das Set	des Sets	die Sets
das Shampoo	des Shampoos	die Shampoos
das Sideboard	des Sideboards	die Sideboards
der Sieg	des Sieges	die Siege
der Sieger	des Siegers	die Sieger
das Signal	des Signals	die Signale
das Silber	des Silbers	-
die Single	der Single	die Singles
der Sinn	des Sinn(e)s	die Sinne
die Sirene	der Sirene	die Sirenen

der Sittich	des Sittichs	die Sittiche
der Sitz	des Sitzes	die Sitze
das Skateboard	des Skateboards	die Skateboards
das Skelett	des Skelett(e)s	die Skelette
der Slowake	des Slowaken	die Slowaken
der Smaragd	des Smaragds	die Smaragde
der Smoking	des Smokings	die Smokings
das Sofa	des Sofas	die Sofas
die Sohle	der Sohle	die Sohlen
der Sohn	des Sohn(e)s	die Söhne
der Soldat	des Soldaten	die Soldaten
die Sorge	der Sorge	die Sorgen
die Soße	der Soße	die Soßen
das Souvenir	des Souvenirs	die Souvenirs
die Spange	der Spange	die Spangen
der Spanier	des Spaniers	die Spanier
der Spaten	des Spatens	die Spaten
der Spatz	des Spatzen	die Spatzen
die Speise	der Speise	die Speisen
der Spezialist	des Spezialisten	die Spezialisten
der Spiegel	des Spiegels	die Spiegel
das Spiel	des Spiel(e)s	die Spiele
das Spielzeug	des Spielzeug(e)s	die Spielzeuge
die Spinne	der Spinne	die Spinnen
die Spitze	der Spitze	die Spitzen
der Spitzer	des Spitzers	die Spitzer
der Sportler	des Sportlers	die Sportler
die Sprache	der Sprache	die Sprachen
das Spray	des Sprays	die Sprays
der Sprecher	des Sprechers	die Sprecher
die Spritze	der Spritze	die Spritzen
der Sprung	des Sprung(e)s	die Sprünge
die Spüle	der Spüle	die Spülen
die Spur	der Spur	die Spuren
der Staat	des Staates	die Staaten
der Staatsstreich	des Staatsstreich(e)s	die Staatsstreiche
der Stab	des Stab(e)s	die Stäbe
das Stadion	des Stadions	die Stadien
die Stadt	der Stadt	die Städte

der Städter	des Städters	die Städter
der Stadtstreicher	des Stadtstreichers	die Stadtstreicher
der Stamm	des Stamm(e)s	die Stämme
der Ständer	des Ständers	die Ständer
die Stange	der Stange	die Stangen
der Star *(person)*	des Stars	die Stars
der Star *(bird)*	des Stars	die Stare
der Start	des Start(e)s	die Starts
die Statue	der Statue	die Statuen
der Stau	des Staus	die Staus
der Staubsauger	des Staubsaugers	die Staubsauger
das Steak	des Steaks	die Steaks
der Stecker	des Steckers	die Stecker
der Stein	des Stein(e)s	die Steine
die Stelle	der Stelle	die Stellen
der Stern	des Stern(e)s	die Sterne
der Steward	des Stewards	die Stewards
die Stewardess	der Stewardess	die Stewardessen
der Stich	des Stich(e)s	die Stiche
die Stiel	der Stiel(e)s	die Stiele
der Stift	des Stift(e)s	die Stifte
die Stirn	der Stirn	die Stirnen
der Stock	des Stock(e)s	die Stöcke
der Stoff	des Stoff(e)s	die Stoffe
der Storch	des Storch(e)s	die Störche
der Stoß	des Stoßes	die Stöße
die Strafe	der Strafe	die Strafen
der Strahl	des Strahl(e)s	die Strahlen
der Strand	des Strandes	die Strände
die Straße	der Straße	die Straßen
der Strauch	des Strauch(e)s	die Sträucher
der Strauß	des Straußes	die Sträuße
das Streichholz	des Streichholzes	die Streichhölzer
der Streifen	des Streifens	die Streifen
der Streik	des Streiks	die Streiks
der/die Streikende	des/der Streikenden	die Streikenden
der Streit	des Streit(e)s	die Streite
der Streuer	des Streuers	die Streuer
der Strom	des Strom(e)s	die Ströme

der Strumpf	des Strumpf(e)s	die Strümpfe
die Stube	der Stube	die Stuben
das Stück	des Stück(e)s	die Stücke
der Student	des Studenten	die Studenten
der Studienrat	des Studienrat(e)s	die Studienräte
die Stufe	der Stufe	die Stufen
der Stuhl	des Stuhl(e)s	die Stühle
die Stunde	der Stunde	die Stunden
der Sturm	des Sturm(e)s	die Stürme
der Stürmer	des Stürmers	die Stürmer
der Sturz	des Sturzes	die Stürze
der Sumpf	des Sumpfes	die Sümpfe
die Suppe	der Suppe	die Suppen
die Synagoge	der Synagoge	die Synagogen
das System	des Systems	die Systeme
der Tabak	des Tabaks	die Tabake
das Tablett	des Tablett(e)s	die Tablette
die Tablette	der Tablette	die Tabletten
die Tafel	der Tafel	die Tafeln
der Tag	des Tages	die Tage
die Taille	der Taille	die Taillen
das Tal	des Tal(e)s	die Täler
das Tampon	des Tampons	die Tampons
der Tank	des Tanks	die Tanks
der Tankwart	des Tankwart(e)s	die Tankwarte
die Tanne	der Tanne	die Tannen
die Tante	der Tante	die Tanten
der Tanz	des Tanzes	die Tänze
die Tapete	der Tapete	die Tapeten
der Tarif	des Tarif(e)s	die Tarife
die Tasche	der Tasche	die Taschen
die Tasse	der Tasse	die Tassen
die Taube	der Taube	die Tauben
der Taucher	des Tauchers	die Taucher
die Taufe	der Taufe	die Taufen
das Taxi	des Taxis	die Taxis
das Team	des Teams	die Teams
der Techniker	des Technikers	die Techniker
der TEE	des TEEs	die TEEs

der Teenager	des Teenagers	die Teenager
der Teich	des Teich(e)s	die Teiche
der Teil	des Teil(e)s	die Teile
der Teilnehmer	des Teilnehmers	die Teilnehmer
der Teint	des Teints	die Teints
das Telefon	des Telefons	die Telefone
der Telefonist	des Telefonisten	die Telefonisten
das Teleskop	des Teleskop(e)s	die Teleskope
der Teller	des Tellers	die Teller
die Temperatur	der Temperatur	die Temperaturen
der Teppich	des Teppichs	die Teppiche
der Termin	des Termins	die Termine
der Terminal	des Terminals	die Terminals
die Terrasse	der Terrasse	die Terrassen
der Text	des Textes	die Texte
das Theater	des Theaters	die Theater
die Theke	der Theke	die Theken
das Thema	des Themas	die Themen
das Thermometer	des Thermometers	die Thermometer
der Tiger	des Tigers	die Tiger
der Tisch	des Tisch(e)s	die Tische
der Titel	des Titels	die Titel
der Toaster	des Toasters	die Toaster
die Tochter	der Tochter	die Töchter
die Toilette	der Toilette	die Toiletten
die Tomate	der Tomate	die Tomaten
der Ton	des Ton(e)s	die Töne
die Tonne	der Tonne	die Tonnen
der Topf	des Topf(e)s	die Töpfe
das Tor	des Tor(e)s	die Tore
der Tornado	des Tornados	die Tornados
die Torte	der Torte	die Torten
der Torwart	des Torwart(e)s	die Torwarte
der/die Tote	des/der Toten	die Toten
der Tourist	des Touristen	die Touristen
die Trage	der Trage	die Tragen
der Träger	des Trägers	die Träger
der Trainer	des Trainers	die Trainer
der Tramper	des Trampers	die Tramper

die Träne	der Träne	die Tränen
der Traum	des Traum(e)s	die Träume
das Treffen	des Treffens	die Treffen
die Treppe	der Treppe	die Treppen
der Tritt	des Tritt(e)s	die Tritte
der Trockner	des Trockners	die Trockner
der Tropfen	des Tropfens	die Tropfen
die Truhe	der Truhe	die Truhen
der Tscheche	des Tschechen	die Tschechen
das T-Shirt	des T-Shirts	die T-Shirts
das Tuch	des Tuch(e)s	die Tücher
die Tulpe	der Tulpe	die Tulpen
der Tunnel	des Tunnels	die Tunnel
die Tür	der Tür	die Türen
der Türke	des Türken	die Türken
der Turm	des Turm(e)s	die Türme
das Turnier	des Turniers	die Turniere
die Tusche	der Tusche	die Tuschen
die Tüte	der Tüte	die Tüten
der Überfall	des Überfall(e)s	die Überfälle
der/die Überlebende	des/der Überlebenden	die Überlebenden
der Übersetzer	des Übersetzers	die Übersetzer
das UFO	des UFOs	die UFOs
die Uhr	der Uhr	die Uhren
der Uhrmacher	des Uhrmachers	die Uhrmacher
der Uhu	des Uhus	die Uhus
die Ulme	der Ulme	die Ulmen
der Umfang	des Umfang(e)s	die Umfänge
die Umfrage	der Umfrage	die Umfragen
der Umschlag	des Umschlag(e)s	die Umschläge
das Unentschieden	des Unentschiedens	die Unentschieden
der Unfall	des Unfall(e)s	die Unfälle
der Ungar	des Ungarn	die Ungarn
das Ungeheuer	des Ungeheuers	die Ungeheuer
die Uni	der Uni	die Unis
die Uniform	der Uniform	die Uniformen
die Universität	der Universität	die Universitäten
das Unternehmen	des Unternehmens	die Unternehmen

der Unterschied	des Unterschied(e)s	die Unterschiede
die Unterschrift	der Unterschrift	die Unterschriften
der Urlaub	des Urlaubs	die Urlaube
die Urne	der Urne	die Urnen
das Urteil	des Urteils	die Urteile
der Vampir	des Vampirs	die Vampire
die Vase	der Vase	die Vasen
der Vater	des Vaters	die Väter
die Vene	der Vene	die Venen
der Verband	des Verband(e)s	die Verbände
der Verbündete	des Verbündeten	die Verbündeten
das Verdeck	des Verdeck(e)s	die Verdecke
der Verein	des Verein(e)s	die Vereine
der Vergaser	des Vergasers	die Vergaser
das Vergehen	des Vergehens	die Vergehen
das Vergissmeinnicht	des Vergissmeinnicht(e)s	die Vergissmeinnicht(e)
der Vergleich	des Vergleich(e)s	die Vergleiche
der Verkäufer	des Verkäufers	die Verkäufer
der/die Verletzte	des/der Verletzten	die Verletzten
der Verlierer	des Verlierers	die Verlierer
der/die Verlobte	des/der Verlobten	die Verlobten
der Verlust	des Verlust(e)s	die Verluste
der Vermieter	des Vermieters	die Vermieter
der Verschluss	des Verschlusses	die Verschlüsse
das Versteck	des Versteck(e)s	die Verstecke
der Verteidiger	des Verteidigers	die Verteidiger
der Vertrag	des Vertrag(e)s	die Verträge
der Vertreter	des Vertreters	die Vertreter
der Vetter	des Vetters	die Vettern
das Video	des Videos	die Videos
das Viertel	des Viertels	die Viertel
die Villa	der Villa	die Villen
das Visum	des Visums	die Visa
der Vogel	des Vogels	die Vögel
das Volk	des Vokes	die Völker
das Volumen	des Volumens	die Volumen
der Vorhang	des Vorhang(e)s	die Vorhänge
die Vorhersage	der Vorhersage	die Vorhersagen

die Vorliebe	der Vorliebe	die Vorlieben
der Vorstand	des Vorstand(e)s	die Vorstände
der Vorsteher	des Vorstehers	die Vorsteher
der Vorteil	des Vorteils	die Vorteil
der Vulkan	des Vulkan(e)s	die Vulkane
die Waage	der Waage	die Waagen
die Wache	der Wache	die Wachen
die Wade	der Wade	die Waden
der Wagen	des Wagens	die Wagen
der Wagenheber	des Wagenhebers	die Wagenheber
der Waggon	des Waggons	die Waggons
die Wahl	der Wahl	die Wahlen
der Wahrsager	des Wahrsagers	die Wahrsager
die Waise	der Waise	die Waisen
der Wal	des Wal(e)s	die Wale
der Wald	des Wald(e)s	die Wälder
der Waliser	des Walisers	die Waliser
der Walkman	des Walkmans	die Walkmans
die Wand	der Wand	die Wände
die Wange	der Wange	die Wangen
die Wanne	der Wanne	die Wannen
die Warze	der Warze	die Warzen
die Wäsche	der Wäsche	-
die Wäscherei	der Wäscherei	die Wäschereien
das Waschmittel	des Waschmittels	die Waschmittel
das Wasser	des Wassers	die Wasser
das WC	des WCs	die WCs
der Wecker	des Weckers	die Wecker
der Weg	des Weges	die Wege
der Wegweiser	des Wegweisers	die Wegweiser
die Weide	der Weide	die Weiden
der Wein	des Wein(e)s	die Weine
die Weite	der Weite	die Weiten
die Welle	der Welle	die Wellen
der Werbespot	des Werbespots	die Werbespots
die Werkstatt	der Werkstatt	die Werkstätten
das Wesen	des Wesens	die Wesen
die Wespe	der Wespe	die Wespen
die Weste	der Weste	die Westen

der Western	des Westerns	die Western
der Wettbewerb	des Wettbewerb(e)s	die Wettbewerbe
die Wette	der Wette	die Wetten
die Wiese	der Wiese	die Wiesen
das Wiesel	des Wiesels	die Wiesel
der Wind	des Windes	die Winde
der Winkel	des Winkels	die Winkel
der Wipfel	des Wipfels	die Wipfel
der Wirt	des Wirt(e)s	die Wirte
die Wirtschaft	der Wirtschaft	die Wirtschaften
der Wischer	des Wischers	die Wischer
der Wissenschaftler	des Wissenschaftlers	die Wissenschaftler
die Witwe	der Witwe	die Witwen
der Witwer	der Witwe	die Witwen
der Wolf	des Wolf(e)s	die Wölfe
die Wolke	der Wolke	die Wolken
der Wolkenkratzer	des Wolkenkratzers	die Wolkenkratzer
das Wort	des Wort(e)s	die Wörter
die Wunde	der Wunde	die Wunden
der Wunsch	des Wunsch(e)s	die Wünsche
der Würfel	des Würfels	die Würfel
die Wurst	der Wurst	die Würste
die Wurzel	der Wurzel	die Wurzeln
die Wüste	der Wüste	die Wüsten
die Zahl	der Zahl	die Zahlen
der Zahn	des Zahn(e)s	die Zähne
die Zahnpasta	der Zahnpasta	die Zahnpasten
der Zapfen	des Zapfens	die Zapfen
der Zauberer	des Zauberers	die Zauberer
das Zebra	des Zebras	die Zebras
die Zehe	der Zehe	die Zehen
der Zeichner	des Zeichners	die Zeichner
der Zeiger	des Zeigers	die Zeiger
die Zeit	der Zeit	die Zeiten
der Zeitvertreib	des Zeitvertreib(e)s	die Zeitvertreibe
die Zelle	der Zelle	die Zellen
das Zelt	des Zelt(e)s	die Zelte
der Zentner	des Zentners	die Zentner
das Zentrum	des Zentrums	die Zentren

der Zettel	des Zettels	die Zettel
der Zeuge	des Zeugen	die Zeugen
das Zeugnis	des Zeugnisses	die Zeugnisse
die Ziege	der Ziege	die Ziegen
der Ziegel	des Ziegels	die Ziegel
die Zigarette	der Zigarette	die Zigaretten
das Zigarillo	des Zigarillos	die Zigarillos
die Zigarre	der Zigarre	die Zigarren
das Zimmer	des Zimmers	die Zimmer
der Zimmermann	des Zimmermann(e)s	die Zimmerleute
der Zirkel	des Zirkels	die Zirkel
das Zitat	des Zitat(e)s	die Zitate
die Zitrone	der Zitrone	die Zitronen
die Zone	der Zone	die Zonen
der Zoo	des Zoos	die Zoos
der Zufall	des Zufall(e)s	die Zufälle
der Zuhälter	des Zuhälters	die Zuhälter
der Zuhörer	des Zuhörers	die Zuhörer
die Zunge	der Zunge	die Zungen
der Zuschauer	des Zuschauers	die Zuschauer
der Zuschlag	des Zuschlag(e)s	die Zuschläge
der Zweig	des Zweig(e)s	die Zweige
der Zwerg	des Zwerg(e)s	die Zwerge
die Zwiebel	der Zwiebel	die Zwiebeln
das Zwinkern	des Zwinkerns	-

INDEX

Note that entries refer to chapter numbers rather than page numbers

INDEX